THE SELF-SUFFICIENT KITCHEN

PRESERVING

DR. KAREN K. BREES

Publisher: Mike Sanders
Editor: Christopher Stolle
Book Designer: William Thomas
Cover Designer: Lindsay Dobbs
Compositor: Ayanna Lacey
Proofreaders: Gail Stein & Mira Park
Indexer: Beverlee Day

First American Edition, 2022
Published in the United States by DK Publishing
6081 E. 82nd Street, Suite 400, Indianapolis, IN 46250

Published in the United States by Dorling Kindersley Limited.
Library of Congress Catalog Number: 2022934276
ISBN 978-0-74406-177-2

Note: This publication contains the opinions and ideas of its author. It is intended to provide helpful and informative material on the subject matter covered. It is sold with the understanding that the author and publisher are not engaged in rendering professional services in the book. If the reader requires personal assistance or advice, a competent professional should be consulted. The author and publisher specifically disclaim any responsibility for any liability, loss, or risk, personal or otherwise, which is incurred as a consequence, directly or indirectly, of the use and application of any of the contents of this book.

Trademarks: All terms mentioned in this book that are known to be or are suspected of being trademarks or service marks have been appropriately capitalized. Alpha Books, DK, and Penguin Random House LLC cannot attest to the accuracy of this information. Use of a term in this book should not be regarded as affecting the validity of any trademark or service mark.

DK books are available at special discounts when purchased in bulk for sales promotions, premiums, fund-raising, or educational use. For details, contact: DK Publishing Special Markets, 1745 Broadway, 20th Floor, New York NY 10019. SpecialSales@dk.com

Printed and bound in the United States of America

Reprinted and updated from *The Idiot's Guide® to Preserving Food*

For the curious
www.dk.com

Contents

Introduction 6

How to Use This Book 6

Acknowledgments 8

About the Author 8

Part 1: To Your Health 9

Chapter 1: A Warm Welcome 11

Chapter 2: Food Safety Basics 19

Part 2: Freezing 29

Chapter 3: Freezing Basics 31

Chapter 4: Freezing Fruits 43

Chapter 5: Freezing Herbs & Vegetables 61

Chapter 6: Freezing Meat, Poultry, Seafood & Game ... 79

Chapter 7: Freezing Dairy Products, Eggs & Bakery Products 103

Chapter 8: Freezing Convenience Foods & Meals 117

Part 3: Canning...**127**

Chapter 9: Canning Basics.................................**129**

Chapter 10: Canning Fruits & Fruit Products..............**153**

Chapter 11: Canning Vegetables.........................**171**

Chapter 12: Canning Meat, Poultry, Seafood & Game.................................**187**

Part 4: Pickles, Relishes & Fermented Foods........**205**

Chapter 13: Pickling, Relish & Fermenting Basics.....**207**

Chapter 14: Pickling Fruits & Vegetables...................**215**

Chapter 15: Pickling Meats, Fish & Eggs...................**229**

Chapter 16: Relishes..**245**

Chapter 17: Fermenting **261**

Part 5: Fruit Spreads..**275**

Chapter 18: Jams, Jellies & Marmalades **277**

Chapter 19: Butters, Conserves & Chutneys **295**

Part 6: Drying, Salting, Smoking & Root Cellaring

Part 6: Drying, Salting, Smoking & Root Cellaring 307

Chapter 20: Drying 309

Chapter 21: Salting 335

Chapter 22: Smoking 351

Chapter 23: Root Cellaring 369

Appendixes

Appendix A: Glossary 387

Appendix B: Syrup Chart 391

Appendix C: Processing Times Reference Charts 393

Appendix D: Freezer Storage Chart 397

Appendix E: Best Preserving Methods for Specific Foods 399

Appendix F: Resources 403

Index 405

To my mother-in-law, the late Frances Briggs Brees, who showed me how to begin

Introduction

Home food preservation is enjoying a remarkable surge in interest as people look for ways to cut costs, eat healthier foods, and eliminate unnecessary additives and preservatives from their diets. Combined with the increased interest in home gardening, the expansion of bulk foods warehouses, and the burgeoning growth of farmers' markets, the timing couldn't be better to begin preserving food at home.

Some of us learned to preserve foods by watching our mothers and grandmothers, asking questions, and peeling countless apples and pears while we apprenticed in this art. Others of us didn't have that early experience and came to home food preservation via books or classes taught by experts in the field.

However it happened, we got hooked.

The saying "Life is hard by the yard; it's a cinch by the inch" applies nicely to learning how to preserve foods. Take it one step at a time, follow the directions, use tested and approved recipes, and you'll be a pro before you know it.

It's fun. Sometimes that part of putting up food gets overlooked. It's a hobby that pays you back instead of costing you bucks. It lets you get creative with gift possibilities. And not to put too fine a point on it, it lets you play with food.

Whatever your reasons for perusing this book, you've come to the right place if you want to get started "putting food by," as the old phrase used to say. If you have any questions about preserving and you don't find them answered here, drop me a line and I'll do my best to answer them. That's what a food safety advisor and master food preserver for the Cooperative Extension Service does. You can reach me at karenbrees@gmail.com. I look forward to hearing from you. Happy preserving!

How to Use This Book

The chapters in this book are organized into six main parts, with each one representing one aspect of food preservation:

Part 1, "To Your Health," discusses the many reasons for preserving food at home. You'll discover the many methods available for putting up food, plus important safety procedures for protecting your preserved foods.

Part 2, "Freezing," provides a great starting place for the novice home food preserver. You'll learn essential procedures, get experience, and gain confidence. Pick your own produce or patronize the farmers' market and you'll start with the freshest ingredients—the key to great-quality frozen foods.

Part 3, "Canning," raises the ante. With the basics under your belt, you're ready to move to the next level. You'll learn how to fill your pantry with nutritious foods at a fraction of the cost of their grocery store counterparts.

Part 4, "Pickles, Relishes & Fermented Foods," shares the secrets of pickling and fermenting and gives you choices of traditional or quick recipes to add just the right touch to complete your main courses.

Part 5, "Fruit Spreads," celebrates the wonderful world of jams and jellies, conserves and chutneys. Get the whole family involved and start a new family tradition.

Part 6, "Drying, Salting, Smoking & Root Cellaring," takes you on a quick trip through time. You'll explore ancient methods of preserving foods, although with a decidedly modern twist. Complete your food preserving repertoire with one or more of these methods.

Following the chapters, you'll find some helpful information in the appendixes:

Appendix A is the glossary. If you're stumped by an unfamiliar term, here's where you'll find the answer.

Appendix B is the syrup chart, which gives you exact amounts of sugar and water to create different syrup strengths.

Appendix C gives you the recommended processing times for different foods. It includes recommendations for when to use boiling water or the pressure canner.

Appendix D is a handy reference for the recommended freezer storage times for different foods.

Appendix E gives you the best methods for preserving different types of foods.

Appendix F provides additional resources to help you expand your food preserving knowledge and skills.

Acknowledgments

I'd like to thank Joey Peutz, Extension Educator, Food and Consumer Science, for answering all my questions; Bob Hill and Rita Peders, from May Hardware, McCall, Idaho, for the loan of the modern pressure canner; L & L Custom Meats, New Meadows, Idaho, for the meat-wrapping lesson; C & M Lumber, New Meadows, Idaho, my local source for canning supplies; John W. Brees, my husband, for his patience in formatting photos; Andrea Hurst, my literary agent; and Christopher Stolle, my editor at DK.

About the Author

Dr. Karen K. Brees grew up in the inner city (New Haven, Connecticut), but weekend jaunts to the country in search of native corn and vine-ripened tomatoes in the summertime turned into a lifetime passion for gardening. Preserving the bounty from her own gardens over the years was the logical next step and her mother-in-law was the expert teacher. The final step in her food preservation education was becoming a master food preserver and food safety advisor for the University of Idaho—and that came courtesy of the Extension Service. Now she's happy to share what she's learned over a lifetime of gardening and putting food by.

To Your Health

Food nourishes our bodies, provides comfort, and binds us together in shared traditions. Of all the reasons to preserve food, the most important is health. In this first part of the book, we'll look at what food preservation is and we'll review some basic principles of food safety.

A Warm Welcome

What is food preservation? The easy answer is that food preservation is saving surplus food for a time when you'll need it. Each time you return the milk carton to the fridge or close the twisty tie on a loaf of bread, you're practicing the ancient art of food preservation. You're extending the life of the food product. If you left the milk on the counter, it wouldn't take too long for it to get warm, for bacteria to grow, and for the milk to sour. It would go bad. The bread without its protective wrapper would get hard and stale. It would also go bad. Granted, these are simple examples, but the basic idea holds for whatever food you have that you don't need to use all at once. We look for ways to preserve it—to make it last longer.

Since the beginning of our existence, we've sought ways to keep our foods edible beyond the immediate moment and we've developed some sound practices that will do just that. This book will give you an introduction to a variety of methods for preserving food so it will be there for you when you need it. We've become used to a safe and reliable food supply. We've come to expect it and take it for granted. This isn't guaranteed, however, and recent developments have driven the point home. The pandemic has shown us we can't really take anything for granted. It's shown us that the old-fashioned virtue of self-sufficiency is timeless. Home food preservers understand this very well, and for those of us who freeze, can, pickle, root cellar, salt, and dry, empty shelves in grocery stores are just a minor inconvenience. We're prepared to take care of our families and weather the storms that come, however unexpected they might be.

The ideal situation is to grow your own food. Gardening is a wonderful hobby, and if you don't intend to be totally off the grid, you don't need 40 acres and a plow to grow a considerable amount of produce. A windowsill, a back deck, or a portion of the backyard can yield an astounding harvest. If this isn't your cup of tea, seek out the many farmers' markets that have sprouted in cities and rural areas alike. Buy farm direct and you eliminate many hands from touching what you eat. Farmers' markets go back to the foundations of colonial America. In 1643, Hartford, Connecticut, was ordered by the general court of the colony to provide a public market and the idea took off.

Additionally, preserving food is fun! This book will introduce you to the equipment you need for each form of food preservation. It will then walk you through every step you need to take and be your confident companion along the way. This isn't a cookbook, but there are some recipes included at the end of many of the chapters to give you some ideas for how you can use your preserved foods. They're there to prime the pump.

Added benefits of becoming a home food preserver are knowing just what's in your food. You'll follow approved methods, knowing that your food is safe to eat and free of contaminants that can cause foodborne illness. The Cooperative Extension Service is your essential go-to source for any questions you might have. You'll find your local branch with an easy online search. It's also a great idea to bookmark the National Center for Home Food Preservation's website: nchfp.uga.edu.

What You're Really Eating

The next aspect of home food preservation follows naturally from the previous section, with emphasis on the word *natural*. In addition to what's *on* your food, what's *in* the food you eat? Or to phrase it a bit differently, "When isn't a can of beans a can of beans?"

Read the labels on the canned foods you generally buy and you'll get an education about what's included along with the principal ingredients. Ingredients on labels are listed in order from most to least. For example, here's the list of ingredients on a can of a national brand of beef stew:

- Beef broth
- Beef
- Potatoes
- Carrots
- Tomatoes (water, tomato paste)
- Peas
- Beef fat
- Wheat flour
- Potato starch
- Salt

- Modified food starch

- Flavoring

- Caramel color

- Monosodium glutamate

- Spices

Here's the list of ingredients for a can of home-preserved beef stew:

- Beef

- Carrots

- Onions

- Potatoes

- Beef stock

- Spices

You can draw your own conclusions. If you or someone in your family has special dietary considerations—whether a food allergy or a need to reduce salt or sugar intake—or if you simply want to eliminate additives, which can of stew will you choose? There's no magic or mystery to canning stews and other foods at home, and it's a great way to create foods using the recipes your family enjoys.

Produce has its own concerns. We've become conditioned to demand perfect-looking fruit. We don't want bruises or blemishes of any kind, and bigger is always better. But is it really? Here's the journey one apple has taken from the tree to your kitchen:

1. Sprayed with pesticides approved for use on foods

2. Picked too early to ensure it doesn't get overripe before it's bought and boxed

3. Removed from the box and washed and waxed (to replace the wax lost during washing—sort of like your car)

4. Boxed

5. Shipped to the store, where it's handled (again), unboxed, and placed in a display

6. Handled by consumers while it's waiting to be bought

By a conservative count, at least six people—and potentially a great many more—have handled your apple. Now take a look at what transpires with an apple that's organically grown and offered for sale at a farmers' market:

1. The apple is picked and boxed.

2. You purchase the apple.

By any count, the number of handlings is markedly decreased, there's no pesticide residue or chance of residue, and the apple hasn't traveled any greater distance than from the tree to the roadside stand or the nearest farmers' market.

Is the fruit perfect? It all depends on how you define perfect. Is the fruit guaranteed to be mega-sized, blemish-free, and picture-perfect? No. Or as the organic farmer says, "No—and proud of it."

You won't get the image of perfection; you'll get the real deal. This apple will have crunch, flavor you haven't tasted in years, and a guarantee that it's not older than your great-aunt Tillie. And when you make applesauce, apple butter, apple jelly, or spiced apples, you'll have something truly special. (See Part 5 for some tasty fruit recipes.)

What is food preservation? It's using fresh, healthful ingredients when putting up fruits and vegetables, fruit spreads, pickles, relishes, and so much more.

Waste Not, Want Not

Thrift is a charter member of the virtues. To paraphrase Shakespeare, "Some are born thrifty, some achieve thrift, and some have thrift thrust upon them." Whether we're thrifty because it's a personal characteristic or because economic circumstances have required us to become thrifty, the end result is the same. The home food preserver practices thrift.

We waste a great deal. We live in a throwaway society that seems to have a foundation of built-in obsolescence. Technology is proof of that. Today's must-have component is tomorrow's landfill nightmare. Home food preservation can reconnect us to what has stood the test of time. It can reconnect us to our roots and our traditions and teach us respect for the bounty of Mother Earth.

Food preservation was born out of necessity: how to keep foods from spoiling while maintaining their nutritional value. The heat of the sun provided one answer. In hot climates, the heat was sufficient to dry all the moisture out of food before the spoilage microorganisms could spring into action and cause the food to rot.

Salting, which you'll read about in Chapter 21, was another early method. Especially in seafaring regions, salt was readily available and could be used to dry fish. This worked best in dry climates where the humidity didn't conspire to reconstitute the dried foods and cause them to spoil. Later, salt mines were developed inland and this spurred the use of salt for drying meats and vegetables.

Smoking, covered in Chapter 22, was the final form of early food preserving, reserved primarily for fish, meats, and the occasional cheese. The smokehouse doubled as a processing plant and storage facility—the earliest form of multitasking.

This remained the state of food preservation for many centuries until canning entered the picture in the early 19th century. Again, it was an invention of necessity, spurred on by the need to feed armies on the move.

Freezing (see Part 2) was dependent on the discovery of refrigeration principles. Early on, this was the exclusive province of the commercial sector. Most urban residents had electricity, but it took the creation of the Rural Electric Administration (REA) in 1935 to bring electricity to the 90% of rural Americans without it.

State-of-the-art technology today would astound someone for whom salting was modern technology. Portable food dehydrators, freezer bags, two-piece adjustable canning lids, and pressure canners have revolutionized this ancient practice into a modern-day form of art.

What is food preservation? It's a commitment to keep in with the past and to invest in the future.

Partnership with Experts

The home food preserver's best friend is the Cooperative Extension Service, which has been offering expert advice and tested recipes to the home food preserver for many, many years. In fact, the origins of the service go back to the time of Abraham Lincoln and an important piece of legislation he signed in 1862, the Morrill Act, which established the land grant colleges that became part of the West.

Half a century later, in 1914, the Smith-Lever Act established a link between these land grant colleges and the US Department of Agriculture (USDA), and the Cooperative Extension Service was created as a result. Its mission was to provide education and practical demonstrations in state-of-the-art technology in agriculture.

During both world wars, extension agents helped people deal with food shortages by helping with gardens and preserving foods grown in these gardens. The famous "victory gardens" of World War II were a result of these efforts.

There are nearly 3,000 extension offices around the country and you can reach the one closest to you by simply looking it up online. Check out Appendix F for resources available from the Extension Service.

What is food preservation? It's partnering with experts to learn the latest techniques and safest methods for safeguarding your food supply.

Personal Satisfaction

Food has many qualities—texture, flavor, color, and aroma—but it's the last quality that's the most powerful. Catching a whiff of bread baking, lasagna in the oven, or an apple pie cooling on the counter can bring back memories that span a lifetime.

Food is so much more than sustenance. Think of any ceremony, tradition, or family custom—and food is there. We mark milestones, celebrate achievements, and offer comfort with gifts of food. Each family has its own traditional dishes and each culture its traditional fare. Recreating those recipes and preserving those foods to enjoy at a time of your choosing is just one more benefit to home food preserving.

When people are asked why they're home food preservers, a sense of achievement is one of the most commonly given answers. It's a sense of control over what you eat. You don't need to accept a commercial product that has less of what you want or too much of what you don't want. You decide what goes into what you serve your family.

"I made it myself." There are few sentences that better sum up the pride and sense of accomplishment involved in creating something. What would you like to make? The possibilities are endless when you're a home food preserver.

What is home food preservation? It's passing down traditions. It's celebrating food and all that food can do.

Giving Food as Gifts

Home food preservation is an almost endless source of gift-giving possibilities. As you expand your skill set, you'll undoubtedly discover your particular penchant. Will you be the jam or jelly expert? The pickle person? Will it be your clam chowder that becomes your signature dish? If you cook it, you can preserve it.

The beauty of putting up foods as they come into season is you've got a wide variety to choose from when it comes time for giving gifts. There are other benefits to giving gifts of home-preserved foods:

- It gets eaten.

- Nobody has to dust it.

- No last-minute frantic shopping is involved.

- There are no returns or exchanges.

There are more benefits, but you get the idea. All you need to do is gather a supply of small or large baskets, some bows, and some decorative wrap, and you're set for the year. Always include the recipe. Punch a hole in the card and attach it to the jar rim with a ribbon.

Welcome to the ranks of home food preservers! I've been one for more than 50 years!

Food Safety Basics

Chapter
2

Product safety recalls and foods contaminated by unclean handling practices are important concerns for all consumers. Dealing with these issues after the fact is small comfort if you've contracted a foodborne illness or been sickened as the result of improper processing procedures.

Many of our food products are imported. In some cases, these countries don't have the same types of controls our government places on food handling. An example is garlic. When you purchase garlic at the store, check to be sure the root remains are still there and the bulb hasn't had them whacked off. Why? China uses human excrement for fertilizer and they must chop off the roots to clean up the product before shipping. Roots, good. No roots, not good. Buy locally whenever you can.

However, even at home, it takes just one careless or uncaring individual to cause harm to many others. Safe food handling and processing are essential to producing high-quality preserved foods—whether in the commercial arena or at home.

Much is beyond our control—and that includes nature. Being prepared to handle emergency situations is also important. Fortunately, there's no mystery to proper food management techniques. As a home food preserver, you can take steps to provide your family with nutritious foods that have been prepared with your family's health in mind.

Safety & Food Preparation

Cleanliness might be next to godliness, but in the kitchen, it stands alone. There's nothing more important and essential than cleanliness. So what does *clean* mean? First, it means you wash your hands in warm, soapy water for at least 20 seconds (or as long as it takes to recite the alphabet) before you pick up a kitchen utensil; before you handle food; and after you've handled raw poultry, meat, or seafood.

Next, take a critical look at your work area. You're going to be preparing food here, so everything should sparkle—but sparkle isn't enough.

Scrub the countertops with a commercial cleaning product designed for the particular surface you have—granite, tile, Formica—or sanitize with a solution of 1 teaspoon of chlorine bleach to 1 quart of water. Then scrub the sink. While you're at it, what does your kitchen sink drain look like? Be sure it's free of residual food particles and then sanitize it. You can also run the removable kitchen plug or drainer through your dishwasher to give it an extra good cleaning.

Toss the kitchen sponges. They're a petri dish of bacteria and other organisms that can make you sick. As for popping them in the microwave to disinfect them, there are some safety hazards involved—fire primarily. Use kitchen dishcloths and wash them at the end of the day.

With the counters and sink ready for work, it's time to take a cleanliness inventory of your kitchen equipment. The cutting board will get a great deal of use while you're preparing food for processing, so be sure it's not a source of contamination for that food. Cutting boards made from hard woods, plastic, and marble are easy to clean and sanitize. Check to be sure there are no cracks or splits in them, as these places harbor bacteria. Clean and sanitize them thoroughly after they've been used for cutting meats, poultry, and seafood. Having two cutting boards will cut down on the work. You can use one for meats, poultry, and seafood, and use the other for other foods. You can purchase sets of cutting boards with four labeled colors per set: one each for meat, poultry, seafood, and other foods. That way, there's less chance of cross-contamination. You'll come across these at kitchen supply stores or at the big chains.

Safety & Food Storage

Food safety means keeping foods at safe temperatures. It's counterproductive to keep everything clean and sanitary while you're preparing foods, only to have them spoil on the counter or in the fridge afterward.

Keep a thermometer in your refrigerator and consult it periodically. It should register no higher than 40°F.

Think two! Two hours is the recommended maximum time perishable foods should be left out of the refrigerator and it's less in warm weather. Cold foods should be kept cold (below 40°F) and hot foods hot (above 140°F). If you're going to be traveling with perishable foods that need to be kept cold, take along a cooler and fill it with ice or frozen gel packs. Hot foods should be stored in insulated carrying containers and used as soon as possible.

Frozen foods should be kept frozen, dried foods dry, and canned foods stored away from light and heat. These are the basics, but a great part of safe food storage is keeping food available in case of an emergency.

Food Safety in Emergencies

The difference between an emergency and a disaster is often preparation. The best time to prepare is now because an emergency can quickly become a disaster if you haven't made preparations to deal with it. A three-day emergency supply of food and water is the bare minimum, and ideally, you should plan for a week of total self-sufficiency. As a home food preserver, you're already ahead of the curve.

Emergency supplies need to be stored in watertight containers in a place you'll be able to access. This means having an emergency preparedness plan in place. In addition to food and water, you'll need some other essentials. The US Department of Homeland Security has a website devoted to helping families prepare for emergency situations: www.ready.gov.

As a home food preserver, you're prepared, resilient, and forward-thinking. You understand the importance of planning and you pride yourself on being self-sufficient. All these qualities will serve you well if you're faced with an emergency.

People often wait for others to help them. Sometimes, however, that help doesn't come right away. If you're prepared to help yourself, you'll be able to deal with the curveballs until help does arrive.

Preserved Foods & Floods

Flood waters are doubly deadly. First, they destroy life and property and then they cause havoc with your food and water supply. What can you do to protect your home-preserved foods? Think higher. That's the operative word when the weather forecast warns of possible flooding in your area. Do everything you can to raise your food supply above the level of flood waters. Refrigerators and freezers can be elevated by placing blocks (preferably of concrete, which won't move that easily) under the four corners.

Move your preserved foods to higher shelves. If they're in the basement, move them to the main floor or a second floor if necessary. Think closet shelves and even tabletops. If your home-canned foods come into contact with flood water, the US Cooperative Extension Service considers them not safe to eat.

In fact, foods that come in contact with flood waters should be discarded. The reason is that flood waters might be contaminated with sewage, chemicals, and other substances that might be poisonous or harbor disease.

So what's safe? It might hurt to discard food you believe is safe to eat, but it's a lot cheaper to toss a can of food than to deal with a foodborne illness that has the potential to be fatal. Only undamaged, commercially canned foods can be considered safe after coming into contact with flood waters—and then only if the outsides of the cans are sanitized. To do this, the Cooperative Extension Service recommends these steps:

1. Fill one bucket with a strong detergent solution.

2. Fill another bucket with a solution made from 1 teaspoon of chlorine bleach per 1 quart of water.

3. Put on rubber gloves.

4. Using an indelible marker, write the contents of the can on the lid.

5. Take the label off the can and dispose of it in the trash. Paper can be contaminated with bacteria and other harmful agents.

6. Place the can in the detergent solution and scrub it thoroughly with a scrub brush.

7. Take the can from the detergent solution and place it in the bucket containing the bleach solution. Leave it there for 15 minutes.

8. Remove the can from the detergent solution and allow it to air-dry before opening.

What else should you discard if it comes in contact with flood waters? Again, the Cooperative Extension Service comes to the rescue:

- Meat, poultry, fish, and eggs. An eggshell doesn't protect bacteria from entering the egg.

- Any fresh fruits or vegetables.

- Any fruit spreads preserved with paraffin. Paraffin can crack or separate from the glass and allow harmful bacteria to enter.

- Commercially produced glass products with a waxed cardboard seal inside the lid, corks, pop tops, or peel-off tops. These include most mayonnaise jars and salad dressings. Even if you haven't opened them before, contaminants can work their way inside.

- Anything in a cardboard box (such as cookies, crackers, and cereals), foil, cellophane, paper, or any combination of these.

- Spices, extracts, and seasonings.

- Any opened containers or packages.

- Anything you've put in a canister, such as coffee, flour, sugar, etc.

- Cans that are dented, bulging (which you shouldn't even think about using under any conditions, let alone after a flood), or rusted.

Unfortunately, what you have left might not be much. That's why preparing ahead of time is important. In addition to food, you'll need water. There are a few ways to ensure that your water supply is safe. If you've used up the water you've set aside, you'll need to purify the water that's available to you.

Purifying Your Water Supply

Water filters and water purification tablets contain iodine, halazone, or chlorine. The US Department of Agriculture (USDA) recommends that because these tablets will kill most waterborne bacteria, viruses, and some parasites—but not all—a water filter must also be used. A water filter works on a very simple premise: the barrier's micropores allow water molecules to pass through but are so small that they keep bacteria—which are bigger—from passing to the other side. Some filters are so small, they can even keep viruses from passing through.

Read the labels carefully before you purchase a water filter. The recommendation is that these devices must be 1 micron absolute or smaller. This information will be on the label. A micron is $1/125,000$ of an inch. That's small! Water purification tablets can lose potency over time, so you should replenish your supply regularly. Water sanitizing tablets aren't the same as water purification tablets. The former are used for washing dishes, not for purifying drinking water. You can find these supplies at camping and outdoor supply centers.

You can add liquid bleach, such as Clorox or Purex, to your water supply to purify it for drinking purposes. This procedure calls for 16 drops of bleach (about ¼ teaspoon) per 1 gallon of water. Thoroughly mix the water and bleach and then let it sit for 30 minutes before using. If the water is cloudy or cold, increase the time before using to 60 minutes. The water should have a slight chlorine odor. If it doesn't, repeat the entire process and let it stand an additional 15 minutes.

Chlorine bleach won't kill *cryptosporidium* cysts that might be present in flood waters. Boiling is the best means of dealing with these.

If you suspect your water is harboring harmful bacteria, boiling provides the best means of purifying. Pour water into a clean pot and bring it to a full, rolling boil. Continue to boil for 1 to 3 minutes. This is the recommended procedure at sea level. You'll need to adjust for altitude by increasing the boiling time several minutes at higher elevations. Keep the pot covered while the water cools. When cool, pour the water into clean containers.

Preserved Foods & Fires

Fire and the chemicals used to fight it can damage your preserved foods and make them unsafe to eat. Heat can activate bacteria inside jars and commercially canned foods, and heat can also cause jars to crack and split, allowing air and harmful bacteria to enter.

Burning materials release toxic fumes. These fumes can penetrate many types of food packaging, including cardboard, plastic wrap, and screw-top containers. These foods aren't safe to eat and should be discarded. Additionally, these fumes can penetrate refrigerator and freezer seals as well as contaminate the food stored inside. If the food has an off-putting odor or off-putting taste, dispose of it.

Any raw foods that have come in contact with fumes from a fire should be discarded. This includes potatoes, onions, or fruits.

The chemicals used in fighting fires also contain toxic materials that can't be washed off food. Any foods that have come into contact with these chemicals should be discarded. These include foods with screw-top lids as well as foods stored in plastic, paper, or cardboard containers.

To decontaminate canned goods and cooking utensils that have come in contact with chemicals, first wash them in a strong detergent solution. Then immerse them in a solution of 1 teaspoon chlorine bleach per 1 quart of water for 15 minutes. Remove items from the solution and allow them to air-dry before using.

Preserved Foods & Earthquakes

If floods mean higher in terms of salvaging home-preserved foods, earthquakes definitely mean lower—but not basement level. Store your canning jars on low, sturdy shelves at ground-floor level, preferably in a sturdy cabinet with doors that close securely. If they lock, so much the better. This added protection can help keep the doors closed if the ground action gets violent. Have the key secured to the outside of the door so it stays put and is accessible.

Not being able to get to your food is one problem; having all that hard work destroyed just compounds the situation. Earthquakes strike without warning, so preparation is essential. After an earthquake, broken glass is everywhere—and this might include your canning jars.

You'll need to check the jars if they've ended up on the floor or have fallen over on the shelf. Use sturdy gloves when handling jars. Pick up each jar and check the seal. If the seal is intact and the glass doesn't appear cracked, dip the jar in a bucket of water and scrub to remove any residue that might be sticking to it from other jars that have broken. Then re-examine the jar carefully to be sure it's intact. Dry the jar and store it in a safe location, as aftershocks are common and are capable of causing as much damage as the original earthquake.

Preserved Foods & Power Outages

There are two types of power outages: scheduled and unscheduled. You'll receive a notice from the utility company for a scheduled power interruption. They're generally scheduled during the workday to allow utility workers to make repairs or upgrade the system. While inconvenient, they shouldn't pose any hazard to your refrigerated or frozen foods.

Common sense applies here. Limit the number of times you open and close your refrigerator and freezer. If possible, remove items from the freezer that you'll need that day and keep them in the refrigerator. Then think before you open the refrigerator door. "Is this trip really necessary?" should be your mantra for the day.

A small, gasoline-powered generator can supply power to keep your freezer operating and safeguard the food inside. It's a useful item to have on hand. They're relatively inexpensive and available at hardware stores.

It's the unscheduled power outages that can threaten your food supply. Again, preparation is key to handling them. That means knowing how to determine what's safe to eat and what's not and stocking up on supplies you'll need during the outage.

Your refrigerator and freezer(s) should have thermometers inside them. If they don't, it's time to get one for each of these appliances and put it in a place where you'll be able to read it easily and without keeping the door open too long.

Keep the refrigerator door closed. That's the first rule. If you absolutely must open the door, take out everything you'll need for the next 2 hours. Then close the door quickly and leave it closed. Warmth is the enemy here, as harmful bacteria grow in the danger zone, which begins above 40°F.

If you can keep the inside temperature of the refrigerator between 34°F and 40°F, properly stored food should be safe to eat. Generally, if the power is out for no longer than 4 hours, your refrigerated items should be safe; however, never taste food you think might have spoiled. If the food has an off-putting odor or color or if the texture seems different than it should, discard it without tasting it.

It might be prudent to gather up your insulated food coolers and put in a good amount of ice or frozen gel packs if you're getting close to the 4-hour mark and the power still hasn't come back on. Put the food in the ice, along with a thermometer, and close the lid securely. Add more ice as needed to keep the temperature at 40°F or below.

Getting ice when the power's out can be difficult, and if the outage is widespread, for all practical purposes, it can be impossible. Having a supply of gel packs in your freezer is one way to prepare for this emergency situation. Your local grocery store might also have a supply of ice, but it will probably go quickly.

Dry ice is also an option if you can find a resource for it. A good time to find that resource is now—before you need it. The USDA advises that a 50-pound block of dry ice will keep a full 18-cubic-foot freezer at a safe temperature for 2 days. Wear gloves or use tongs when handling dry ice, as it will give you a severe burn. Dry ice has a temperature of –216°F.

It's human nature to want to check on things to see what's happening, but every time you open the refrigerator or freezer door or the cooler lid, cold air escapes and warm air enters. Resist this impulse.

If the outage occurs during the winter and outside temperatures are below freezing, you can put containers filled with water outdoors to freeze. When they're frozen, you can use them to keep your cooler cold. Don't store food outdoors, though, as sunlight and temperature fluctuations might cause it to spoil. Also, nocturnal animals can settle in for a feast and you'll awaken to the remains of their picnic.

Your freezer is designed to keep foods at 0°F. It functions most efficiently when full. A full freezer will hold food safely for about 2 days, provided you don't open the door.

When the power comes back on, it's time to check the freezer. If food still contains ice crystals, it can be safely refrozen. Also, if the temperature is 40°F or below, the food can be safely refrozen. The quality might not be as good, but it's safe.

If the temperature is 40°F or below but there are no ice crystals, you can cook the food and then freeze the cooked food or can it.

The Cooperative Extension Service recommends that the following foods be discarded if they've been exposed to temperatures above 40°F for 2 or more hours:

- Raw or cooked meats, including lunch meats, hot dogs, poultry, and fish
- Dairy products, including milk, creams, soft cheeses, yogurt, and custards
- Eggs (including egg substitutes)
- Any products with cream or custard fillings
- Creamy salad dressings
- Soups and stews
- Casseroles
- Refrigerated cookie dough
- Custard, cheese, or chiffon pies

Opened jars of mayonnaise, tartar sauce, or horseradish should be discarded if they've been held at temperatures above 50°F for more than 8 hours. You might have read that mayonnaise doesn't need to be refrigerated. This is true—until you open the container. In a perfect world, you could keep the mayo unrefrigerated even after that, provided you never touched it. The moment you introduce a knife, a spatula, a spoon, or anything into the mayonnaise, you're introducing bacteria. Keep the mayo in the fridge.

Food products that should be safe at room temperature for a few days include:

- Butter, margarine, and hard and processed cheeses
- Fruit pies
- Opened jars of vinegar-based salad dressings
- Jellies
- Relishes, barbecue and taco sauces, mustard, ketchup, olives, and peanut butter

If anything develops mold or an off-putting odor, it should be discarded.

Power outages that occur during the winter in colder climates can create other problems with your food supply. Your house will become cold. In extreme climates, your canned foods might actually freeze. Canned foods that have frozen might still be safe to eat. Metal cans that have frozen are safe if they've not split and allowed their contents to become exposed to air. If the seam has split and the contents have thawed, the food should be discarded.

Broken or cracked glass canning jars should be discarded. If the jars and their seals are intact, the food is safe. Allow them to thaw gradually at room temperature. As with all home-canned foods, check to be sure the seal is intact before using the food. If the seal has failed and the contents have thawed, the product should be discarded.

Freezing

Here's your opportunity to make the most of your food dollar. Buy in bulk, buy in season, and preserve nature's bounty for your use all year long. Freezing is a relative newcomer to the home food-preservation scene and it's one area in which the technology has made some incredible advances in ease and practicality. This part of the book will teach you all you need to know about freezing foods.

Freezing Basics

Freezing is the newest addition to the field of home food preservation. It had to wait for refrigeration to become economical and that meant there needed to be a steady and reliable supply of electricity. And therein lies the greatest weakness of this modern miracle. When the power goes out, it doesn't matter how high tech your freezer or refrigerator is, time is the enemy and you hope the power will be restored quickly before your food spoils. However, hope isn't a good survival strategy and the basic tenet of home food preservation is self-sufficiency.

What's surprising is to read numerous reports that the average household only has between 3 to 7 days' worth of food on hand. In the event of any disruption in delivery of food supplies or breakdown of the infrastructure, this reality quickly goes from disturbing to catastrophic. The fact you're reading this means you're not average! You have a plan and you're ready to put that plan into action.

Thinking ahead is important, so many home food preservers who live in rural and suburban areas have backup generators. Indeed, many new homes come with the capability of being generator-powered in case of a natural disaster or another emergency. Even if you're a city dweller, you can still ensure your food supply will see you through.

As with each method of food preservation we'll discuss, freezing has its pros and cons. "Don't put all your eggs in one basket" is time-honored advice and it bears repeating and adhering to.

The Science Behind Freezing

There's some interesting science behind how freezing works to preserve food and this chapter will take a look at how to put that science to work for you. We'll discuss the equipment and supplies you need to begin freezing foods, and we'll cover the basic procedures involved.

In 1924, Clarence Birdseye invented a method of quick-freezing foods and ended up revolutionizing the food-preservation industry. He got the idea while fishing in Canada, and as with most ingenious discoveries, he just simply became aware of what was happening around him. It was so cold that the fish froze about as soon as he hauled them out of the water. When thawed months later, he noted that the quality was good. Quick-freezing, he decided, was the way to go.

Up until this time, freezing foods wasn't an especially quick process, and because of this, large ice crystals formed in the foods. This caused rupturing of the cell membranes of the foods being frozen. This wasn't good. When the foods were thawed, all the ice melted, water drained from the food, and the flavor and texture suffered.

Birdseye got busy and developed a couple of ways to quick-freeze foods. One method used calcium chloride and the other used ammonia. Ammonia—or, more specifically, evaporating the ammonia to get a temperature of –25°F—allowed fruits and vegetables to be frozen in about 30 minutes and a 2-inch-thick (5cm) package of meat to be frozen in about 90 minutes. The rest, as they say, is history and the frozen food industry we take for granted today owes its existence to an observant fisherman. The Birdseye brand of frozen foods became a supermarket staple and is still a staple today.

How Freezing Works

When you freeze foods, you're freezing the water content of that food. Water expands as it freezes and creates ice crystals inside the food. These ice crystals can rupture the cell walls of the food being frozen, but freezing the food quickly will result in smaller ice crystals and less damage to the cell walls.

Maintaining a temperature of 0°F or below also keeps ice crystal formation in check, but constant temperature fluctuations will result in larger ice crystal formation and more damage to the texture of the food. Keep opening and closing the freezer door to a minimum to prevent this from happening!

The home food preserver can use a vacuum sealer to come close to this method and we'll discuss that later on in this chapter.

The Spoilers

Air, microorganisms, chemical changes, and enzymes are the enemies of frozen foods. Proper processing, packaging, and storage are necessary for dealing with these potential food spoilers.

Freezing stops microorganisms from growing, but it's just temporary. It doesn't destroy them; they're just in a state of suspended animation, so when foods begin the thawing process, those microorganisms start to multiply again and can cause food to spoil.

The presence of air can result in oxidation as well as freezer burn. Both adversely affect the texture and flavor of frozen foods. The oxidation process causes fats in frozen meats to go rancid in the presence of air. In freezer burn, air causes moisture loss from the frozen foods—ice crystals evaporate from the product, and when you unwrap it, you'll see frost on top of whatever you've frozen. The surface will look dry and brown or sometimes white. The food is safe to eat, but it will definitely be less than good.

Enzymes control the ripening process in fruits and can cause light-colored fruits to turn brown when their cut surfaces are exposed to air. Freezing slows down the enzyme process but doesn't stop it. Ascorbic acid or commercial antidiscoloration products can keep these fruits from turning brown (see Chapter 4) and blanching will protect the quality of vegetables. (Blanching is discussed later in this chapter. Specific blanching times for vegetables are covered in Chapter 5.)

Benefits of Freezing Foods

All methods of preserving foods have their benefits, but freezing definitely has quite a bit going for it as far as the home food preserver is concerned:

- Freezing temporarily stops the growth of organisms (such as bacteria, yeast, and molds) that cause spoilage in foods. It doesn't kill them but essentially puts them in a state of suspended animation.

- Freezing inactivates enzymes responsible for controlling the ripening process.

- Properly frozen foods generally keep more of their nutrients, flavor, and texture than foods preserved by other methods.

- Freezing foods saves space. Frozen foods can be stacked in the freezer, whereas glass canning jars can't be stacked.

The Freezer

When it comes to freezing foods, the biggest and most expensive item to consider is, of course, a freezer, but it's an investment you'll amortize over time. The other supplies and equipment you'll need are relatively inexpensive and, like the freezer, most will last for years with proper care.

Freezer capacity is measured in cubic feet, ranging from 5 to 25 cubic feet. You might be tempted to buy the biggest freezer you can find, but before you plunge ahead and purchase a mega-freezer, stop to consider how you'll use this appliance.

Keeping a smaller freezer full will be more energy-efficient than running a larger freezer that's less than half full. Modern, smaller freezers have more storage capacity than older, bigger freezers. This is because of improvements in insulation technology that have reduced the need for thicker walls.

Smaller units generally use less electricity than larger ones, but the difference isn't huge. What *is* huge is keeping your freezer as full as possible to get the most return on your food-preserving dollar. Freezers are designed to run more efficiently when full, so keeping your freezer at least half (and preferably three-quarters or more) filled is the way to go.

If you have a large or growing family, the larger freezer might make sense. Also, if you're planning on stocking up for the year, a larger freezer will store that much for you. However, if your family is small or if you're also planning on preserving foods by other means, such as canning or drying, a smaller unit might make more sense. Many families have two freezers and put them to different uses, such as one for meats and the other for bulk-food purchases.

Important Features

There are certain features you'll want to look for in a freezer. Most of them are standard in newer models. These include the following:

- **A power-on light.** This light tells you the freezer is working. Checking this every day can save you a lot of headache and expense if something goes haywire (such as, the power going out or a mouse chewing through the cord or any other weird occurrence). If your freezer is in the garage, just make it a habit to check the light each day as you walk to the car.

- **A locking mechanism with a key.** This is an essential item, especially in homes with children. I know a friend's child who was playing hide-and-seek and hid in the freezer. She couldn't get out, but fortunately, she was found in time.

- **An adjustable temperature control dial with a "fast freeze" setting.** This quickly gets your foods to the optimum temperature. Once the food has frozen, you can then return the freezer to 0°F.

- **An internal light.** Especially with chest freezers, peering into the dark abyss can be frustrating. Holding a flashlight in one hand while you're rummaging with the other is annoying. The second best option is a headlight that makes you look like someone out to explore the Carlsbad Caverns.

- **ENERGY STAR designation.** The Environmental Protection Agency (EPA) developed the ENERGY STAR program to promote energy-efficient products.

- **A defrost drain.** This is found in the bottom for manual defrost units.

Automatic or Manual Defrost?

Of the two, automatic defrost is definitely the easier way to go. You don't have to devote a morning or afternoon to scraping, wiping, draining, and especially moving all your frozen foods into boxes while you clean out their home.

On the other hand, manual defrost units are generally less expensive than automatic defrost units. Also, if you have a tendency to drop items haphazardly into the freezer instead of carefully entering them on an inventory sheet and putting them in their proper place, a semiannual investigation of your freezer's contents can yield some interesting discoveries. Additionally, it will prompt you to use those items that are nearing the end of their recommended storage times. (See Appendix D.) It can be quite refreshing to perform this chore on an especially hot summer day—just remember to keep your storage containers stacked and covered, and return them to the freezer as quickly as possible.

Making the Decision

When purchasing a freezer, consider the initial capital outlay, along with the cost to operate. Making an informed choice about which kind of freezer to purchase will require some research and careful study. You have a choice of two types of freezers: upright and chest. Each has advantages and drawbacks. An upright freezer has a smaller footprint than a chest type. It's vertical with shelves. The chest type is horizontal with a vast amount of open interior space. It also has baskets that fit across the opening to hold smaller items. The following are some further pros and cons.

Upright Freezers	
Pluses	**Minuses**
Adjustable shelving	Less energy-efficient (large air loss each time the door is opened)
Suitable for smaller quantities of food	Larger items might be difficult to store
Door storage for easy access to frequently used foods	10 to 15% less usable space than a chest freezer
Pullout drawer at the bottom	Costs more than a chest freezer
Same footprint as a refrigerator	

Chest Freezers	
Pluses	**Minuses**
Uses less energy because less air escapes each time you open the door	Requires reaching, bending, and lifting to retrieve items
Tends to last longer than other model types (especially if you buy a manual defrost chest model)	Requires careful organization (can use cardboard boxes to help with organizing)
Best for bigger items and bulk purchases	No shelves, although it does have baskets
The entire unit is usable space	Bigger footprint

Ultimately, you'll make the decision based on your own needs, available space, and budget. Do some comparison shopping before you buy.

Situating the Freezer

The main requirements are a dry, level space that's not subject to extremes in temperature. If your garage is heated or if winters in your area are mild, this might be the best place. The basement is another option, but only if you live in areas where earthquakes don't occur. A personal story: The Loma Prieta earthquake of October 17, 1989, in the Santa Cruz Mountains of California destroyed more than 500 homes and damaged more than 18,000 others. My home was toast. Unfortunately, the freezer and all the year's canning were in the basement. The house came to rest on top of all this and all was lost. Bottom line: Know where you live and plan accordingly.

Other Equipment & Supplies

There are several options when it comes to deciding which type of containers you'll use for freezing foods and new technology has expanded your choices. Whether you choose to be traditional or modern, you'll easily find just what you want.

Freezer Containers & Freezer Bags

Freezer containers are made of rigid plastic with tight-fitting lids, and they're moisture- and vapor-resistant to prevent freezer burn. Some are designed to allow you to raise one corner of the lid after packing and burp out the extra air. You won't eliminate all of it, but every little bit helps. Pint and quart sizes are the most versatile. These containers stack nicely and take up less space in your freezer than glass canning jars. Like glass jars, they're reusable and reasonably priced.

Yes, you read that correctly. You can use glass canning jars for freezing. We'll cover all aspects of these jars in Part 3 of this book.

There are different types of freezer bags: envelopes with slides that help lock the bag, envelopes without slides but with tracks that fit together to create a tight seal, and soft bags that can be secured with a twisty tie.

You might find it easier to expel air from the softer bags because they conform more easily to the shape of the food in them. With the stiffer bags, you might be able to fold them over, starting at the bottom and pushing out the air as you go up to the seal. These have a greater tendency to cause freezer burn because it can be difficult to expel enough air. If your food product will permit it, first wrap it tightly in plastic food wrap before putting it in the freezer bag.

Vacuum Sealer Packaging Machines

Vacuum packaging machines or vacuum sealers are handy appliances designed to remove air from packages of food and thereby increase their storage life. Different kinds of systems are available and prices vary widely. They work well when used for their specified purpose, but they're not intended to take the place of the freezer. They're simply another form of packaging to get food *ready* for the freezer. Make them the last step before schlepping your foods to the freezer.

But the air is gone, you think. Why can't I store the packages in the pantry, you ask. Most bacteria that cause food spoilage thrive in the presence of oxygen. When food is going bad because of these microorganisms, there's a better than good chance you'll find out about it. The food will smell bad, it might get slimy, and the color will look definitely "off." You'll notice all this and should dispose of the food so no one gets sick.

It would seem logical, then, that removing this oxygen from the food's environment would solve the problem—and it does for those bacteria that love oxygen.

The problem is there's another genus of bacteria, *Clostridium*, that thrives in the absence of oxygen and this *anaerobic* bacteria is potentially lethal. It's responsible for tetanus, gas gangrene, and botulism. Food that's contaminated with *Clostridium* might not smell bad, look bad, or taste bad, but it *can* kill you.

If you're using a vacuum-sealing system, you must be aware of proper food storage for low-acid, perishable foods, such as vegetables, meats, poultry, and seafood. Vacuum packaging isn't a replacement for proper pressure canning of low-acid foods nor is it a replacement for proper refrigeration and freezing of foods that would otherwise require refrigeration and freezing. You must also be aware that perishable food always carries the potential for contamination with pathogens, such as bacteria. Previously frozen foods that are thawed will spoil more quickly than their fresh counterparts. After thawing, keep them refrigerated until ready for use.

Bottom line: If the food won't keep at room temperature without spoiling, it must be refrigerated or frozen after being vacuum-sealed. Nonperishable food items (such as dried nuts, crackers, lentils, or other dried foods) are good candidates for vacuum sealing because they have very little moisture content. However, these items store very well in regular storage containers with tight-fitting lids and you can remove the product as needed and replace the lid. Once you open the vacuum-sealed package, you must go through the resealing process again.

Freeze & Cook Bags

These are nifty for doing just what the name says. You can freeze foods in them and then transfer them directly from the freezer to a pot. They're designed to handle from below 0°F to above boiling. They're pricey but convenient. Plus, you can save on cleanup.

You can buy these bags in 1½ pint or quart size and they also come in a roll so you can cut whatever size you need. This is handy for odd-shaped items that won't fit in standard freezer containers. You'll need a heat sealer if you go the roll route. These are sold separately and are available at most larger department or chain stores.

General Supplies

You've decided which freezer will serve your needs, you've stocked up on freezer containers and other necessary items for prep work and storage, and you're ready to preserve food. But there are still some other supplies you also need:

- Cutting boards in various sizes (especially ones with rims)
- Good knives (meaning sharp)
- Pots and pans
- A colander or sieve
- Utensils (slotted spoon and regular spoons, vegetable peeler, spatulas, ladle)
- Measuring cups and spoons
- Clean dishcloths and towels
- Potholders and/or mitts
- Sugar (if you're freezing fruits in a sugar or liquid pack)
- A timer
- Scales
- Plastic wrap, freezer wrap, and aluminum foil
- Freezer tape, permanent marker, and Freezer Inventory Sheet

General Procedures for Freezing

Examine all your containers and jars. Discard any plastic containers with cracks or chips. Examine your glass freezing and canning jars, and discard any with chips or cracks. Run a finger around the rim to detect any small nicks and dispose of any jars that don't pass muster into the recycling bin.

Cleanliness is the order of the day. Wash all containers and jars in hot, soapy water, rinse, and invert them on a clean towel.

Now you can focus on what you'll be freezing. Wash fruits and vegetables in cool water. Cut the items according to how you plan to use them (cubes, slices, etc.). Packaging instructions for various types of foods are discussed in the following chapters.

Blanching

Most vegetables will need to be blanched in order to stop enzyme action from causing the food to deteriorate during storage. Blanching doesn't destroy these enzymes, but it does inactivate them. Blanching means to put vegetables in boiling water or to steam them for a specified period of time and then plunge them into ice-cold water for rapid cooling. Different vegetables require different blanching times. (See Chapter 5.)

Blanching in the microwave is possible if you're working with small quantities of vegetables. It doesn't save any time, but it does require electricity, so you're not saving energy. Also, most charts only give blanching times for boiling water, so unless you've kept the instructions for your microwave, you'll end up guessing and might produce less than satisfactory results. After blanching and cooling, vegetables need to be drained to remove as much water as possible before being packed for the freezer.

Headspace

Water expands when it freezes, so you must allow enough room for that expansion when you're packing foods for the freezer. The room between the food and the lid is called *headspace*. Headspace requirements vary according to the type of food being frozen and whether it contains syrup or liquid. Proper amounts of headspace for freezing fruits and vegetables are discussed in the following chapters.

Preventing Discoloration

Light-colored fruit oxidizes in the presence of oxygen. This means it turns brown. Apples and peaches are especially vulnerable. You can prevent this by using ascorbic acid or a commercial antidiscoloration product. (See Chapter 4.)

Storing Frozen Foods

During the initial freezing process, packages or jars should come in direct contact with the freezing unit. This will hasten freezing. Leave some air space between packages or jars of food being frozen. This keeps the cold air on the move and more able to do its job. Once everything is frozen, you can stack, cram, and arrange to your heart's content.

Thawing Procedures

For every safe way of doing something, someone will come up with a creative but totally unsafe way of accomplishing the same task. The US Department of Agriculture (USDA) warns against defrosting foods in any of the following ways:

- In the basement
- In your car
- In plastic garbage bags
- In the dishwasher
- Outdoors
- On the porch
- In a pan of hot water
- On the kitchen counter

You probably wouldn't dream of trying any of these methods, except perhaps for the last one. So what's wrong with setting a package of meat out on the counter to defrost? Could be plenty. As food thaws, the bacteria that are present (and that were inactive while the food was frozen) begin to get frisky. They multiply when any part of the meat gets to 40°F or above. So while the interior section of the meat is still frozen, the outer layers have passed into the danger zone, which begins at 40°F and extends to 140°F.

Thawing in the Refrigerator

Planning ahead is best. If you know what you'll want for dinner, take the package out of the freezer the night before and put it in the refrigerator to thaw. Temperatures vary throughout the refrigerator, so take advantage of the warmer portions when you want something to thaw. Generally, the lower shelves are best for thawing if your freezer unit is on top.

Put the package of frozen food on a plate or inside a bowl to contain any liquid that leaches through the wrappings. This is especially important for meat or poultry juices that shouldn't come in contact with other foods stored in the refrigerator. Plan on using thawed ground meats within a day or two. The same goes for poultry. Solid cuts of beef, such as roasts or steaks, should keep up to 5 days. If your plans change, you can refreeze foods that have thawed, although the quality won't be as good.

Thawing in Cold Water

This works more quickly than the refrigerator method, but it does require you be on hand to keep changing the water to be sure it stays cold. It can also be messy, especially if the freezer bag is leaking. Not only can bacteria enter through the opening, but water can turn your food product into a soggy mess. If in doubt, put the package in another freezer bag (double-bag it) just to be sure. Change the water about every half hour. You can expect a 1-pound package to thaw in about 1 hour. Once the food has thawed, it must be cooked right away. If you change your mind about using the product right away, it should still be cooked before refreezing.

Thawing in the Microwave

Microwaves are probably used more for reheating coffee and defrosting foods than for any other purpose. However, you'll need to keep a close eye on the defrosting process when you use the microwave because outer portions of the food can begin cooking while the interior is still hard as a rock.

Once food has thawed by this means, it should be cooked right away to prevent bacteria from growing. If you decide to refreeze the food, it should still be cooked before you return it to the freezer. Again, there will be some loss of quality in a refrozen product.

Now that you've got the basics under your belt, let's get started freezing foods.

Freezing Fruits

If you're new to preserving food, freezing fruits is the place to start. It's fast and it's easy! It's almost impossible to make a mistake, you need very little in the way of equipment and supplies, and you get an instant return on your efforts. You have a great deal of latitude regarding whether to use sugar, and you can learn some tricks of the trade to make peeling a breeze and to ensure your fruit doesn't darken during storage.

Berries

Berries are versatile (great for jams, jellies, cobblers, and pies), they're healthful (high in antioxidants and other good things), and they're fun to eat. Berries come in a variety of sizes and shapes and in a rainbow of colors. Berries are generally broken down into two categories: hard and soft.

Hard Berries

Hard berries include blueberries, cranberries, huckleberries, and youngberries. These berries are firm and round, and a cranberry in prime condition will actually bounce. In fact, cranberries were originally called *bounceberries*.

Blueberries are generally available from May through October and cranberries are available during the holiday season.

Blueberries contain oxalates, which are naturally occurring substances. When oxalates become too concentrated in body fluids, they can crystallize and cause problems. Folks with kidney or gallbladder problems should avoid eating large amounts of blueberries. As always, if you have any suspected or diagnosed health issues, consult your physician before changing your diet.

Blueberries come in clear plastic cartons with ventilation holes. Cranberries come in plastic bags, also with ventilation holes. Cranberries and blueberries should be loose inside the container. There should be no moisture, mold, or browning to the berries. Healthy blueberries have a whitish "blush" that protects them from breaking down.

Berries used in baked goods sometimes take on a greenish tinge. This isn't harmful. When the recipe calls for baking soda, this creates an alkaline environment, which causes the yellow pigments in the blueberries to turn green. The products are still safe to eat.

There's no special handling involved for these berries, and preserving blueberries and cranberries couldn't be easier. Just put them in the freezer as is (in the bag or carton) and they'll keep for 1 year. This is a good way to take advantage of seasonal special prices. Take out what you need as you go along. Don't wash the berries until you're ready to use them.

Soft Berries

Soft berries include blackberries, raspberries, loganberries (a cross between raspberries and blackberries), and boysenberries (a cross of loganberries, raspberries, and Pacific blackberries). There are many other soft berries, but most of them are the result of crossing various strains of blackberries and raspberries.

Pick-your-own berry farms have become popular places for families to gather all kinds of soft berries. Even if you live in the city, you'll probably not be too far from one. If you're worried about thorns and getting scratches, most of these commercial, open-to-the-public places have thornless bushes and canes. Still, long sleeves and thin gloves are a good idea, and don't forget the sunblock and insect repellent.

You bring your own containers. They shouldn't be too deep—you don't want to crush the bottom layer. Coffee cans work well. Berries are fragile, so handle them with care. Blackberries and raspberries are ripe when they easily slip from their caps. The more you have to tug, the greener (less ripe) the berry.

To find a complete listing of all pick-your-own fruit and vegetable farms in the US, the UK, Canada, and various other countries, go to www.pickyourown.org.

Preserving soft berries is just one step more advanced than freezing blueberries and cranberries: It's time for those cookie sheets. Here are the step-by-step instructions:

1. Wash berries with cool water. The spray nozzle on your sink works well. You don't want to blast the berries—just give them a gentle shower.

2. Set berries aside to drain; you can spread them on paper towels to absorb any excess water. You'll use a dry pack (more about that in the next section) and you'll want them to be dry for step 3.

3. Spread the berries in a single layer on cookie sheets. Don't crowd them.

4. Pop the trays into your freezer. When the berries are hard, take the cookie sheets out of the freezer, use a spatula to loosen the berries, scoop them into freezer bags (prelabeled and dated), and seal. Return the sealed bags to the freezer.

When you need some, take out what you need and either thaw them in the microwave or let them thaw at room temperature. Use berries on cereal and yogurt and in muffins, fruit salads, and smoothies—or just eat them plain. When you're ready to make jams and jellies on a cold or rainy day (see Chapter 18), you'll have a supply of berries on hand.

Before we get started, let's deal with a myth once and for all. You've probably heard the old saying "Bruises are the sweetest part of the fruit." This isn't true—just a handy old lie children have been told to be sure they eat everything up. Bruises are damaged flesh. Cut them out and throw them away.

Blackberries on a cookie sheet

Strawberries

Strawberries are almost a category of their own. They're firm (but not hard) when ripe but require gentle handling and can become overripe (and too soft) very quickly. You can store them in the fridge for a few days, but they're best used quickly. Strawberries make excellent jams and jellies (see Chapter 18), and if your jelly doesn't set the way you'd like, you've got wonderful strawberry syrup.

Strawberries have a nice long season, and when you've eaten your fill, you can freeze a bunch for the fall and winter seasons. You have a few options when it comes to preserving strawberries. The texture of thawed strawberries will differ depending on which method you choose for your needs, but the taste will be great.

- **Dry pack.** This method of preserving food doesn't use any additional liquid, such as juice or water, when packing food in freezer bags or containers. Food is packed as is. You can use the cookie sheet method and dry-pack strawberries the same way you freeze blackberries or raspberries, but the berries will tend to lose their shape as they thaw.

- **Sugar pack.** This option expands your preserving skill set. It's nothing more than rolling strawberries in superfine sugar. Superfine sugar (referred to as "castor sugar" in Great Britain) is finely granulated sugar that dissolves almost instantly without leaving a granular residue at the bottom of the bowl. It's manufactured by Domino and should be available at your local grocery. Then put the strawberries on cookie sheets and pop them in the freezer. When they're frozen, remove them with a spatula, place in freezer bags, and return to the freezer. When thawed, the sugared berries will keep their shape better.

- **Syrup pack.** The other method of putting up strawberries uses syrup, which is a mixture of differing proportions of sugar and water that are heated until boiling, then cooled and poured over fruit before the container is sealed. See Appendix B for instructions on making different strengths of syrups.

To prepare strawberries for a syrup pack, wash the berries and remove the green caps. Some people prefer to keep digging and also remove the core, but it really isn't necessary. A short paring knife works well for this. Just make a circular incision and remove the stem and cap. Slice the berries directly into a freezer container (usually a hard plastic container with a tight-fitting lid) and cover them with the syrup of your choice, leaving about ½ inch (1.25cm) of headspace to allow for expansion during the freezing process. Then secure the lid, label and date, and store in the freezer.

Fruits packed without added sugar or liquid, such as syrup or juice, need ½ inch (1.25cm) of headspace. That applies to any container of any size. If you've puréed or crushed the fruit or packed it in liquid, allow a headspace of 1½ inches (3.75cm) for wide-mouth pint jars and 1 inch (2.5cm) for wide-mouth quart jars if you're going the glass jar route. If you're using regular (narrow-mouth) jars, allow ¾ inch (2cm) for pints and 1½ inches (3.75cm) for quarts. And yes, as already noted, those glass canning jars are also fine for freezing. Once you've packed, sealed, labeled, and dated your containers, it's time to take them to the freezer. Spread your containers around in a single layer until the fruit has frozen. A good rule is to keep them spread overnight and then stack them the next morning.

Cherries

Cherries are generally divided into sweet (eating) and tart or sour (pie). Both types can be frozen as well as canned. Cherries can be frozen by the cookie sheet method or packed in liquid. Frozen cherries don't need to be pitted, but the use you have in mind for them will determine if you pit them or not. For example, if you're going to be snacking, it's no trouble to spit out a pit. If you're going to make a pie, pitting is definitely the way to go. Always double-check to be sure the pits have been removed before proceeding to pack the cherries. Biting down on a pit can break a tooth.

Pitting used to be tedious work, but for under $20 you can have a lifetime of pitting ease. Cherry pitters are remarkable little devices. You drop cherries into the hopper, depress a plunger that neatly divests the cherries of their pits (two at a time), and the pits are pushed out into side trays while the pitted cherries slide down a little ramp and into your waiting receptacle. This is a great job for the younger apprentices in your preserving kitchen. Still, one last check to be sure a wayward pit hasn't moved back into one of the cherries is a good idea.

If you've come home with a box of cherries, plan on putting them up right away. They have a habit of turning soft quickly. Wash and sort the cherries. Trim any bruised portions, toss the bruises, and set the trimmed fruit aside to make jam. (See Chapter 18.) Remove the stems and pits if desired. Pack into freezer containers.

If you've decided to pack the cherries in syrup, determine the strength of the syrup you'll use and prepare it according to the directions given in Appendix B's syrup chart. Cover the cherries with syrup, allowing enough headspace for expansion during the freezing process. Wipe the rims of the containers to remove any syrup. Seal, label, date, and freeze them. When the cherries have frozen, you can stack the containers.

Cherries in freezer containers

Apricots, Peaches & Nectarines

These fruits can be frozen, canned, or dried—and pickled peaches are a wonderful accompaniment to holiday meals. (See Chapter 14.) Each method produces a good product with different textures suitable for different uses.

Apricots

Apricots don't require any special preparation and they hold their shape better if frozen with their skins on. Wash them carefully, checking for bruises and blemishes. Trim the damaged portions and set the trimmed fruit aside to make jam. (See Chapter 18.) Slice the apricots in half, remove the pits, and pack into freezer containers. Freeze without sugar or freeze using syrup in the strength of your choice. Allowing proper headspace, seal, label, date, and freeze.

Peaches & Nectarines

These fruits differ from berries and cherries in that they have skins that must be dealt with and their pits are quite a bit larger. They also tend to discolor quickly when their cut surfaces are exposed to air. However, taking it one step at a time makes the job easier.

Peaches are either clings or freestone. Clings do just that; the pits are firmly attached to the skin and can be difficult to remove without mangling the fruit. Freestones separate more easily. You slice around the fruit and then twist the two halves in opposite directions. Voilà! The fruit separates—one side has the pit and the other side is free. The pit should separate easily. However, if freestones are picked green, the pit might not work the way it's supposed to and you'll be faced with a clinger.

Clings are the first peaches to ripen in the spring, and unless you've got access to a commercial pick-your-own orchard, you'll probably not find them readily available. Most of them are marked for commercial packers. Later on, the freestones ripen and these are the ones you're more likely to find at the grocery store or farmers' market.

Nectarines are peaches that lack fuzz. In fact, a peach tree can bear nectarines and vice versa. Once peaches and nectarines have been picked, sugar production ceases and the ripening process stops. The fruit will soften, but it won't ripen any further. All the more reason to buy tree-ripened fruit at the local farmers' market.

Ripe peaches are fragrant. Early Elberta, Elberta, Improved Elberta, and O'Henry are good varieties for freezing. Check with your local Extension Service for recommended peach and nectarine varieties in your area. (See Appendix F.) Ripe peaches also have a nice blush and their skin should gently yield to the touch. They shouldn't be soft and definitely shouldn't be hard.

Removing Skins

Unlike apricots, which usually hold their shape better with the skin left on, peaches are frozen without their skins. If you're groaning at the prospect of peeling two or three boxes of peaches, you're in for a very pleasant surprise. You won't have to peel a single peach and the skins will come off so easily, you'll probably decide to buy another box. But first, assemble the needed equipment:

- At least three large bowls (about 15 inches [38cm] in diameter and able to hold 1 gallon or more of liquid)

- Boiling water canner or a pot of similar size

- Ascorbic acid, lemon juice, or a commercial antidarkening agent for light-colored fruits
- Slotted spoon
- Colander
- Paring knife
- Grapefruit spoon
- Prepared syrup
- Freezer containers (pints or quarts)

1. Wash and sort the fruit. Here's where a couple of large bowls will come in handy. Perfect fruit goes into one bowl; fruit with blemishes goes in another. You'll be preserving your perfect peaches first. Later, you can cut up the damaged fruit and save the good parts to make jam or purée them for fruit leather. (See Chapter 20.)

2. Fill your pot or canner about half full of water, turn the heat to high, and bring the water to a boil.

3. Mix up your antidiscoloration solution (see the next section) in a large bowl and set it to one side of your sink. You'll be working with 2 to 3 pounds of fruit at a time.

4. Fill the sink with cold water and add ice cubes to get it even colder.

5. Once the water in the pot has come to a boil, use a slotted spoon to carefully lower the peaches into the water. Leave the peaches in the water for 10 to 20 seconds. You'll see the skins begin to separate.

6. Once you've seen the first signs of the skins separating, use the slotted spoon again to remove the peaches and plunge them into the ice water.

7. Keeping each peach underwater as you work, gently rub the skin with your fingers. The skin will separate easily from the peach.

8. Place each whole peach in the bowl containing the antidiscoloration solution.

9. Make a 360° cut around the peach, starting at the stem and proceeding to the bottom. Use your paring knife to gently coax the halves apart and use your grapefruit spoon to nudge the pit away from the half it's still attached to. Then you can either cut the halves into slices or keep them as is. Hold them in the antidiscoloration solution until you're ready to put them into containers.

Peaches with a buffer protection

Most of the prep work is now done. You can use plastic freezer containers or glass canning and freezing jars. If you're planning on freezing halves and want to use jars, wide-mouth quart jars are an easier way to go. With slices, it doesn't matter, although it's easier to neatly arrange the slices if you've got some room to work with.

Slice the peaches into the freezer containers and add syrup in the strength of your choice. There's one additional step to ensure your peaches won't rise up and greet the air in the headspace: Tear off a small piece of plastic wrap, crumple it up, and place it on top of the fruit. This will keep the peaches in their place. Seal, label, date, and freeze.

Apples

You can freeze apple slices and use them later in pies. Put slices in boiling water for 2 minutes. Remove them from the boiling water, drain, and plunge into ice water. When cooled, drain and pack in freezer bags.

That's one way, but if you have some extra room in the freezer, why not line a pie pan with aluminum foil—leave plenty for folding back over—arrange your apple slices in the pan until you're happy with the height, and then fold the foil securely around the apples? Place the pan with the apples in the freezer. When the apples have frozen, lift out the pie-shaped foil from the pan and return your preshaped pie to the freezer. When you're ready to bake your pie, all you need do is unwrap the foil, remove the frozen apples and transfer them to the crust, add spices, and bake.

You can also freeze applesauce. Prepare your favorite recipe (or see Chapter 10 on canning fruits for some suggestions) and pack it into freezer containers, leaving ½ inch (1.25cm) of headspace. Seal, label, date, and freeze.

Pears

Good old Bartletts freeze nicely. They're by far the most popular and readily available pear and the one most used by commercial and home food preservers. You can freeze them as halves or quarters or put them up as a purée. Wash fruit in several changes of cool, clean water. To pare pears is a matter of preference. They tend to hold their shape better if you leave the skins on.

Use a grapefruit spoon to gently remove the stringy center. A neat twisting motion followed by a scrape will clean up the pear half quite neatly. Pack halves or slices into freezer containers and add syrup (in your choice of strength) to cover, leaving proper headspace. Seal, label, date, and freeze.

Plums

Plums freeze nicely whole, halved, or quartered. They hold their shape better if frozen with their skins on. If you're planning to make jam later, don't use a sugar or syrup pack. Choose plums with a deep, rich color. Wash in several changes of cool, clean water.

To pack unsweetened, pack whole plums into containers, leaving proper headspace. Seal, label, date, and freeze.

To pack in syrup, slice the plums in half or in quarters. Remove the pits. Select the syrup strength of your choice. Cover the fruit with the syrup, leaving proper headspace. Seal, label, date, and freeze.

Citrus

If you have your own citrus trees, it's worth the time and effort to freeze these fruits, but it's a bit more work than putting up other kinds of fruit. Of course, this is why grapefruit spoons were invented. When you're freezing oranges, lemons, or limes, save some rind for making marmalade. (See Chapter 18.)

Grapefruit & Oranges

Wash the fruit, peel away the white membrane, and use a sharp knife to make the first cut and remove the first section. The rest will be easier. Separate each section and clean up the extra membranes that cling to the segments. Remove the seeds as you go along.

This is a juicy process, so be sure to collect the juice as you work and save it for packing. You can sweeten the juice to your taste or leave it unsweetened. Pack the fruit into freezer containers and cover with juice or a light or extra light syrup, leaving proper headspace. Seal, label, date, and freeze.

If you want to freeze juice and have enough fruit to make it cost-effective, consider investing in a juice extractor to make the job easier. Freezing juice in glass canning and freezing jars makes for a more attractive product. Leave the appropriate headspace, seal, label, date, and freeze.

Lemons & Limes

You'll want to freeze lemons and limes for their juice. Use your juice extractor (or you can use the old tried-and-true hand juicer) and pour the juice directly into freezer containers. Leave the appropriate headspace, seal, label, date, and freeze. No need to worry about these products darkening!

Grapes

Seedless grapes freeze well if you treat them the same way you do berries. They make great snacks and are good additions to fruit salads. Arrange them in a single layer on a cookie sheet and pop them in the freezer. When they're frozen, loosen them with a spatula and pack them into freezer bags. Return to the freezer. If you're handling grapes with seeds, slice the grapes in half lengthwise and remove the seeds before committing them to the cookie sheet.

To freeze with liquid, pack freezer containers with grapes and cover with a syrup in your choice of strength. Leave the appropriate headspace, seal, label, date, and freeze.

You can also freeze grape juice. Wash the grapes in several changes of cool, clean water. Remove the stems and use a potato masher to crush the grapes. Pour the mixture into a jelly bag and allow it to drip at its own pace. The sediment will settle to the bottom of the receiving container, so carefully pour off the clear juice so you don't disturb the sediment.

Melons: Cantaloupe, Honeydew, Casaba & Watermelon

All these freeze well—with the exception of watermelon. You can try using your melon baller on watermelon, but this fruit tends to get mushy. After all, it's mostly water. If you do decide to give it a shot, take a close look at the thickness of the rind. If it's thick, put it aside to make watermelon rind pickles. (See Chapter 14.)

For other melons, you want to use the firm flesh for melon balls, so remove the seeds and any of the soft, flaky parts. Scoop away, arrange on cookie sheets in a single layer, and freeze. When the melon balls are frozen, use your spatula to loosen them and then pour them into freezer bags. Seal, label, date, and freeze. If you prefer slices or cubes, they'll also do fine. Just be sure to cut off all the rind and any dark green coloring close to the rind.

Avocados

Preparation involves mashing. (Think guacamole and bases for dips.) Peel and smash away. If you're planning on using the avocados for something sweet, add ⅛ teaspoon of crystalline ascorbic acid (vitamin C) to each quart of purée. Otherwise, 1 tablespoon of lemon juice for every 2 avocados will keep them from turning dark.

Coconut

Puncture the eye and pour out and save the coconut milk. Crack open the shell with a hammer and separate the meat from the shell. You can grate it by hand or use a food processor. Put the coconut in a freezer container and cover with the coconut milk. Seal, label, date, and freeze.

Dates

Dates are fruit of the date palm. They're about 1½ inches (3.75cm) long, a dark reddish brown, and oval. Their skins are wrinkled and coated with a sticky, waxy film. They're very sweet when ripe. These are as easy to freeze as cherries. Wash, drain, dry, pit, and pack. Seal, label, date, and freeze.

Figs

Sort, wash, and cut off the stems. You can peel the figs if you prefer them that way. You can slice them or leave them whole. Pack them in a 35% syrup with ¾ teaspoon of ascorbic acid per quart. (A 35% syrup uses 2½ cups of sugar per 4 cups of water.)

If you prefer the no-sugar method, simply use water. Cover the figs with water to which you've added ¾ teaspoon of ascorbic acid per quart. Seal, label, date, and freeze.

Pineapple

A pineapple is ripe when the top pulls out easily. Pare the pineapple and dig out the eyes. Core it. Then decide how you want to freeze it. Slices? Cubes? Sticks? Pineapple freezes nicely in its own juice, but if you want a sweeter syrup, it's best to go with extra light or light syrup. (See Appendix B.) Ripe pineapple has a rich flavor already and is sweet enough. Pack the pineapple in freezer containers, add liquid to cover, and leave proper headspace. Seal, label, date, and freeze.

Pie Fillings

The main ingredients of pie fillings are fruit and sugar, spices for interest and flavor, and a thickening agent. Thickening agents include tapioca, flour, or cornstarch. Here we'll discuss freezing, but in Part 3, I'll have some recipes for canned pie fillings.

Cornstarch has twice the thickening capacity of flour. You dissolve it in a small amount of cool water before adding it to your pie filling so it won't lump up. Also, unlike flour, cornstarch won't add a white tint to your filling. It sets up clear. Flour and water, of course, make paste. Tapioca is another option.

To make an 8- or 9-inch (20 or 23cm) pie, plan on putting up a quart of filling.

- **Apple pie filling:** One apple pie uses about 6 to 8 apples, ½ cup of sugar, cinnamon, nutmeg, and lemon juice.
- **Berry pie filling:** One berry pie uses 1 to 2 quarts of berries, ⅔ cup of sugar, and 1½ tablespoons of tapioca.

- **Cherry pie filling:** One cherry pie uses 1 to 2 quarts of sour cherries, 1 to 2 cups of sugar, and 2 tablespoons of cornstarch or flour.

- **Peach pie filling:** One peach pie takes about 1 to 2 quarts of peaches, 1 cup of sugar, ¼ cup of flour, cinnamon, nutmeg, and lemon juice.

Whatever your favorite pie recipe, you can freeze it. Gently mix all the ingredients together in a medium-sized pot. Cook over low heat until the juices begin to flow from the fruits and the mixture begins to thicken. Pack it into quart freezer containers or glass canning and freezing jars, allowing the proper headspace. Seal, label, date, and allow the filling to cool down before placing it in the freezer.

Recipes

Frozen berries, cherries, peaches, apples, and pears that have been dry-packed all work well with these recipes. There's no need to thaw berries or cherries before using them in cooking, but if you want to use fruit that's been frozen in liquid, you'll want to thaw first and drain before using.

Blueberry Grunt or Slump

This was a colonial favorite, although this version uses baking mix, something colonial cooks didn't have unless they made their own. Some say this dessert got its name from the "grunts" of satisfied eaters or the fact it didn't hold its shape when served!

Serves	Prep time	Cook time
8	10 minutes	25 minutes

2 cups buttermilk baking mix

⅔ cup milk of choice

for the blueberry mixture

½ to ¾ cup granulated sugar

1 quart blueberries

1 tsp lemon juice

⅛ tsp ground nutmeg

¼ tsp ground cinnamon

2 cups blueberries

1 cup water

cream or ice cream, for topping

1. In a medium bowl, combine all the blueberry mixture ingredients. Mix well. Transfer the mixture to a large cast-iron skillet on the stovetop over low heat. Simmer for 10 minutes, stirring occasionally.

2. Prepare the buttermilk baking mix according to the package directions. Add the milk and stir until thoroughly moistened. Drop this mixture in by spoonfuls over the blueberry mixture.

3. Cover and cook on low for 10 minutes more or until the drop biscuits are done.

4. Use a large spoon to scoop out each serving. Invert onto a plate and cover with another spoonful of blueberry mixture. Serve with the cream or ice cream.

Linda's Crispy Cobbler

This is a real crowd-pleaser and very easy to make.

Serves	Prep time	Cook time
6 to 8	5 minutes	40 minutes

½ cup butter, melted

1 cup sifted all-purpose flour

1 cup granulated sugar

2 tsp baking powder

⅛ tsp salt

¾ cup milk of choice

4 cups fruit (blackberries, raspberries, peaches, apples, and pears are well suited for this dish)

vanilla ice cream (optional)

1. Preheat the oven to 375°F (190°C). Coat the insides of an 8×10×5 inch (20×25×13cm) baking pan with the butter.

2. Sift the flour, baking powder, and salt into a medium mixing bowl. Stir in the milk.

3. Pour the batter into the buttered pan and spread the fruit over the top.

4. Place the pan in the oven and bake for 40 minutes or until the top is very brown.

5. Remove the pan from the oven and serve the cobbler with the vanilla ice cream.

Rice Pudding
with Smashed Fruit Topping

This is a nice dessert that uses leftover rice. Serve it warm on a cold night or serve it chilled on a warm night!

Serves	Prep time	Cook time
6	15 minutes	25 minutes

frozen strawberries, raspberries, or blackberries, for topping

2 cups milk of choice

⅓ cup granulated sugar

1 large egg, beaten

1 tsp pure vanilla extract (if using strawberries) or 1 tsp pure almond extract (if using blackberries or raspberries)

2 cups cooked white rice (Calrose or long grain recommended)

powdered sugar

1. Preheat the oven to 350°F (175°C). Thaw the frozen berries.

2. In a medium bowl, combine the milk, sugar, egg, and extract. Mix well. Add the rice and stir until thoroughly moistened.

3. Grease a medium-sized round baking dish (a round dish makes for a nice presentation). Pour the mixture into the dish.

4. Place the dish in the oven and bake for 25 minutes or until the rice is nicely browned and the filling is bubbly.

5. In a large bowl, use a fork to smash the berries until they make a nice pulp.

6. Remove the dish from the oven and transfer the pudding to individual serving bowls. Spoon the mashed fruit over the pudding. Sprinkle powdered sugar over the top before serving.

Note: Calrose rice makes a creamy pudding; long grain rice makes a firmer pudding.

Cranberry & Orange Muffins

These muffins are great for breakfast or with your morning tea.

Yields	Prep time	Cook time
12 muffins	15 minutes	20 to 25 minutes

2 cups all-purpose flour

⅔ cup granulated sugar

1 tbsp baking powder

¾ cup milk of choice

¼ cup vegetable oil

¼ cup orange juice

1 large egg, beaten

1 cup cranberries

⅓ cup chopped walnuts

1 tbsp grated orange peel

1. Preheat the oven to 400°F (200°C).

2. In a large bowl, combine the flour, sugar, and baking powder.

3. In a separate large bowl, combine the milk, vegetable oil, and orange juice.

4. Add the dry ingredients to the wet ingredients. Stir until just moistened. Spoon the mixture into a muffin tin.

5. Place the tin in the oven and bake for 20 to 25 minutes or until a toothpick inserted in the center of a muffin comes out clean.

6. Remove the tin from the oven and serve the muffins immediately.

Freezing Herbs & Vegetables

Freezing vegetables definitely takes less time than canning them, and the flavor, texture, and quality are often superior to the canned product. If you choose varieties suitable for freezing, you'll be happy with the result and have a good supply to last the entire year. If you're a gardener, you understand the importance of choosing the right variety of vegetable for your intended purpose.

Why not put up vegetable combinations while you're dealing with the garden harvest? Once the blanching is done (see Chapter 3), feel free to mix things up. Then, when you want to make a pot of whatever, you don't have to go on an expedition to the freezer. Just pick a bag of carefully labeled goodness and save time.

While you're at it, add some herbs to your preserving repertoire. Herbs give zip to soups, stews, and all kinds of meat dishes. They're also a snap to freeze!

Asparagus

Asparagus is one of the taste treats of spring. Mary Washington is the standard variety and it's great for freezing. Choose young, tender stalks with tips that haven't begun to blossom out. Hold the stalk with one hand and grasp the base of the stalk with the other. Bend the end of the stalk until it snaps. This should leave you with the tenderest part of the stalk to freeze. You can cut the stalk into sections or freeze it whole.

Blanching times are as follows:

- **Small stalks:** 1½ minutes
- **Medium stalks:** 2 minutes
- **Large stalks:** 3 minutes

After blanching and cooling, drain and pack the asparagus in labeled and dated moisture/vapor-resistant freezer bags or containers and freeze.

Beans

Beans have undergone an explosion as far as new varieties coming onto the market. Those that freeze well include Indy Golden (a yellow wax), Aquadulce broad bean, Roma II (Italian), Matador, and Provider (green).

Green Beans

Also called snap beans or string beans, green beans come in a nice assortment of colors, including yellow wax beans and purple beans that turn green while they cook. You can also use Italian beans (flat and wide). Most catalogs will tell you whether a variety is best for freezing or canning. Blue Lake, Emerite, and Green Crop are good varieties. If your variety isn't recommended for freezing and you try it anyway, you're likely to end up with a rather limp, watery product. But they're still fine for soups.

Select green beans that are firm. They should snap when bent. They should be moist and full inside, not hollow (the sign of an old bean). Beans have a bit of a fuzzy surface that tends to trap pieces of leaves and other garden debris. Washing them doesn't always work and you might need to pick these off by hand or use a soft brush.

Snipping tips and tails comes next. You might choose to do this one bean at a time, but that's time consuming and tedious. Instead, try this: Pick up half a dozen beans and arrange them in your hand. Using your kitchen shears, snip off the tips. Turn the beans around, even them up, and snip off the tails. Then snap them into pieces, slice lengthwise, or leave whole.

Wash the beans in cool water and give them a final quality-control check. Next is blanching. The blanching time for green beans and Italian pod beans is 3 minutes (2 minutes for green bean pieces). Then cool, drain, and pack in labeled and dated moisture/vapor-resistant freezer bags or containers and freeze. Beans also can well. (See Chapter 11.)

Lima Beans

Lima beans are treated like peas for freezing purposes. Select firm green pods without yellowing or blemishes. Snip off the blossom tip of the bean and open the bean along the seam. Remove the beans—there are generally three or four per pod. The blanching time is 1 minute for small, 2 minutes for medium, and 3 minutes for large beans. Pack in labeled and dated moisture/vapor-resistant freezer bags or containers and freeze.

Slicing beets with an egg slicer

Beets

Smaller beets, such as Cylindra or Rodina, are the best choice for freezing. Clip off the tops, leaving just enough to cover the beet, and clip most of the root, leaving about an inch. Wash the beets and cook them until tender. Small beets will cook in about 25 to 30 minutes, while bigger ones might take nearly 1 hour.

Remove the beets from the pot and immerse them in cold water to slip the skins. Beets can be frozen whole, as slices, or as cubes. To slice beets, try using your egg slicer. It will give you uniform slices of just the right width. Just be careful to use a sturdy slicer, not one with those fragile metal wires that bend and snap like twigs in the wind.

Broccoli, Cauliflower, Broccoflower & Brussels Sprouts

The only difference between these is that broccoli stalks are also freezable. Blanching and cooling procedures for all are the same and so is the deworming procedure. These vegetables are often hosts for loopers, which are nasty little white or yellow worms. (They won't hurt you, but it's not the hallmark of a good dinner when a guest pulls a yellow worm from their broccoli and then pushes their plate away.)

Loopers are tough to find sometimes, so soaking the vegetables for 30 minutes in a saltwater solution can speed up the process of getting rid of them. Use 4 teaspoons of salt to 1 gallon of water. This kills the worms; they lose their grip and drift to the bottom of the sink.

Broccoli

Choose broccoli with dark green, tightly budded heads. Premium Crop and Arcadia are good choices for freezing. If the heads are beginning to open or yellow, the broccoli is past its prime. You can choose to freeze just the florets or stalks with the florets attached. Wash the broccoli and remove the leaves. The young, tender leaves are quite tasty, similar to collards.

If you're using the stalks as well as the heads, peel the hard outer skin away. Examine the heads carefully for worms. If the heads are overly large and difficult to separate into florets, you can split the stalk down the middle lengthwise and divide the head. Otherwise, break off sections of the head for florets. Blanching time is 3 minutes.

In packing stalks with florets, alternate head first with the stalk end first. You'll get more in the container and won't crush the heads.

Cauliflower & Broccoflower

Broccoflower is a cross between broccoli and cauliflower. It looks like cauliflower, but it's green. Choose heads that are firm and all white for cauliflower and a lime green for broccoflower. Avoid heads with brown or black spots. Cut off the stems, peel away the covering leaves, and break off the florets. Soak the florets in a saltwater solution (4 teaspoons of salt to 1 gallon of water) for 30 minutes to remove worms. Blanching time is 3 minutes. When cool, pack in labeled and dated moisture/vapor-resistant freezer bags or containers and freeze.

Brussels Sprouts

If you find these at a farmers' market, they might still be attached to the stalk. That's good. Leave them that way until you're ready to deal with them. They'll stay fresher and you'll be happier with the flavor.

The heads should be firm and compact. They should be a nice even green without signs of yellowing or drying. Wash and remove the outer leaves. Soak them in a saltwater solution (4 teaspoons of salt to 1 gallon of water) to remove worms. Blanching time is 4 minutes for small heads and 5 minutes for bigger ones. When cool, pack in labeled and dated moisture/vapor-resistant freezer bags or containers and freeze.

Carrots

Carrots are fairly straightforward to freeze. Touchon is a good variety to use. Cut off the tops and any trailing roots. Scrub or scrape, as it suits you, and slice into pieces or lengthwise depending on their future intended use. Blanching time is 2 minutes. When cool, pack in labeled and dated moisture/vapor-resistant freezer bags or containers and freeze. Carrots also can and root cellar well. (See chapters 11 and 23, respectively).

Corn

There are many good varieties for freezing and corn that matures in mid- to late summer is generally better than the earlier-ripening varieties. Corn should be picked and processed quickly. The sugars turn to starch faster than you can blink. If you must hold the corn for a day or so, keep it refrigerated. Ears should be well filled with kernels that shouldn't be overly large. Large kernels generally indicate old, tough corn.

Shucking corn is messy business that's best done outside. It's a good task for children and any other family members who want to help. After the corn is shucked and most of the silk removed, haul the lot inside and give it a good washing under cool, running water. This should help get the last of the silk.

Blanching comes before cutting. Blanch for 4 minutes and then plunge the ears into cold water. When the corn has cooled, use a sharp knife or a corn slicer to cut the kernels from the ears. Don't scrape all the way to the cob. If you aim for about two-thirds of the kernel, you'll get plenty.

Keep the board dry when you're slicing corn off the cob. You'll decrease the chances of the cob slipping out from under your hand and you getting a nasty cut with the knife.

For creamed corn, cut from the cob at about one-half of the kernel and then use a kitchen knife to scrape the milk and the rest of the kernel pieces from the cob.

For corn on the cob, the blanching time is 7 minutes for small ears, 9 minutes for medium ears, and 11 minutes for large ears. Cool the corn quickly and thoroughly to help prevent it from having a "cobby" taste.

Then pack the corn in labeled and dated moisture/vapor-resistant freezer bags or containers and freeze. Corn also cans well (see Chapter 11) and makes excellent relish (see Chapter 16).

Greens

Some plants are grown strictly for their tender leaves (chard, spinach, collards, and kale). Mustard, beets, and turnips are dual-use vegetables, with the leaves being a tasty bonus. Regardless of the type of greens you'll be harvesting, try to pick them early in the morning when they're at their freshest. As the day wears on, the sun's heat causes them to wilt, dry, and otherwise be less than perfect for picking. Whether picking your own or buying at the farmers' market, choose young, tender leaves. It doesn't make sense to struggle with tough, spotted, insect-damaged greens. What you work with is what you'll have available to eat and the freezing process won't improve the quality.

Wash the greens thoroughly in a few changes of cool water. Greens are sand magnets and you don't want to taste grit with your greens. Grits perhaps—but not grit. The easiest way to get the job done is to fill the sink with cool water, add an armful of greens, and swish them around. Repeat this until you don't see any telltale grains at the bottom of the sink. Then drain the greens in a colander. They don't have to be dry; after all, they're headed to boiling water shortly. You just want to remove the excess water that will lower the temperature in the blanching pot.

During the rinsing process, check for yellowed leaves or other blemishes and discard the rejects. You can also trim the stems on chard if your family isn't partial to them.

Next comes blanching. The boiling water canner works very well as a blanching kettle, so fill it two-thirds full of water, put the lid on, and turn the heat to high. When the water has reached a boil, take a double handful of greens and submerge them in the boiling water, using your long-handled slotted spoon to get them totally underwater.

Don't overfill the pot; it will take too long for the water to return to a boil and you'll end up with cooked mush. This is where that old saying "Make haste slowly" bears considering. You're not saving any time by cramming the pot full and you're actually stepping on your own foot if you do so. Replace the lid and wait for the water to boil again. Then set the timer. Blanching times for greens are as follows:

- Beet greens: 2 minutes

- Chard: 2 minutes

- Collards: 3 minutes

- Kale: 2 minutes

- Mustard: 2 minutes

- Spinach: 1½ to 2 minutes (depending on the size of the leaves)

- Turnip: 2 minutes

While the greens are blanching, rinse out the sink and refill it with cold water. You can add some ice cubes to help lower the temperature. When the timer buzzes, remove the lid from the canner (being careful to turn it away from you to avoid a steam burn) and use a slotted spoon, fried food lifter, or whatever handy kitchen utensil will help you lift the greens from the pot and transfer them to the cold water in the sink.

Swish the greens around in the cold water. You want to stop the cooking process as quickly as you can. While the vegetables are cooling down, you can label your freezer bags or freezer containers.

When the greens are sufficiently cool, transfer them to a colander and allow them to drain. You can gently press to remove excess water, but be careful not to mash the greens. When they've drained, transfer them to freezer containers.

When you've blanched the last load, turn off the heat, replace the lid on the canner, and allow it to cool down. Don't move it unless you absolutely have to. Remember, you've got a very big pot of boiling water and it takes time to cool down. As you gain experience, you'll find it easy to develop a good rhythm. You'll have one batch in the blancher, another in the cool water, and another draining.

Kohlrabi

Kohlrabi belongs to the cabbage family, although in this case, we eat the stem rather than the flower. Kohlrabi comes in white, green, and purple varieties. Choose young kohlrabi for freezing. Cut off the tops and the roots. Scrub, peel, and either leave whole or cut into cubes. The blanching time for whole kohlrabi is 3 minutes and just 1 minute for cubes. When cool, pack in labeled and dated moisture/vapor-resistant freezer bags or containers and freeze.

Mushrooms

Select mushrooms without spots or signs of decay. Wash them in cool water. Cut off the stem ends and either leave the mushrooms whole if they're small or cut them into slices or quarters. Mushrooms more than 1 inch (2.5cm) in diameter should be cut or sliced.

To prepare for blanching, mushrooms should be treated to prevent darkening. Use either 1 teaspoon of lemon juice or 1½ teaspoons of citric acid per 1 pint of water. Immerse the mushrooms in the solution for 5 minutes. Then either steam-blanch or sauté. Steam-blanching times are as follows:

- 5 minutes for whole mushrooms

- 3½ minutes for buttons or quarters

- 3 minutes for slices

Steam-blanching takes longer than regular blanching, but if you prefer not to partially cook your vegetables, you might find this is a good alternative. You place a single layer of vegetables in a basket and hold the basket in place over boiling water. The steam generated by the boiling water blanches the vegetables. This method works for broccoli, pumpkin, sweet potatoes, winter squash, and mushrooms.

If you prefer not to steam-blanch, you can sauté the mushrooms in butter until they're nearly done. Then cool them. With either method, when cool, pack in labeled and dated moisture/vapor-resistant freezer bags or containers and freeze. Mushrooms are also suitable for canning. (See Chapter 11.)

Okra

If you love gumbo, you need okra. Wash and cut off the stems. Be careful not to cut too deep and expose the seed cells. Blanch small pods for 3 minutes and large pods for 4 minutes. Cool and pack in labeled and dated moisture/vapor-resistant freezer bags or containers and freeze.

Peas

Peas are a spring vegetable and one of the first to become available at the grocery store or farmers' market. There are three basic types of fresh peas: pod peas, snap peas, and snow peas. All can be frozen. Good varieties of shelling peas include Frosty, Green Arrow, Wando, Mr. Big, and Dakota. Oregon Sugar and Oregon Dwarf Sugar Pod are excellent varieties for pod peas.

If you disliked peas as a youngster, it might be because the ones you were served were tough and mealy. This does the pea a disservice because it's tender and delicious when picked young. The English might be to blame for this travesty because sprouted peas (peas so old that they're actually trying to get about the business of reproducing) are a staple of their cuisine.

Young peas come from young pods. When you're selecting peas for freezing, choose pods that are a uniform green with no yellowing. Pods that are an intense green are generally immature. The peas should be bumps you can feel on the outside but shouldn't be so big that the pod looks like it's stretched to the max trying to hold them in.

You can expect about 7 to 9 peas per pod and opening the pod is simple to do if the peas are at the right stage of ripeness. Hold the pod in your palm and press down on the seam by the tail tip. The pod will pop open and you can then split it the rest of the way down the seam and run your finger along the back of the pod to extract the peas.

You don't need to wash pea pods before shelling them unless they're absolutely filthy for some reason. It just makes them difficult to handle. They get slippery or slimy, and it's quite frustrating. If they're that dirty, it's probably best not to buy them anyhow. If you've grown them, hose them off before bringing them into the kitchen.

Snap peas should snap firmly when bent. If they bend but don't break, look elsewhere. They should be plump and juicy on the inside. Snow peas should be a nice green with barely visible little pea bumps showing through the outer skin.

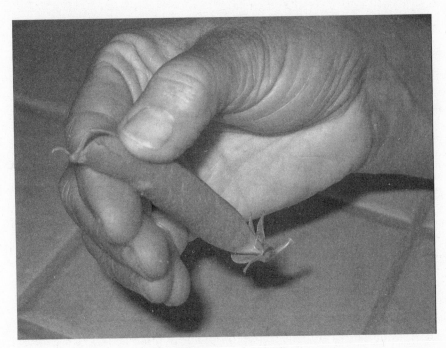

Popping a pea pod

Shelling peas is a great way to get your family involved in home food preservation. You get the job done, and at the same time, you get to talk together—something that's tough to come by these days. The most streamlined process for shelling involves three pans: one to hold the pea pods, one to hold the shelled peas, and one to hold the empty pods. It actually works like a shell game!

While the shelling is going on, get the boiling water canner ready for blanching and the sink ready for cooldown. When the peas have been shelled, place them in a colander or steam basket and submerge them in the boiling water. Replace the lid on the canner and wait for the water to return to a boil. When it's boiling, set the timer for 1½ to 2 minutes depending on the size of the peas. Snow peas and snap peas also blanch for 1½ to 2 minutes.

When the timer buzzes, remove the lid, lift out the basket or colander, and dump the peas into cold water. Swirl the peas around a bit to get them started cooling. When cooled, snare the peas with a slotted spoon and return them to the colander to drain. Then place them in labeled and dated freezer containers or moisture/vapor-resistant freezer bags and freeze. Peas also can well. (See Chapter 11.)

Bell Peppers

Bell peppers are easy to freeze. Look for thick-walled peppers—Orange Sun is a good variety. It starts out green and turns orange as it matures. They require no blanching. Wash the peppers, cut them open, and remove the seeds and pith. Then slice and package them in labeled and dated moisture/vapor-resistant freezer bags or containers. They're a bit soft when thawed, but they do quite well in stir-fries and other recipes calling for cooked peppers.

Summer Squash

There are many varieties of summer squash, although crookneck and zucchini are the most popular. They can be frozen, although they tend to get watery and are best used in soups and stews after thawing.

Select young squash. Don't peel them or you'll end up with mush. Cut off and discard the blossom ends and stalk ends. Slice or cube the squash. Blanching time is 2 minutes. When cool, pack the squash in labeled and dated moisture/vapor-resistant freezer bags or containers and freeze. If you have an abundance of zucchini or other summer squash, consider shredding it for future service in zucchini bread.

Use your food processor or the vegetable shredder. Shred the squash (skin on) and pack it in 2-cup portions in moisture/vapor-resistant freezer bags or containers. (See page 73 for a zucchini bread recipe.)

Freezing Herbs

Get out a cookie sheet! You can freeze herbs using the cookie sheet method. This works especially well for the more tender herbs with a higher water content. Mint, basil, and tarragon do very well frozen. Clip the herbs and place the stems with leaves on the cookie sheet. When they're frozen, pick leaves from the stems and pack the leaves in labeled and dated moisture/vapor-resistant freezer bags or containers and freeze.

Another option is to place herb leaves in ice cube trays, fill the trays with water, and pop them in the freezer. When the cubes have frozen, tip them out of the ice trays and pack them into freezer bags.

Shredded zucchini

Recipes

Frozen vegetables are basic ingredients in most of what we prepare. Treat your freezer as if it were the produce section of the grocery store and get into the habit of seeing what you've got before heading out to the store. Keep your inventory sheet up to date and you won't have to wonder what's in the freezer.

Zucchini Bread

Zucchini bread is moist and dense. When accompanied with a scoop of vanilla ice cream, it's a complete rich, chewy, and flavorful dessert. The squash adds moisture and texture.

Yields	Prep time	Cook time
1 loaf	20 minutes	40 minutes

3 cups all-purpose flour

1 tsp kosher salt

2 tsp baking soda

2 tsp ground cinnamon

½ tsp ground nutmeg

¼ tsp ground cloves

3 large eggs

2 cups granulated sugar

1 cup vegetable oil

2 tsp pure vanilla extract

2 cups shredded zucchini

1 cup cranberries or raisins

1 cup chopped walnuts

1. Preheat the oven to 350°F (175°C).

2. In a large bowl, combine the flour, salt, baking soda, cinnamon, nutmeg, and cloves. Mix well.

3. In a separate large bowl, beat the eggs until light. Add the sugar, vegetable oil, vanilla, and zucchini. Stir well.

4. Add the dry mixture to the wet ingredients. Stir until all the ingredients are moistened. Fold in the cranberries or raisins and the walnuts. Pour the mixture into an 8½×4½×2½ inch (22×11×6cm) loaf pan.

5. Place the pan in the oven and bake for 1 hour or until a toothpick inserted in the center of the loaf comes out clean.

6. Remove the pan from the oven and allow the bread to cool slightly.

Asparagus & Beef Stir-Fry

As with most Asian fare, a majority of the work for this dish is in the preparation, with minimal cooking time. You can use broccoli or bok choy instead of asparagus. Slice them on the diagonal before combining them with the other ingredients.

Serves	Prep time	Cook time
4	45 minutes	10 minutes

½lb (225g) flank, round, or sirloin
  steak, sliced thinly across the grain

1lb (450g) asparagus spears, sliced
  into 1-inch (2.5cm) pieces

4 tbsp peanut oil, divided

1 large slice of ginger

½ tbsp dry sherry

¼ tsp baking soda

½ tsp kosher salt

2 tbsp water

for the marinade

2 tbsp soy sauce

1 garlic clove, minced

1 tsp granulated sugar

1 tbsp cornstarch

½ tsp baking soda

2 tbsp water

1. In a large bowl, make the marinade by combining the soy sauce, garlic, sugar, cornstarch, baking soda, and water. Add the steak to the marinade and allow to marinate for 30 minutes.

2. Heat 2 tablespoons of peanut oil in a wok on the stovetop over high heat. Add the asparagus, ginger, dry sherry, baking soda, and salt. Stir quickly.

3. Add the water, then reduce the heat to medium. Cover the wok and steam for 2 minutes. Transfer the food to a large serving bowl and cover to keep warm.

4. Add the remaining 2 tablespoons of peanut oil to the wok and raise the heat to high. Add the meat and spread it evenly. Don't stir until the meat has slightly browned, about 2 minutes. Flip and allow the other side to brown, about 1 minute.

5. Reduce the heat to low and add the cooked asparagus. Stir to mix well. Remove the wok from the heat. Transfer the beef and asparagus to the large serving bowl. Serve with white or brown rice.

Sweet & Sour Pork

This is a tasty way to use your frozen green peppers.

Serves	Prep time	Cook time
4	25 minutes	10 minutes

4 tbsp peanut oil, divided

1 medium onion, sliced

frozen green pepper slices,
 equivalent to a green pepper

1lb (450g) pork, cut into ½ to ¾ inch
 (1.25 to 2cm) strips

1 tbsp soy sauce

20oz (560g) pineapple tidbits in
 pineapple juice

1 to 2 garlic cloves, smashed

1 tbsp dry sherry

for the sauce

⅓ cup granulated sugar

⅓ cup ketchup

⅓ cup apple cider vinegar

1 tbsp cornstarch

1. In a small bowl, combine the sauce ingredients. Mix well and set aside.

2. Heat 2 tablespoons of peanut oil in a wok on the stovetop over high heat. Add the onion and peppers. Sauté for 2 minutes. Transfer the vegetables to a plate.

3. Add the pork, soy sauce, and the remaining 2 tablespoons of peanut oil. Sauté the pork until crispy.

4. Return the peppers and onions to the wok. Add the sauce, pineapple tidbits, pineapple juice, garlic, and dry sherry. Reduce the heat to low and cook until the sauce has thickened and is bubbly, stirring frequently.

5. Remove the wok from the heat and transfer the sweet and sour pork to a large serving bowl. Serve with white rice.

Ham, Cheese, Potato & Broccoli Casserole

This meal is a good way to use leftover ham, frozen broccoli, seasoned breadcrumbs, and root-cellared potatoes.

Serves	Prep time	Cook time
4	45 minutes	40 minutes

3 cups cooked ham, sliced

2 medium potatoes, sliced (Yukon gold or red Pontiac recommended)

1 (10.5oz [300g]) can of cream of chicken soup

1 (10.5oz [300g]) can of cream of mushroom soup

½ cup milk of choice

1½ cups shredded cheddar cheese

1 small onion, diced

2 cups broccoli florets

½ cup seasoned breadcrumbs

1. Preheat the oven to 350°F (175°C). Spray a 9×13 inch (23×33cm) baking dish with cooking spray.

2. Evenly space the ham slices in the dish to fill the bottom. Place the potato slices on top of the ham.

3. In a large bowl, combine the cream of chicken soup, cream of mushroom soup, milk, cheddar cheese, onion, and broccoli florets. Spread the mixture over the potatoes and top with the breadcrumbs.

4. Place the dish in the oven and bake for 40 minutes or until bubbly and the potatoes test done.

5. Remove the dish from the oven and serve immediately.

Peas & Pearl Onions in Cream Sauce

Depending on your preference, any thickness of white sauce works. This recipe uses a thin sauce. For a thicker sauce, add 1 tablespoon each of flour and butter.

Serves	Prep time	Cook time
4	20 minutes	10 minutes

1 tbsp butter

1 tbsp all-purpose flour

1 cup hot milk of choice

2 cups frozen peas, thawed

2 cups frozen pearl onions, thawed

kosher salt, to taste

freshly ground black pepper, to taste

1. Melt the butter in a large saucepan on the stovetop over low heat. Add the flour, stirring constantly to make a roux. Scald the milk and add to the roux, stirring constantly until thickened.

2. In a large bowl, combine the roux, peas, and pearl onions. Season with salt and pepper to taste.

3. Add the mixture to the saucepan and cook until the sauce has thickened, stirring constantly.

4. Remove the saucepan from the heat and transfer the peas and pearl onions to a serving bowl.

Freezing Meat, Poultry, Seafood & Game

This is by far the most common reason for purchasing a home freezer. These items make the biggest dent in your food budget and also take up a considerable amount of storage space. Buying in bulk can be an excellent cost-cutting decision, and knowing how to properly wrap and store these foods will ensure your purchases are fresh and flavorful when you're ready to use them. In this chapter, we'll consider where, when, and how to purchase and store these high-end items.

Checking Out the Sources

Farmers grow fruits and vegetables, but ranchers grow meat. If you want the best beef, pork, or lamb, go to the places where these products are grown and buy direct. You don't even have to visit them in person because many ranches have a virtual presence. You contract with the grower and make arrangements with the butcher, where you pick up the cut and wrapped meat. Check to see if the supplier is a member of the Better Business Bureau and ask for references from customers who have patronized the supplier.

Another method is to contact your local Cooperative Extension Office for information on 4-H and Future Farmers of America (FFA) county fair livestock auctions. You can support the youngsters who participate in 4-H and FFA by buying an animal they've raised for sale. Again, you make arrangements with the butcher (you'll be provided a list of names in your area) and you'll pick up the cut and wrapped meat there.

Finally, you can contact your local meat locker. It often has special purchase plans for families interested in buying a quarter, half, or whole animal.

The preceding options can help you eliminate the costs incurred with an intermediary. You can also take advantage of buying in bulk at warehouse clubs and stocking up on specials at your local grocers. Allow 1 cubic foot of freezer space for each 35 to 40 pounds of cut and wrapped meat. Not all packages will be uniformly sized and odd-shaped packages might require slightly more space.

Making the Decision

You can buy beef, pork, and lamb as a whole, half (side), or quarter. You can also purchase special cuts (which are more expensive) either wholesale or retail. You might find it economical to go in with someone else and each of you gets a side. If a quarter is sufficient for your family, then you'll want to have a few people involved in the purchase.

The main factor is buying cuts of meat your family enjoys. It doesn't make sense to buy a whole beef, hog, or lamb if your family only likes rump roast, leg of lamb, or spare ribs. However, if your tastes are more varied and you're open to creating new recipes, then buying the whole, side, or quarter might be the logical and economical choice.

When you buy a beef or part of a beef, you'll be getting ground beef made from that one animal, whereas a package of ground beef purchased at the store might have been made from many animals. The meat is done up in big lots. That raises the possibility of contamination as well as lesser-quality meat in that package.

It's a Wrap!

If your meat comes to you via the butcher or meat locker, it will already be wrapped. If you buy in bulk, you'll need to do your own wrapping. It's the same basic procedure as wrapping a gift. Double-wrapping helps prevent freezer burn. This means using moisture/vapor-resistant wrap (usually plastic) and freezer wrap or aluminum foil.

Place the cut of meat in the center of the moisture/vapor-resistant wrap. Wrap the meat securely, pressing out any air. If you're wrapping chops, place a piece of freezer wrap between them so they'll separate more easily when you defrost them. If there's a sharp bone, place a wadded piece of wrap around it. Now you're ready for the overwrap (as shown on page 79), known as the "diaper wrap," for which you'll use freezer wrap or aluminum foil. Secure the ends with freezer tape. Label, date, and freeze.

The other method is the familiar gift-wrapping method. Position the meat in the center of the foil or freezer paper. Bring the two ends of the wrap together over the center of the meat. Fold them together and then fold again, this time bringing them down to the meat and making a tight fit. Secure this with a piece of freezer tape. Fold each other edge by pressing the top layer of wrap toward the bottom and creasing each edge, making a triangle. Bring each folded edge up and secure it with freezer tape. Label, date, and freeze.

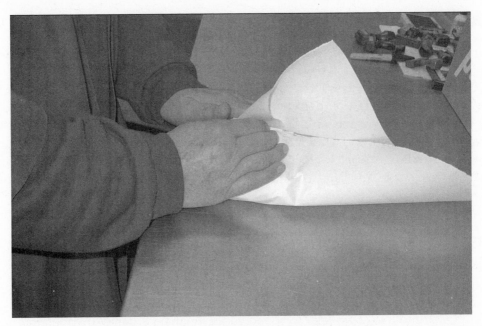

Beginning the diaper wrap for butchered meat

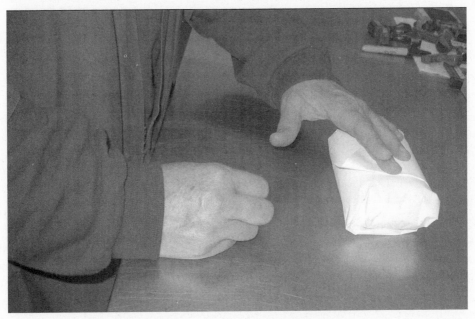

Wrapped meat ready for securing with tape

About Beef

On average, a beef carcass weighs around 600 pounds. That means a side (the hanging weight—or the weight of the beef right after slaughter) is going to be in the vicinity of 300 pounds. It's the carcass after the head, hide, and entrails have been removed. If you buy a whole, half, or quarter beef, you'll be paying hanging weight price. Also, you'll be charged for cutting and wrapping. You might also pay a kill fee. After hanging, the meat is cut, trimmed, and wrapped. You can expect around 25% weight loss during this process. That means you'll wind up with about 350 pounds from a whole and about 225 pounds from a side. You'll get about one-third of this meat in steaks, one-third in ground beef and stew meat, and one-third in roasts.

Coming to Terms

There's some basic terminology that's helpful to know:

- *Beef* refers to meat from fully grown cattle that are about 2 years old.

- *Calf* and *baby beef* refer to young cattle weighing around 700 pounds. They've been raised on milk and grass.

- *Veal* refers to meat from a calf weighing about 150 pounds that's been mostly milk-fed.

A *cow* is a female who's given birth, a *heifer* is a cow in training, a *steer* is a castrated male, and a *bull* is the daddy. Because most purchases involve either a steer or a heifer, they're referred to as "beef" for simplicity's sake. All cattle are initially grazed on grass. Some continue on grass until slaughter, while others are transported to feedlots, where they're finished on grain. This involves feeding them grain, usually free choice, in concentrated rations. The goal is to get them to market weight as quickly as possible.

Consumer Concerns

One important consideration is whether the beef you're purchasing has been exposed to hormones, antibiotics, or additives. Antibiotics are used to prevent or treat disease in cattle. However, there's a specific withdrawal time required before the animals can be legally slaughtered. The Food Safety and Inspection Service (FSIS), which is the public health agency of the US Food and Drug Administration (FDA), conducts random tests to sample tissues from cattle at slaughter to ensure the law is complied with.

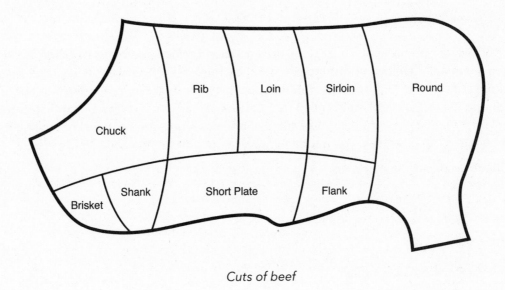

Cuts of beef

Hormones are permitted to be used in cattle to promote efficient growth. Estradiol, progesterone, testosterone, zeranol, and trenbolone acetate might be implanted in the animal's ear. These are time-released over a period of 90 to 120 days.

Melengesterol acetate, used to prevent cows from coming into heat or to improve weight gain and efficient use of feed, is permitted to be used as a feed additive. For additional information, consult the FDA website at www.fda.gov.

Making the Grade

While USDA inspection of all meat is mandatory under the law, grading of the meat is voluntary. A meat plant must pay a fee to have its meat graded. USDA grades of beef are prime, choice, and select. Other grades include standard, commercial, utility, cutter, and canner—cuts used primarily in ground or processed meat products.

USDA prime is the most tender and flavorful cut with the most marbling. *Marbling* is the term given to the white flecks of fat in the muscle. Higher grades have more marbling, which increases the tenderness and flavor of the meat.

Cuts

Beef has four primal cuts: chuck, loin, rib, and round. When you buy a package of beef, you'll generally see two terms: the cut and the product. For example, *chuck roast* or *loin chops*. Chuck and round are less tender cuts; loin and rib are more tender. You might be used to hearing a cut of meat called by a certain name. This is regional and that same cut might be called something else somewhere else. For example, if you're looking for a boneless top loin steak, you might find such a cut also being called a strip steak.

Chuck produces the following:

- Chuck eye roast
- Boneless top blade steak
- Arm roast
- Boneless chuck roast
- Cross rib roast
- Blade roast
- Under blade roast
- 7-bone roast (because it's shaped like the number 7)
- Short ribs
- Flanken-style ribs

Loin produces the following:

- Boneless top loin steak
- Top loin steak
- T-bone steak
- Tenderloin roast
- Porterhouse steak
- Tenderloin steak
- Sirloin steak (pin, flat, round, wedge, boneless)
- Top sirloin steak

Rib produces the following:

- Rib roast
- Rib eye roast
- Rib steak
- Rib eye steak
- Back ribs
- Skirt steak

Round produces the following:

- Round steak
- Top round roast
- Top round steak
- Boneless rump roast
- Bottom round roast
- Tip roast
- Eye of round roast
- Tip steak

The brisket and shank are cuts from the lower chest below the shoulder and the neck; the short plate is located below the primal rib; and the flank is cut from the belly.

In addition, there are the liver, kidneys, heart, and tongue.

The Skinny on Beef

Beef is a marbled meat, which means it contains fat. The leaner the beef, the less fat it has, but fat is what adds flavor and tenderness. The amount of fat in ground beef is based on what cut of meat was ground up. For example, ground chuck or ground round will generally have a lower fat content than ground scraps of various other cuts.

The difference between ground beef and hamburger is simple: Ground beef doesn't contain added beef fat, but hamburger does. The cuts are generally not trimmed of excess fat before grinding and the USDA has established a maximum amount of fat that can be added. Hamburger or ground beef can have *up to* 30% fat by weight. That means it's 70% meat.

Hamburger and ground beef can have seasonings added but not water, phosphates, extenders, or binders. Both must be labeled according to federal standards and carry a USDA-inspected label. Even though most ground beef is made and packaged at the local grocery store, it still must comply with federal labeling laws on fat content.

What About Color?

Freshly cut meat is purplish. That bright red color you see on prepackaged meats comes about when oxygen reacts with pigments on the surface of cut meat. Underneath the surface, the meat is generally a gray-brown color. If the meat in the package is more gray or brown than red, spoilage could be underway. Dispose of the package.

If you're buying ground beef at the market, you might be surprised to find the meat seems to be bicolored. This often occurs when less fresh (but still not past the *use by date*) is carefully covered with fresher, pinker-colored meat. It makes a more attractive presentation and you're none the wiser until you open it up. You'll often encounter this if you buy ground beef in those plastic tubes that are convenient to use and store but conceal the contents. One safety note: Because ground beef has more surface area exposed to air than solid cuts of beef, there's greater opportunity for bacterial contamination. This is why you should never eat raw or partially cooked ground beef and never use it to make jerky.

Pork

An average hog at butchering time weighs about 250 pounds. The hanging carcass will weigh about 180 pounds. From that you can expect to get about 145 pounds of meat for the freezer. Pork can give you fresh cuts in addition to smoked cuts. The smoked cuts will give you hams, ham hocks, and bacon. Bacon comes from the side of the hog.

Many people have the hind quarters smoked for hams and leave the forequarters for roasts. A whole ham is rather large, and unless you have an army to feed, it will probably do best if you have it cut in half. From this you can have smaller hams, ham slices, and ham cubes (for stir-fry, kabobs, or casseroles and soups).

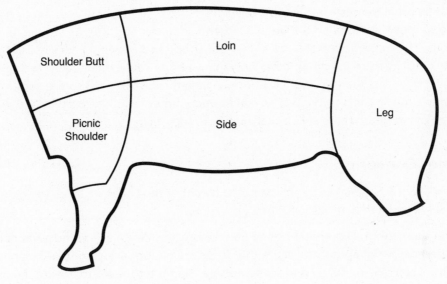

Cuts of pork

Shoulder produces the following:

- Shoulder butt, roast, steak

- Blade steak

- Boneless blade Boston roast

- Smoked arm picnic, picnic shoulder

- Smoked hock

- Ground pork for sausage

Loin produces the following:

- Boneless whole loin

- Loin roast

- Sirloin roast

- Tenderloin

- Chops

- Country style ribs

If you're partial to roasts and chops, consider purchasing a whole bone-in or boneless loin cut. The loin is located between a leg and shoulder and weighs around 15 to 18 pounds. The center loin gives you center-cut chops and roasts, and it's usually a good value. You'll need to tell the butcher how many chops you want in each package and how thick you like them—generally about an inch thick works well so the chops don't dry out when you're cooking them. This can happen if they're either too thin or they need to be cooked to death to be safe because they're too thick.

Consumer Concerns

All pork sold in stores has been inspected by either the USDA or by state agencies with standards equal to that of the federal government.

Antibiotics might be given to hogs to treat or prevent disease. A withdrawal period is required before slaughter to ensure the drugs are no longer present in the animal's system. The FSIS conducts random samples at slaughterhouses to ensure the law is complied with.

No hormones are permitted in the raising of hogs.

Making the Grade

The grading process is simple for hogs: They're either acceptable or utility. Acceptable quality is the only grade sold in retail stores.

Lamb

Lamb refers to a sheep that's less than 1 year old. Mutton refers to an animal older than 1 year. A lamb at slaughter weighs about 125 pounds and yields about 60 to 75 pounds of meat. Lamb doesn't take up a lot of space in the freezer. You'll need about 2.5 cubic feet of freezer space per lamb.

Lambs aren't very difficult animals as far as cuts of meat are concerned. Shoulder, leg, shank, rack, and loin are referred to as the "primal cuts." Unlike pork, where you can have bone-in or boneless hams, lamb legs keep the bone. This gives added flavor.

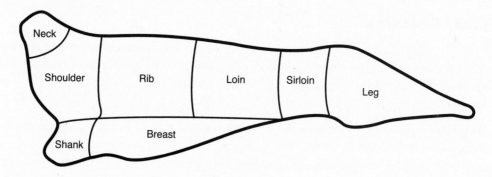

Cuts of lamb

Shoulder produces the following:

- Shoulder roast (bone-in or boneless)
- Shoulder steaks and chops
- Shoulder arm chop
- Ground lamb or cubes
- Shoulder blade chops (bone-in or boneless)

Leg produces the following:

- Leg roast or steaks
- Cubes or strips
- Ground

The *neck* is the cut above the shoulder. The *rib* is the cut directly behind the shoulder and next to the loin. It produces rib roast and rib chops.

The *breast* is the cut below the rib and loin. The *loin* is the cut between the rib and the leg. It produces chops and roast.

The *sirloin* is the cut directly behind the loin. The *shank* is the cut below the shoulder and below the leg.

When packaging lamb for the freezer, trim the excess fat from chops and other smaller cuts, but don't remove the *fell*—the covering on the outer fat—from roasts or legs.

Consumer Concerns

All lamb is USDA inspected. Antibiotics might be given to prevent or treat disease in lambs. A withholding period is required before the animals can be slaughtered. This is to permit the antibiotics to pass through the animal's system. The FSIS conducts random samples at slaughter to ensure compliance with the law.

The synthetic hormone zeranol is permitted to be used as an implant to promote efficient growth in feedlot lambs. The hormone is time-released over a 30-day period. A withholding period of 40 days is required before the animals can be slaughtered. This withholding period allows the hormone to pass out of the animal's system.

Making the Grade

There are five grades of lamb: prime, choice, good, utility, and cull. Prime and choice are the grades you'll usually find at the meat counter. Prime has more marbling than choice, but both grades give good-quality meat.

Game Meat

The essentials of preparing game meat for the freezer involve strict cleanliness and cold temperatures. Game meat must be cooled to a temperature below 40°F (preferably 32°F to 36°F) within 24 hours after harvesting to prevent souring or spoiling. For more information, HGIC 3516, "Safe Handling of Wild Game Meats," can be downloaded from hgic.clemson.edu/factsheet/safe-handling-of-wild-game-meats.

Poultry

We generally think of chicken or turkey when the word "poultry" comes to mind; however, the term is a bit broader and also includes domestic duck and goose.

Coming to Terms

The local market might have a super sale on poultry (chicken usually) and you want to stock up while the price is right. Poultry is also usually a good buy at food warehouse outlets. However, is the bird fresh or frozen? It could be tough to tell.

The USDA allows any poultry that's never been below 26°F to be labeled as fresh. It could be worth your while to ponder that for a moment in light of the fact that freezing occurs at 32°F. Frozen or previously frozen refers to poultry that's been held at 0°F. If the poultry has been stored at temperatures between 0°F and 25°F, the label doesn't have to tell you. You can ask the butcher or the person behind the counter, but they probably won't know. So the truth is that you won't know if your bird was killed yesterday or 2 weeks ago.

Consumer Concerns

Antibiotics might be used to prevent disease. They also might be used to increase the poultry's efficient use of feed. This means the grower wants the most return in poundage of bird per pound of grain consumed.

Chickens that have been given antibiotics must be held from slaughter until the antibiotics have passed out of their system. FSIS conducts random samples of poultry at slaughter to ensure compliance.

No hormones are permitted to be used in the raising of poultry.

Bacterial Concerns

Bacteria associated with poultry can include *Salmonella enteritidis*, *Staphyloccus aureus*, *Campylobacter jejuni*, and *Listeria monocytogenes*. To deal with these bacteria, the FSIS has approved the use of an antimicrobial agent called *trisodium phosphate* (TSP). It's either sprayed in a dilute solution on chickens or is used as a dip at slaughter to reduce levels of bacteria that might be present. TSP falls into the category of substances generally recognized as safe by the FSIS.

Irradiation

Irradiation exposes foods to radiation or radiant energy in order to control bacteria that might be present. This practice was approved for poultry by the USDA in 1992. Irradiated chicken sold in stores must carry the international symbol for radiation and must bear the statement "treated with irradiation" or "treated by irradiation." To learn more about how irradiation works, consult www.fsis.usda.gov/food-safety/ safe-food-handling-and-preparation/food-safety-basics/irradiation-and-food-safety-faq.

You can also help protect your family's health by observing strict cleanliness when preparing poultry. Keep poultry juices from coming in contact with other foods. Avoid cross-contamination by cleaning and sanitizing your cutting board and utensils after working with poultry—and wash your hands frequently. (See Chapter 2 for more.)

Freezing Poultry

You can freeze chicken in the grocery store bag, but it's better to clean the bird and repackage it. You'll see that the bag contains an absorbent diaper that's been placed in the vicinity of the bird's posterior. This is to sop up the moisture that develops during the chilling process after slaughter. There might be a slight pink tinge to this liquid, but it's mostly water. Birds that aren't bled thoroughly after slaughter are condemned and don't continue on the path to your grocery store.

Remove the bird from the bag and dispose of the paper diaper. Clean and rinse out the cavity to remove all the internal organs. Find a plastic bag big enough to accommodate the bird—be sure there aren't any holes in it—and put the bird inside. You're going to force out nearly all the air.

Dip the bag into a dishpan filled with enough water to nearly cover the bird, but don't let the water seep into the bag. Rest the bird on the bottom of the dishpan and gently press the air out of the bag, starting from the bottom and working up. Then secure the top with a twisty tie. After this, pack the bird in a moisture/vapor-resistant freezer bag and label, date, and freeze. Package the heart, gizzard, and liver separately.

It's easy to turn a whole chicken into parts. It's generally a lot cheaper than buying select parts, and cutting and/or boning a chicken takes only a few minutes. All you need is a sharp knife and a little patience. YouTube has an excellent video on the process: www.youtube.com/watch?v=sy6P3E84Dqs.

Game Birds

Game birds, such as quail, duck, dove, and pheasant, should be field dressed and gutted as quickly as possible. They should then be cleaned thoroughly and cooled immediately. Removing excess fat from wild duck and goose helps prevent the bird from turning rancid. They're frozen in the same manner as poultry. For additional information on processing game birds, consult HGIC 3515, "Safe Handling of Game Birds," which can be downloaded from hgic.clemson.edu/factsheet/safe-handling-of-wild-game-birds.

Freezing Seafood

Seafood is always best served fresh, but proper freezing techniques can give you an excellent product. For best results, freeze seafood as soon as possible after the catch. Fish is highly perishable.

Fish

The initial procedures are the same, regardless of how you'll eventually freeze the fish. Begin by washing it in cool water. Then scale it and remove the entrails, gills, head, and fins. After that, you can freeze the fish whole or cut it into steaks (cutting across the body) or fillets (making lengthwise slices). Small fish are usually frozen whole.

You can then wrap the fish in moisture/vapor-resistant freezer wrap and place it in a labeled and dated freezer bag or you can choose to first glaze the fish. This helps prevent drying out and flavor loss. To glaze it, simply place the fish on a cookie sheet and put the sheet in the freezer. When the fish is solidly frozen, remove it from the freezer and dip the fish into cold water for about 20 seconds. The water will freeze; this is called an "ice glaze." Return the fish to the freezer to ensure the water has frozen. Then you can wrap the fish for freezing as previously described.

See Appendix D for recommended freezer storage times for different varieties of fish.

Freezing Smoked Fish

Wrap the fish for freezing as soon as they come out of the smoker. You can apply a thin coat of olive oil to help retard oxidation and moisture loss during freezing. Wrap as previously discussed.

Freezing Roe

Roe is the term for fish eggs. Wash the roe in cool, running water. Pack it in freezer containers, leaving ¼ inch (0.5cm) of headspace. Label, date, and freeze.

Scaling

Fish tend to be slippery, so you don't want to use a sharp knife for scaling. If the fish slips out of your grasp, you could end up with a nasty cut. A regular dinner knife or even a teaspoon works fine. Grasp the fish by the tail, and with the knife blade or edge of the spoon, scrape down the fish. You might find this easier to do under cool, running water.

Gutting

To gut the fish, make a knife cut along the length of the fish's belly. Then spread the sides apart, scoop out the innards, and rinse the cavity thoroughly.

Removing the Head, Backbone & Fins

Off with their heads! This is the easy part. Just slice through above the collarbone. You can give the backbone a sharp smack on the counter or cutting board. That will break it so it will be easier to ease out.

You might be accustomed to clipping off the fins with your kitchen shears, but this leaves some bones still stuck to the fish where the fins are attached. It's better to make a small incision alongside each fin and lift it out.

Crab

Crab purchased from the store has already been cleaned. That is to say, it's been scrubbed to remove sea debris. If you've harvested your own crab, you'll find it much easier to scrub it after you've killed it. That brings us to the pressing issue of how to humanely kill a crab.

Tossing a crab into a pot of boiling water has been the traditional method of killing and cooking a crab, but it's not all that humane. If you've used this procedure, you might have noticed that occasionally one or more of the legs will detach from the body. That's caused by the crab going into shock. If the water isn't at a rolling boil, it's neither a quick nor a pleasant death.

So what do you do if you're concerned about this? You'll need a screwdriver. Really. Using tongs, flip the crab onto its back. You'll notice a triangular flap near the base of its shell. Lift the flap, and with a sharp motion, jam the screwdriver all the way in and then shove it toward the head. Immediately, fluid will be released and the crab will be dead.

You can then scrub it before putting it in the hot water.

An alternate method involves using the sharp edge of a kitchen counter (that's not in danger of breaking if you whack something against it) or some other sturdy, solid-cornered object. Wearing thick gloves, grasp the crab so the midsection going from top to bottom straddles the sharp edge. Raise the crab and then quickly bring it down on the counter edge so the body separates into two equal halves. The crab is now dead. This requires a bit of practice and also a bit of nerve. Many folks who go crabbing use this method at the dock.

It might help to keep in mind that a crab doesn't have an evolved nervous system—just a mess of ganglia—so it doesn't experience pain the way a human does. Still, it doesn't hurt to be humane.

Boil the crab for 10 minutes, remove it from the water, and allow it to cool. You don't need to pick it before freezing. When cooled, pull off the legs and the back shell. Then remove the gills and entrails. Wrap the prepared crab securely in moisture/vapor-resistant freezer wrap and then put it into a labeled and dated freezer bag. Be sure to press out as much air as you can. Crab has a relatively short freezer life, about 3 months.

Lobster

Freezing lobster uncooked is the best choice and it's also the best way to kill the lobster humanely. Put the lobster in a bowl or pan that's freezer friendly and place it in the freezer. After about 20 to 30 minutes, remove the lobster, which by now is very, very cold and not feeling much of anything. Then insert a sharp knife into the abdomen just behind the smallest set of legs and push down hard. Slice from this point up through the head and sever the body in half. Then rinse the lobster, wrap it in moisture/vapor-resistant freezer wrap, place it in a freezer bag, label, date, and freeze. Freezer life is about 4 to 6 months.

Scallops

Scallops are frozen after being shucked. To shuck a scallop, hold the scallop in the palm of your hand and then insert a thin, strong knife into the slit close to the hinge. Twist. Don't force it open or you'll damage the muscle. Open the shell carefully and cut the muscle free from the top shell. Cut the muscle free from the bottom shell and remove the white scallop meat. Rinse in cool, running water to remove all the sand, pieces of shell, and viscera.

You can place the scallops on a cookie sheet and freeze them. When the scallops are frozen, remove them with a spatula, place them in moisture/vapor-resistant freezer bags, label, date, and freeze. Freezer life is about 4 to 6 months.

Shrimp

You can freeze shrimp raw or cooked and also in the shell or shelled. They'll keep longer in the freezer if you remove the heads but keep the shells on.

Shrimp you buy at the store might be shelled and deveined. If not, you'll need your kitchen shears. Hold the shrimp in one hand so the swimmerets are on the bottom. Insert the shears into the sand vein and cut straight up so the shell comes off. The bluish vein will peel right off. Then rinse the shrimp in cool, running water. You can freeze shrimp by the cookie sheet method. Then package them in labeled and dated moisture/vapor-resistant freezer bags or containers and freeze. Freezer life is about 4 to 6 months.

Clams & Mussels

You can freeze these shellfish in their shells, but you might be disappointed with the result. There's air inside those shells and your shellfish can dry out.

Clams and mussels should be shucked before freezing. Wash them in cool, running water. Holding the shell in the palm of your hand, insert a thin, sturdy knife into the slit. Twist. Then remove the meat. Clean out the contents of the stomach. Rinse the meat. Place the clams or mussels on a cookie sheet and place them in the freezer until they're frozen solid. Then remove them from the freezer and dip them in cold water. Return them to the freezer until they're firmly frozen. Then repackage them in moisture/vapor-resistant freezer bags. Label, date, and freeze. Freezer life is about 4 to 6 months. Freezer life for clams in the shell is only about 1 month.

Oysters

The same principle that applies to clams and mussels applies to oysters. If you freeze them in the shell (and you can), prepare to be disappointed with the result. Air trapped in the shell can cause the oysters to dry out. In any case, frozen oysters lack the mystery and sensuous nature of their raw counterparts. You'll probably want to use them in dishes where they're just one of several ingredients, as they tend to be a bit tough.

It's best to shuck them. First, be sure you're dealing with live oysters. If the oyster is live, the shell will be closed or it will close immediately when you handle it. Discard dead oysters. Then rinse the live oysters in cool, running water. You'll need your oyster knife because these shells are tough to crack. You'll also need a pan to work over because you definitely want to capture the liquor that's inside the shell.

Insert the oyster knife into the dip by the hinge. Twist. This severs the hinge. You might need some help getting the oyster knife into the shell. A wooden mallet works well to help you make the first incision. Then slide the knife around the oyster until you've cut the abductor muscle that controls the shell movement. Take off the upper half of the shell and cut the muscle away from the bottom half of the shell. Remove any pieces of shell from the oyster.

Place the shucked oysters and liquor in a freezer container, leaving ½ inch (1.25cm) of headspace. Label, date, and freeze. You can also freeze the oysters in ice cube trays. Add water to cover them and then pop them in the freezer. When they've frozen, repackage them in moisture/vapor-resistant freezer bags. Label, date, and freeze. Freezer life is about 4 to 6 months.

Recipes

Meat, poultry, and seafood often provide the structure around which meals are built. With a freezer full of choices, the possibilities are endless.

Perfect Scallops

The secret to this dish it to not overcook the scallops.

Serves	Prep time	Cook time
6	5 minutes	4 minutes

2 tbsp butter   24 large sea scallops

1. In a large skillet on the stovetop over medium heat, melt the butter. Add the scallops and sauté on one side for 2 minutes. Flip and sauté the other side for 1 to 1½ minutes. They'll be a light golden brown on both sides and still moist inside.

2. Remove the skillet from the heat. Serve the scallops over pasta with a marinara or teriyaki sauce.

Karen's Lasagna

This is a favorite Italian meal. Serve it with crusty bread and a green salad.

Serves	Prep time	Cook time
6	25 minutes	30 to 40 minutes

1 (10oz [285g]) package of frozen spinach

1 tbsp olive oil

1 to 2 garlic cloves, minced

1lb (450g) hamburger

6 lasagna noodles

1 quart thick spaghetti sauce (not marinara)

1 quart reduced-fat cottage cheese

1 small brick of mozzarella cheese (8 to 10oz [225 to 285g])

grated parmesan cheese

1. Preheat the oven to 350°F (175°C). Thaw the spinach and squeeze out any excess moisture. Set aside to drain.

2. Heat the olive oil in a skillet on the stovetop over medium heat. Add the garlic and hamburger. Cook until the hamburger has browned. Drain the excess fat. Add the spaghetti sauce and mix thoroughly.

3. Fill a large pot two-thirds full of water. Place the pot on the stovetop over high heat and bring the water to a boil. Add the noodles and cook for 2 minutes. Drain.

4. Spoon half the meat and sauce mixture into the bottom of an 11×15 inch (28×38cm) baking dish. Place 3 lasagna noodles lengthwise on top of the meat sauce. Spread the cottage cheese evenly over the noodles.

5. Pull the spinach apart and place it on top of the cottage cheese. Slice the mozzarella about ¼ inch (0.5cm) thick and arrange the slices in rows on top of the cottage cheese and spinach. Place the remaining 3 noodles over this layer.

6. Spoon the rest of the meat sauce over the noodles, covering thoroughly. Sprinkle the parmesan cheese over the top.

7. Place the dish in the oven and bake for about 30 to 40 minutes or until bubbling. Remove the dish from the oven and allow the lasagna to rest for about 10 minutes.

Beef Stroganoff

This is an easy version of the classic dish. Don't skimp on the cut of beef. You want a rich, flavorful piece of beef.

Serves	Prep time	Cook time
6	25 minutes	15 minutes

pasta of choice

1 rib eye steak, approximately 1½lb (680g), cut into 2-inch (5cm) strips

2 tbsp vegetable oil, divided

2 tbsp salted butter

1 garlic clove, minced

8oz (225g) white mushrooms, thickly sliced

1 medium white or yellow onion, sliced

1 tbsp Worcestershire sauce

1 tbsp Dijon mustard

1½ cups beef stock or beef broth

2 tbsp all-purpose flour

¾ cup sour cream

kosher salt, to taste

freshly ground black pepper, to taste

1. Prepare the pasta according to the package directions.

2. Divide the beef into two batches. Heat 1 tablespoon of vegetable oil in a large skillet on the stovetop over high heat. Add half the beef strips and quickly sear on both sides. Keep the skillet on the heat, but transfer the beef to a large bowl and set aside.

3. Add the butter, garlic, mushrooms, onion, Worcestershire sauce, mustard, and the remaining 1 tablespoon of vegetable oil. Sauté for 2 to 3 minutes or until the onions are translucent and the mushrooms have browned.

4. Add the flour and mix thoroughly. Reduce the heat to low. Gradually add the beef stock or broth, stirring constantly until the mixture has thickened. Fold in the sour cream.

5. Return the beef strips and any juices from the bowl to the skillet. Stir until everything has blended, about 2 minutes. Remove the skillet from the heat.

6. Serve the beef over your favorite pasta.

Curried Chicken

Curry is flavorful, hearty, and an excellent way to use up leftover chicken or other poultry. You can also use tuna. This dish is excellent with rice and chutney.

Serves	Prep time	Cook time
4	15 to 20 minutes	10 minutes

¼ cup butter or olive oil

1 apple, pared and diced

1 cup cooked carrots, diced

1 to 2 small onions, chopped

1 garlic clove, minced

1 stalk of celery, diced

2 tbsp all-purpose flour

1 tsp kosher salt

1 tsp curry powder

½ tsp ground mustard

1½ cups chicken broth or stock

1 bay leaf

½ cup milk of choice

3 cups chopped cooked chicken

1. In a large saucepan on the stovetop over medium heat, melt the butter (or heat the olive oil). Add the apple, carrots, onions, garlic, and celery. Sauté for 5 minutes or until the onions have become transparent.

2. Add the flour, salt, curry powder, ground mustard, chicken broth or stock, and bay leaf. Heat to boiling.

3. Add the milk and chicken. Stir well.

4. Remove the saucepan from the heat. Remove and discard the bay leaf. Serve the curried chicken over rice. Top the dish with coconut flakes, cashews, raisins, and candied ginger.

Chicken Breasts in French Dressing Sauce

Prepping a chicken dish doesn't get much easier than this,

Serves	Prep time	Cook time
4	10 minutes	45 minutes

¼ cup finely chopped onions

1 tsp Worcestershire sauce

3 tbsp light brown sugar

1 garlic clove, minced

8oz (225g) French salad dressing

kosher salt, to taste

freshly ground black pepper, to taste

4 chicken breasts

1. Preheat the oven to 350°F (175°C). Spray a large baking dish with cooking spray.

2. In a large bowl, combine the onions, Worcestershire sauce, brown sugar, garlic, French salad dressing, salt, and pepper.

3. Dip each chicken breast in this mixture, turning the chicken over to evenly coat. Place the chicken in the dish and pour any remaining mixture over the top. Cover the dish with aluminum foil.

4. Place the dish in the oven and bake the chicken for about 45 minutes or until the chicken is no longer pink inside.

5. Remove the dish from the oven. Serve the chicken with rice and a colorful salad.

Breaded Pork Chops

Breadcrumbs help seal in all the flavorful juices of the pork chops.

Serves	Prep time	Cook time
4	5 minutes	40 minutes

4 pork chops of your desired
 thickness, trimmed of fat

1 large egg

1 cup seasoned breadcrumbs

1. Preheat the oven to 350°F (175°C). Spray a large baking dish with cooking spray.

2. In a large bowl, beat the egg. Add the breadcrumbs to a separate large bowl.

3. Dip each pork chop in the egg and then dip into the breadcrumbs, turning the chop over to evenly coat. Place the chops in the dish.

4. Place the dish in the oven and bake for 30 minutes or until the chops are no longer pink in the middle.

5. Remove the dish from the oven and serve the pork chops with cranberry applesauce, oven-browned potatoes, and a green vegetable (for color).

Freezing Dairy Products, Eggs & Baked Goods

7

Here's where you can really take advantage of bulk sales, supermarket specials, and day-old bakery markdowns. The secret to keeping these items fresh is proper packaging and storage. If you're freezing your own baked desserts, doubling or tripling your batches will make good use of your freezer space.

Dairy Products (plus Margarine & Cooking Oil)

Freezing will change the consistency or texture of many dairy products and these items also have a shorter freezer life. Previously frozen dairy products are generally fine in cooking but might not be satisfactory for table use. Freezing eggs and dairy in amounts required for specific recipes will give you a head start on holiday baking and you won't have to run out to the store for last-minute supplies.

Butter & Margarine

Whenever you see these on sale, grab as much as you can for freezing. You don't need any special packaging. Just transfer the waxed boxes to your freezer, being careful to spread them around until they're thoroughly frozen. Then stack them up.

If you buy solid 1-pound (450g) blocks as opposed to quarters, you can cut them into usable portions first. Wrap with moisture/vapor-resistant plastic wrap and then place them in plastic freezer bags.

Unsalted butter has a shorter freezer life than salted butter, and margarine and whipped spreads don't freeze well because they tend to break down. Some brands work better than others, so if you prefer margarine to butter, you'll need to experiment.

Cooking Oil

Cooking oil can be frozen. If you don't use it often enough to keep it from going rancid, freezing is a good way to preserve it for when you do need some. Freeze in smaller containers than the big bottles or jugs. The oil will be cloudy when it's frozen, but it will return to its clear state after it thaws.

Milk, Cream, Yogurt, Buttermilk & Homemade Ice Cream

Quarts or half-gallons of milk, including low and nonfat, are the best sizes for freezing and you can freeze them in their original containers. Gallons take too long to freeze and too long to thaw. You'll need to pour out about 1½ inches (3.75cm) of milk from the container to allow adequate headspace. Then close the container securely before placing it in the freezer. Pasteurized and homogenized milk might separate out their water content during freezing. When the milk has thawed, use a whisk to thoroughly remix it. You might be disappointed in the texture for drinking, although it certainly won't hurt you.

Heavy cream with 40% or more butterfat freezes well, although if you're planning on using it for whipping, you might be disappointed in the volume. Plan to use it in cooking or in coffee. To freeze, heat to 170°F (75°C) for 10 minutes. Add ⅓ cup of granulated sugar to each quart, pour into rigid freezer containers, and leave 1 inch (2.5cm) of headspace. Seal, label, date, and freeze. (Note: Half and half doesn't freeze well.)

One way to solve the decreased volume problem is to sweeten and whip the cream first. Then haul out your cookie sheet and drop dollops of the whipped cream on it, being sure to keep some space between each dollop. Place it in the freezer, and when frozen, remove the dollops and place them in a labeled and dated plastic freezer bag.

Changes in texture are the biggest problems when you freeze sour cream, buttermilk, or yogurt. They might not be palatable for consumption because they get grainy and can separate. But they're fine for cooking.

Homemade ice cream doesn't freeze well. It gets grainy. Commercially processed ice cream has milk solids and gelatin included in the ingredients, and these are responsible for its smooth texture.

Cheeses

Hard and semihard cheeses tend to crumble when thawed, and this can make slicing frustrating. If you're going to use them in cooking (such as for mac and cheese), then this isn't a problem. Think smaller chunks—about ½ pound (225g)—when freezing cheese. Creamed cottage cheese can separate after thawing and get mushy. Ricotta, processed cheeses, cheese sauce, cream cheese (again, better when used in cooking), and cheese dips freeze well. Cheese sauces and processed cheeses also tend to freeze well.

Eggs

Eggs keep very well for up to 1 month in the refrigerator, but if you want to freeze some with specific recipes in mind, you can prepare whole eggs, egg whites, and egg yolks. You can't freeze eggs in the shell because expansion while freezing will rupture the shell. The following directions are based on using a dozen eggs.

- **Whole eggs:** Mix whites and yolks thoroughly with a fork, being careful not to whip air into the mixture. If you'll use them in desserts, add 1 tablespoon of granulated sugar. If you'll use them in cooking, add ½ teaspoon of kosher salt. This keeps them from getting grainy or gummy. Strain through a colander, food mill, or sieve to get a good uniform texture. Pour into rigid freezer containers and leave ½ inch (1.25cm) of headspace. Seal, label, date, and freeze. (Note: 3 tablespoons of beaten whole eggs is the equivalent of 1 egg.)

- **Yolks:** Separate the eggs and stir gently. It's best to have certain recipes in mind as you freeze these. If you'll be working with something sweet, add 2 tablespoons of granulated sugar. If the yolks are destined for a recipe that's more for a main course, add 1 teaspoon of kosher salt. Strain and pour into a rigid freezer container, leaving ½ inch (1.25cm) of headspace. Seal, label, date, and freeze. (Note: 1 to 1½ tablespoons of yolks equals 1 egg.)

- **Whites:** Separate the eggs and stir gently. Strain and pour them into a rigid freezer container, leaving ½ inch (1.25cm) of headspace. Seal, label, date, and freeze. (Note: 2 tablespoons of egg whites equals 1 egg white.)

Pour the required tablespoons of a mixture into each cell of an ice cube tray and place the tray in the freezer. When frozen, transfer the cubes to a plastic freezer bag and seal, label, date, and return them to the freezer. When your recipe calls for an egg, thaw the proper cube and you're ready to go!

Breadcrumbs

Breadcrumbs come in handy for all kinds of dishes—from toppings to breading mixtures—and you can make your own breadcrumbs for a fraction of the store price. This is an excellent, thrifty use for end slices or for bread that's gone too stale for regular use. You can use all kinds of leftover baked goods to make crumbs for use in toppings. Don't limit those crumbs to just stale breads.

There are a couple of ways to go about making breadcrumbs: One is messy and the other isn't. The messier method involves dumping chunks of stale bread into your food processor or blender, whirring away, and then pouring the crumbs into gallon freezer bags. There are a few problems with this method:

- You might find that the bread on the bottom has pulverized into fine dust, while the chunks still floating on top are way too big to be called crumbs.

- You've got to clean the processor or blender container, which means soap and water and drying.

- Some crumbs might end up on the kitchen counter or on the floor—and that means more cleaning.

The less messy and more convenient way consists of just one step and involves putting chunks of stale bread into a gallon freezer bag. Don't overfill it; you want plenty of room inside. Close the freezer bag, place it on a bread board or other hard surface, get out your rolling pin, and roll away. You can move the contents around easily to be sure you're getting to all the bread chunks. When you're satisfied with the result, press out as much air as you can, seal the bag, and put the labeled and dated freezer bag in the freezer. No mess and nothing to clean up.

Quick Breads

Quick breads encompass an entire family of baked foods that includes loaves, scones, biscuits, muffins, waffles, popovers, cornbread, spoon bread, and donuts. Quick breads differ from regular breads in that they don't use yeast to make them rise—a process that takes some time. Instead, they use either baking powder or baking soda to achieve loft while they're baking in the oven. In fact, they begin to rise as soon as the baking soda or powder meets the liquid in the recipe. They rise again while they're baking and this is why you'll see the "double acting" note on the baking powder label.

If you've run out of baking powder, you can make your own! Mix 2 teaspoons of cream of tartar and 1 teaspoon of baking soda. If you decide you want to make a big batch, add 1 teaspoon of cornstarch before you store the baking powder in a covered container in your pantry or cupboard.

Quick breads are also quick to assemble and that's an excellent reason to make double or triple batches when you're in the mood to bake. You can eat one batch and freeze the others for future use.

Preparing for the Freezer

When your quick breads have thoroughly cooled, wrap them securely in plastic wrap and then wrap them again in aluminum foil. This double wrapping keeps them fresh. You can then put them in labeled freezer bags if you're so inclined, but the double wrap should be sufficient.

If you wrap them in foil first, you'll find that little pieces of the foil might stick to the quick breads and picking them out is a chore. You'll probably only do it that way once!

Using Quick Breads

Everything about quick breads is quick, including their storage life. For best quality, you'll want to keep them in the freezer for 2 to 4 months. Muffins max out at about 3 months. After that, they'll still be safe to eat, but you might be disappointed in their texture and flavor.

Remove them from the freezer and allow to thaw at room temperature while still wrapped. If you slice them before they're entirely thawed, you'll reduce crumbling.

For biscuits or muffins, preheat the oven to 350°F (175°C) and warm them for 15 to 20 minutes. If you want to use the microwave, it takes about 10 to 15 seconds per biscuit or muffin (depending on size).

Pie Crusts & Pastries

Pie crusts are generally made with flour, salt, fat, and water, although you'll find a wide selection of different possibilities as you rummage through cookbooks. The secret to a good pie crust is gentle, quick handling and ice water. General procedures for making pie crusts are similar and you'll find a recipe for one at the end of this chapter.

Baked pie crusts and pastries yield better results when frozen than unbaked ones. First of all, they'll freeze more quickly than the raw dough because they're less dense, and the quicker you can freeze something, the better the quality will be. They also keep twice as long in the freezer as their unbaked counterparts.

You can freeze pie crust dough, but it will need to be thawed (but still chilled) before you can roll it out. Overhandling the dough will make the crust tough. Freeze dough in portions that will make either an 8-inch (20cm) or 9-inch (23cm) pie, whichever suits your pie pans. You can keep it rolled up or flatten it to size. The flattened dough will thaw more quickly.

Wrap each piece individually with moisture/vapor-resistant plastic wrap. You can stack flattened crust dough to save freezer space. Place a sheet of freezer wrap between doughs to help you remove each one easily. Place in gallon freezer bags and press down to expel the air before sealing.

Another potential difficulty with freezing unbaked crusts is that the water in them will expand during the freezing process and will play havoc with the crust. If you must freeze pie crusts unbaked, use a fork to prick a few holes in the bottom and sides. The key is in secure packaging so your crusts don't fall apart during storage. They have a relatively short freezer life (about 2 months), so be sure to use them while they're at their prime.

Foods get jostled around in the freezer even in the best storage conditions, so you'll be happier with your pie crusts if you freeze them in their pans—that's why saving those aluminum pie pans you accumulate from purchases at the grocery store comes in handy.

Graham cracker crusts also freeze well—with or without pie filling. Add the whipped cream when you're ready to serve.

Wrap each pie crust securely with plastic wrap that's moisture- and vapor-resistant and then wrap in aluminum foil. You can stack pies to save storage space. An optional final step would be placing your wrapped crusts in labeled gallon freezer bags for extra cushioning. To further protect the crusts, you can stack them inside a box, which will keep other foods from intruding on their space.

Pies

There are two schools of thought about freezing fruit pies. One school says to always bake the pie first. The other school says to never bake the pie first. You might have to experiment to discover your preference.

You can freeze filled, unbaked pies, but the crust will most likely get soggy if you do. It's best to lightly coat the top and bottom crusts with shortening to help prevent sogginess. Don't cut air holes in the top crust until you're ready to bake the pie. Add an additional 1 tablespoon of flour or tapioca or 1 teaspoon of cornstarch to fruit pie fillings before freezing. This keeps them from boiling over as they bake.

However, baking pies first will keep the crust flakier. Fruit pies, including mincemeat, freeze very well, as do vegetable pies (pumpkin and squash) and pudding pies. Many standard cookbooks recommend you allow 1 pint of filling for an 8-inch (20cm) pie, although this can be really skimpy. If you like flat pies, that might be enough. However, if you prefer pies with some height, especially if you're dealing with fruit pies, 1 quart of fruit filling will give you a substantial, eye-appealing pie.

If you want to freeze a lemon meringue pie, freeze a lemon pie and add the meringue just before serving. Meringue tends to separate from the edge and adhere to the wrap. Custard and cream pies don't freeze well. Chiffon pies will need to include ½ cup or more of whipped cream if they're to freeze satisfactorily.

You'll take unbaked pie crusts directly from freezer to oven. Don't allow the crust to thaw before baking. Bake at 425°F (220°C) for 12 to 15 minutes or until light brown.

To bake frozen, filled pie crusts, remove the freezer wrap and place the unthawed pie on the bottom shelf of an oven that's been preheated to 450°F (235°C). Bake for 15 to 20 minutes and then reduce the heat to 375°F (190°C) for about 45 minutes or until the pie is done.

To serve a frozen, baked pie, allow the pie to thaw at room temperature if you're serving it cool. This would include pudding pie, pumpkin or squash pie, and chiffon pie. If you want to serve the pie warm, as in fruit pie, remove the freezer wrap, and transfer the pie directly to an oven that's been preheated to 400°F (200°C), and bake for 30 to 40 minutes or until thoroughly warmed.

Cobblers & Crisps

Fruit cobblers are a baked fruit with a pastry base or topping (like dumplings), while crisps are a baked fruit with a crumble/streusel topping. Both are sweet. See Chapter 4 for a fruit cobbler recipe that's rich and flavorful. In both desserts, fruit is either sliced (as in peaches and apples) or left whole (in the case of berries).

Both of these desserts can be made with frozen fruit, with frozen berries working especially well. Don't thaw the fruit. Just take out what you need, arrange it in a baking dish, add the pastry batter or the streusel mix, and bake.

Streusel adds texture and crunch to crisps and coffee cakes. A basic streusel topping consists of flour, sugar, and butter. There are many variations on this, so consider adding oats, substituting brown sugar for white granulated sugar, and adding a bit of ground cinnamon (for apples) or ground nutmeg (for peaches). You'll mix the butter with the sugar, a process called *creaming*. Then add the flour, spices, and oats. Work it with your hands until you've got a good mix of small- and medium-sized clusters. Sprinkle this on top of your fruit and bake.

To freeze cobblers and crisps, cover the baking dish securely with aluminum foil and place it in the freezer. When frozen, remove it from the freezer and remove the dessert from the dish. Wrap the frozen dessert in moisture/vapor-resistant plastic wrap and then wrap it in foil. Label, date, and return it to the freezer.

When you're ready to use these desserts, remove them from the freezer and remove the wrap. Return them to a baking dish and bake unthawed at 375°F (190°C) for 40 to 60 minutes or until thoroughly warmed.

Crackers, Potato Chips, Cookies & Cookie Dough

These are easy to freeze. Commercial products can be frozen in labeled and dated plastic freezer bags. Home-baked cookies can be frozen in either plastic freezer bags or rigid freezer containers. Place a sheet of waxed paper or freezer paper between rows of cookies to keep them from sticking together.

When you're ready to use the cookies, remove them from the freezer and allow them to thaw in their packaging for about 15 to 20 minutes.

You can also freeze cookie dough. If you're making refrigerator cookies, just roll up the dough, wrap it in moisture/vapor-resistant plastic wrap, and then place the rolls in freezer bags. Label, date, and freeze.

Freezing unbaked drop cookies is similar to freezing berries. Drop the dough onto a cookie sheet and place it in the freezer. When the dough has frozen, transfer it to freezer bags. Label, date, and return the dough to the freezer. When you're ready to bake, transfer the cookies to a cookie sheet and bake (without thawing) at 400°F (200°C) for 10 to 15 minutes.

An alternative to freezing individual drop cookies is freezing the batch of dough all at once. Just pack it into the appropriate-sized freezer container and label, date, and store. When you're ready to bake cookies, thaw the dough at room temperature. When you can insert a teaspoon into the dough, it's ready to use. Drop by teaspoonfuls onto a cookie sheet and bake according to your recipe.

Recipes

Finding the perfect pie crust recipe can be difficult, but this first recipe comes close. The remaining recipes can fill your house with different wonderful aromas.

No-Fail Pie Crust

This might seem too good to be true, but it's as close to perfect as you can get! There's practically no way to make this come out any way less than wonderful.

Yields	Prep time	Cook time
Two 9-inch (23cm) crusts	10 minutes	8 to 10 minutes

1 cup shortening

2 cups all-purpose flour

1 tsp kosher salt

6 tbsp ice water

1. Preheat the oven to 400°F (200°C).

2. Add the flour and salt to a medium bowl. Cut the shortening into the flour mixture until well mixed. Add the water 1 tablespoon at a time while continuing to mix.

3. Roll out the pie crust and place it in a pie pan. Bake for 8 to 10 minutes. Remove the pie crust from the oven and place it on a wire rack to cool.

Applesauce & Raisin Loaf

This is a quick bread that's rich and flavorful. Freezing small loaves will get you extra mileage out of one recipe. These also make great gifts.

Yields	Prep time	Cook time
1 loaf	15 minutes	1 hour

½ cup golden raisins

½ cup regular raisins

½ cup butter

1 cup granulated sugar

1 tsp pure vanilla extract

1 large egg

1½ cups applesauce

1 cup walnuts, broken into pieces

¾ tsp apple pie spice

2 cups all-purpose flour

2 tsp baking soda

1. Preheat the oven to 350°F (175°C). Spray a medium loaf pan with cooking spray.

2. To a small saucepan on the stovetop over low heat, add the golden and regular raisins, and cover with water. Simmer for about 5 minutes or until the raisins are plump. Remove the saucepan from the heat and drain the water.

3. In a large bowl, cream the butter and sugar. Add the vanilla extract, egg, applesauce, walnuts, apple pie spice, flour, and baking soda. Mix until well combined. Pour the mixture into the loaf pan.

4. Place the pan in the oven and bake for 1 hour or until a wooden skewer inserted in the middle of the loaf comes out clean.

5. Remove the pan from the oven and allow the loaf to cool for 5 to 10 minutes. Remove the loaf from the pan and place on a wire rack to finish cooling.

Easy Cheesy Biscuits

Tired of the same old same old? Put a bit of a bite into your biscuits with the addition of a bit of parmesan or cheddar cheese

Yields	Prep time	Cook time
about 2 dozen	10 minutes	10 to 12 minutes

2 cups all-purpose flour

1 tbsp plus 1 tsp baking powder

½ tsp kosher salt

2 tbsp shortening

¾ to 1 cup milk of choice

¾ cup grated parmesan or cheddar cheese

1. Preheat the oven to 400°F (200°C). Spray a baking sheet with cooking spray.

2. In a medium bowl, combine the flour, baking powder, and salt. Mix well.

2. Cut the shortening into the flour mixture. Add the milk and cheese. Mix lightly. Depending on the humidity and a host of other things, the amount of milk varies. The goal is a nice, workable dough that's not too stiff.

4. Transfer the dough to a floured surface. Gently roll out the dough until it's about ¾ inch (2cm) thick.

5. Use a cookie cutter or a glass jar to cut the dough into rounds. Place the rounds on the baking sheet.

6. Place the sheet in the oven and bake for about 10 minutes or until lightly browned.

7. Remove the sheet from the oven and serve the biscuits immediately.

Shortcakes

Strawberry season brings memories of homemade shortcakes topped with sweetened whipped cream. The dessert cups sold in the stores can't compare with these. This is a variation of the standard biscuit recipe.

Yields	Prep time	Cook time
1 dozen	10 minutes	12 to 15 minutes

2 cups all-purpose flour

1 tbsp plus 1 tsp baking powder

½ tsp kosher salt

2 tbsp granulated sugar

3 tbsp shortening

¾ cup milk of choice

1. Preheat the oven to 450°F (235°C). Spray a baking sheet with cooking spray.

2. In a medium bowl, combine the flour, baking powder, salt, and sugar. Mix well.

3. Cut the shortening into the flour mixture. Add the milk and lightly mix.

4. Transfer the dough to a floured surface. Gently roll out the dough until it's about ¾ inch (2cm) thick.

5. Use a large biscuit cutter (or a wide-mouth canning ring) to cut the dough into rounds. Place the rounds on the baking sheet.

6. Place sheet in the oven and bake for about 12 minutes or until lightly browned.

7. Remove the sheet from the oven and serve the shortcakes immediately.

Cranberry & Cherry Scones

The trick to good scones is keeping the butter cold—as close to frozen as possible—throughout the mixing process and moving quickly to complete the recipe steps. This puts the "quick" into quick bread.

Yields	Prep time	Cook time
8	20 minutes	15 minutes

2 cups all-purpose flour

1½ tsp baking powder

½ tsp baking soda

½ cup granulated sugar

¼ tsp kosher salt

¼ cup dried cranberries

¼ cup dried cherries

½ cup sour cream

1 large egg

½ tsp almond extract

½ cup frozen butter

1. Preheat the oven to 400°F (200°C). Spray a baking sheet with cooking spray.

2. In a large bowl, combine the flour, baking powder, baking soda, sugar, salt, cranberries, and cherries.

3. Use a grater to add the butter. Quickly mix the ingredients.

4. In a small bowl, combine the sour cream, egg, and almond extract. Add this mixture to the flour mixture.

5. Transfer the dough to a floured surface and work with your hands until the dough forms a ball. The dough will be quite stiff.

6. Pat the dough into a ¾-inch-thick (2cm) circle. Cut the circle into 8 triangles and place the triangles 1 inch (2.5cm) apart on the baking sheet.

7. Place the sheet in the oven and bake for about 15 minutes or until lightly browned.

8. Remove the sheet from the oven and serve the scones immediately.

Freezing Convenience Foods & Meals

8

Saving time, saving money, and making the most of your freezer space are just a few reasons why freezing your own convenience foods makes sense. Concerned about the high sodium and high fat contents of commercially prepared foods? Learn to make your own and eat healthfully!

There are two ways to approach freezing complete meals. You can think in terms of single servings or make plans to feed a crowd. You can also freeze baby foods as well as foods with special dietary requirements in mind.

This is a chapter with nothing but recipes!

Stocks for Soups & Stews

Take a look at the nutritional information of canned or packaged soups or soup mixes and the sodium content is enough to make you put the item back on the shelf. Even with reduced-sodium offerings, you still might not be satisfied.

Another problem with commercially available soups is that there's frequently much too little of the ingredient you're looking for. So if you're tired of fishing for those little bits of beef in the canned beef stew, there's a simple remedy: Use your own recipes, freeze them, and have them on hand. They'll keep in the freezer for up to 1 year.

Soups and stews start with stock, and there are just four basic types. If you haven't made stock before, you're in for a treat. It's very easy, it freezes beautifully, and, best of all, you control what goes into it.

Meat Stock

Meat scraps (with the fat trimmed off) and bones are a wonderful foundation for meat stock. After you've finished up the roast, chops, or ribs, toss the bones into a stock pot (actually a large saucepan whose size will be based on how much meat and how many bones you have), add cold water to cover, and turn the heat to medium. Usually about 5 pounds (2.3kg) of meat and bones make a good stock.

You can roast the bones in a hot oven (400°F to 450°F [200°C to 230°C]) for 30 minutes first. This makes for a darker, richer stock. You can also crack the bones if you're dealing with a shank or leg.

Then add the following:

- 1 bay leaf

- 1 to 2 garlic cloves, minced

- 2 carrots, chopped into 2- to 3-inch (5 to 7.5cm) pieces

- 2 white onions, chopped into quarters

- 2 celery stalks, chopped into 2- to 3-inch (5 to 7.5cm) pieces (include the leaves)

- 2 tomatoes, chopped

- 1 tablespoon each of whichever of the following dried herbs you're partial to: parsley, sage, rosemary, thyme, basil, and oregano

- 1 tablespoon of ground black peppercorns

Bring to a boil, then reduce the heat to low and simmer for 4 to 6 hours. Skim off the gray scum that forms on top of the water during the early cooking. Add water as necessary to keep everything covered.

Remove the pot from the heat. Pour the contents through a colander, capturing all the liquid stock in a large bowl or saucepan. Dispose of the solids. Place the stock in the refrigerator until all the fat has congealed at the surface. Skim off the fat.

Pour the stock into labeled and dated freezer containers or ice cube trays and freeze. If you're using ice cube trays, after the stock has frozen, package the cubes in labeled and dated moisture/vapor-resistant freezer bags. Return them to the freezer.

Poultry Stock

After everyone has picked through the Thanksgiving turkey carcass and there aren't any more meals to be coaxed out of it, it's time to make stock. (This also applies to carcasses from chickens, ducks, and geese.)

Save the necks and backs (freeze them until you've got a good supply), gather up the bones, and you're good to go.

Including poultry livers, hearts, and gizzards in stock is a matter of personal taste. They tend to have a stronger flavor, so if your family doesn't want to eat them when they're first cooked, it's probably best to omit them from the stock.

You'll want about 5 pounds (2.3kg) of poultry bones and parts for the stock pot. Then add the following:

- 1 bay leaf
- 1 large white onion, chopped into quarters
- 2 large carrots, chopped into 2- to 3-inch (5 to 7.5cm) pieces
- 2 celery stalks (plus the leaves), chopped into 2- to 3-inch (5 to 7.5cm) pieces
- 1 to 2 garlic cloves, minced
- 1 tablespoon of ground black peppercorns

Add water to cover. Turn the heat to medium and bring to a boil. Then reduce the heat to low and simmer for 4 to 6 hours, adding water as needed to keep everything covered. Remove the pot from the stove and pour the ingredients through a colander, capturing the liquid stock in a bowl. Dispose of the solids.

Place the bowl in the refrigerator to chill. When the fat has congealed at the top, skim it off. Pour the stock into labeled and dated freezer containers or into ice cube trays. When frozen, pack the cubes into labeled and dated moisture/vapor-resistant freezer bags. Return them to the freezer.

Seafood Stock

Rich, creamy chowders get their aroma and flavor from hearty seafood stocks. Whenever you serve fish with bones, save the bones along with whatever scraps are left over. You can also use shellfish shells, such as crab, lobster, or shrimp.

Fish stock is easy to make. You'll need about 5 pounds (2.3kg) of shells, bones, and scraps. Place the fish parts in a large stock pot, cover with water, and add 1 to 2 teaspoons of kosher salt. Turn the heat to medium and bring to a boil. Then reduce the heat to low and simmer for 1 to 2 hours. Skim off any foam that gathers around the edges of the top of the pot. Remove the pot from the stove and pour the ingredients through a colander with small holes, capturing the liquid stock in a bowl. Dispose of the solids. Strain the stock carefully and thoroughly. Small fish bones can cause serious damage if swallowed.

Place the bowl in the refrigerator to chill. When the fat has congealed at the top, skim it off. Pour the stock into labeled and dated freezer containers or into ice cube trays. When frozen, pack the cubes into labeled and dated moisture/vapor-resistant freezer bags. Return them to the freezer.

Vegetable Stock

This isn't for the faint of heart. You're going to clean out the refrigerator and dump every vegetable that's still edible into the stock pot. This also means using potato peels, beet skins, corn cobs, and just about anything else you can dredge up.

If you're aiming for a generic vegetable broth without any distinguishing flavor or aroma, consider doing without cabbage and cauliflower. Also, a little broccoli and a few tomatoes go a long way. They're powerful.

Add all the vegetables to the stock pot, cover with water, and add 1 bay leaf, 1 to 2 minced garlic cloves, and 1 tablespoon of ground black peppercorns. Add other herbs or spices to suit your tastes (for example, parsley, thyme, and basil). Turn the heat to medium and bring to a boil. Then reduce the heat to low and simmer 1 to 2 hours, checking frequently to be sure the vegetables aren't sticking to the bottom of the pot. Add water as you need to. Then remove the pot from the heat and strain all the ingredients through a sieve. This will catch the bay leaf!

Casseroles

There's certainly no end to the possibilities when it comes to creating casseroles. Casseroles are generally entire meals cooked and served in the same ovenproof dish. They're great time-savers and are convenient ways to use up odds and ends of foods that might otherwise be consigned to the refrigerator until they either dry up or turn green and have to be discarded.

Consider mini-casseroles. Use those microwavable divided dinner trays you might have accumulated and create your own customized meals. Wrap them in moisture/vapor-resistant freezer wrap and then wrap in aluminum foil or place in a large freezer bag. Label, date, and freeze them, and you've got dinner ready for the microwave.

For the price of an additional baking dish, you can save yourself some time and make more economical use of your oven. Cook your favorite casseroles in batches—eat one now and freeze the rest for later. Here are some tips:

- Slightly undercook a casserole destined for the freezer. This keeps the food from becoming overdone while it's reheating. If you'll be including pork or chicken, be sure to allow enough time to finish cooking it thoroughly before you're ready to serve it.

- Add breadcrumb topping as you're preparing the casserole for reheating. Freezing breadcrumbs on top of the casserole will cause them to get soggy.

- Add cheese toppings as you're preparing the casserole for reheating. Freezing cheese makes it dry and brittle.

- If you're freezing a stew, leave the potatoes out. Cook them when you're ready to reheat the stew and add them just before serving. This keeps them from turning to mush.

- Think small! Freeze lemon zest and orange rind for puddings and pies. Crumble leftover bacon and freeze it for topping baked potatoes. Little bits of this and that come in handy as long as they're easily marked and readily accessible in a specifically designated section of the freezer.

- If you're freezing a pasta dish, such as lasagna or mac and cheese, make sure the sauce completely covers the noodles. This prevents freezer burn and tough, dried-out pasta.

To prepare casseroles for the freezer, line the casserole dish with heavy-duty aluminum foil, then add the ingredients and bake. When the food is done, remove it from the oven and allow it to cool. Then place the covered casserole in the freezer. When frozen, you can lift the food out of the dish, wrap it securely in foil, and then return it to the freezer. Casseroles have a relatively short freezer life of about 3 months.

When you're ready to use the casserole, remove it from the freezer, unwrap it, and place the casserole back in the dish. Place it directly in the oven at 350°F (175°C) to reheat. No need to thaw it first.

Meat Loaf & Fish Loaf

To freeze these unbaked, prepare them according to your favorite recipes. Don't top with bacon strips if that's your usual *modus operandi*. Add them when you're ready to cook the loaves. Line a loaf pan with heavy-duty aluminum foil, then place the food in the pan and cover it with foil. Place it in the freezer. When frozen, pop the loaf out of the pan, wrap it securely in moisture/vapor-resistant freezer wrap, overwrap with foil, label and date it, and return it to the freezer. Freezer storage time is 1 to 2 months. When you're ready to use a loaf, remove it from the freezer, unwrap it, place it in a loaf pan, cover it with plastic wrap, and allow it to thaw overnight in the refrigerator. When thawed, remove the plastic wrap, add bacon strips if desired, and bake as usual.

To freeze a baked loaf, wrap it securely in moisture/vapor-resistant freezer wrap and wrap in aluminum foil. Label and date it. When you're ready to use it, allow it to thaw in the refrigerator. Serve it cold or remove the foil and freezer wrap, place the loaf in a loaf pan, cover it loosely with foil, and reheat it in a 350°F (175°C) oven. Always check before you consign a foil-wrapped dish to the oven to be sure you didn't first use plastic wrap and then finish off with foil.

Gravies & Sauces

You can freeze leftover gravy for future use. Pour it into labeled and dated freezer containers and store it in the freezer. It will keep well for 3 to 4 months. When you're ready to use the gravy, remove the desired containers from the freezer and allow them to thaw in the refrigerator overnight. You can also take the gravy directly to the saucepan, turn the heat to low, add 1 tablespoon or so of water to keep it from scorching, and place the lid on the pot. Check frequently and stir to keep the ingredients from scorching or sticking. If you find that the gravy is watery or has separated, grab your whisk and set to work to regain a smooth consistency.

Fried Chicken

Fried foods tend to lose crispness during the freezing process. Still, if you've got leftover fried chicken, it's worth your while to freeze it. You can also partially fry foods and then freeze them. When you're ready to use them, you might find that the final frying process crisps them up nicely. To freeze, wrap them in moisture/vapor-resistant freezer wrap and then either wrap in aluminum foil or place in labeled and dated freezer bags. Freezer storage life is 1 to 3 months.

Cooked Meats & Poultry

Trim as much fat as possible before freezing cooked meats. The fats can turn rancid and this will have a bad effect on the meat. It's best to keep the pieces as large as possible. This reduces the amount of surface area contacting the air and helps prevent freezer burn. For poultry, remove the meat from the bones to help it cool more quickly.

You can choose to freeze cooked meat with or without gravy. Freezing it with gravy helps keep it from drying out, although this makes using a freezer bag difficult. The gravy slops all around, and as the package freezes, it can take on some rather strange shapes if you don't store it flat. Freezer storage life is 2 to 4 months.

When you're ready to use the meat, remove it from the freezer, put it in a bowl to prevent any seepage from spreading across your other foods, and allow it to thaw in the refrigerator. Depending on the size of the package, it might take anywhere from a few hours to overnight. When thawed, reheat the meat in the microwave or in a saucepan on the stovetop over low heat.

To freeze stuffing, cool it quickly in the refrigerator and pack it into rigid freezer containers. Label, date, and freeze it. Storage life is about 1 month. To use, allow it to thaw in the refrigerator. Add to a saucepan with 1 tablespoon of water and reheat over low heat, fluffing occasionally. Keep an eye on it to prevent it from sticking or scorching.

Baked Beans

Baked beans freeze well, provided you slightly undercook them and use bacon, ham, or salt pork sparingly in their preparation. Prepare by your favorite recipe (you'll find a good one at the end of Chapter 20), then cool quickly in the refrigerator and pack in rigid freezer containers. Be sure the beans and any meat are covered with liquid. Leave appropriate headspace. Label, date, and freeze them. Freezer storage life is about 6 months. When you're ready to use the beans, remove them from the freezer and allow them to thaw in the refrigerator. Heat them in a saucepan over low heat.

Pizza

Prepare your favorite recipe, but don't bake it. Wrap it securely in moisture/vapor-resistant freezer wrap and then wrap in aluminum foil. Label and date it. Freezer storage life is about 1 month. When you're ready to use the pizza, remove it from the freezer and place it directly in a preheated 450°F (235°C) oven. Bake for 20 minutes or until the crust is browned, the cheese has melted, and the toppings are cooked.

Sandwiches

If soggy sandwiches don't appeal to you, you're not alone. You can take some steps to prevent this. First, freeze the loaf of bread. Place it in the freezer in its store wrap or wrap a homemade loaf securely in freezer wrap and place it in the freezer.

While the bread is freezing, make the spreads or prepare the meats. Ham, chicken, bologna, tuna (not prepared as tuna salad), and other cuts of lunch meats freeze well. Peanut butter and jelly also does fine. So do cheese spreads or cream cheese with nuts and olives or bits of fruit.

When the bread has frozen, remove it from the freezer and spread a thin layer of butter or margarine across each slice (except in the case of PB&J sandwiches). Then make the sandwiches. Avoid mayonnaise or other oil-based ingredients, such as salad dressings. Wrap them securely in freezer wrap, then place them in labeled and dated freezer sandwich bags. Freezer storage life is about 1 month.

When you're ready to use the sandwiches, remove them from the freezer and allow to thaw in their wrap. Add lettuce or tomato slices just before eating. No soggy bread!

Vegetable Stir-Fry Mix

Make your own vegetable stir-fry mix. You'll have the ingredients you like and won't have to pay grocery store prices. Slice fresh vegetables to your own specifications and follow the blanching times recommended in Chapter 5. Suggestions include carrots, green beans, broccoli, peas, cauliflower, or summer squash. (Peppers don't need blanching.) Cool and package them in labeled and dated moisture/vapor-resistant freezer bags.

Potatoes (White or Sweet)

Raw potatoes don't freeze well, but they do root-cellar beautifully. (See Chapter 23.) Cooked potato dishes are easy to freeze and having a variety of these on hand will help you assemble a tasty and nutritious meal on short notice.

Baked

For baked potatoes, scrub large potatoes to remove all the dirt. Then make a couple of incisions into the skin to allow the steam to escape and to prevent the potato from exploding in the oven. This is a mess you don't even want to contemplate having to clean up.

Rub lightly with butter or shortening, place them on an oven rack, and bake them at 350°F (175°C) until a knife inserts easily all the way through. Cool quickly in the refrigerator. Then wrap them in labeled and dated moisture/vapor-resistant freezer wrap. Overwrap with foil and freeze. Freezer storage life is 1 to 2 months.

When you're ready to use the potatoes, remove them from the freezer and transfer them to the oven. Reheat at 375°F (190°C) until heated through. Baked potatoes left at room temperature have resulted in cases of botulism. Always store foods in the refrigerator if you're not going to be able to get to them within 2 hours.

Stuffed

Bake large potatoes. When done, cut them in half lengthwise and scoop out the white portion. Mash with milk, salt, pepper, shredded cheese, and sour cream. Return the mixture to the hollowed-out potato. Place the potatoes on a cookie sheet and place them in the freezer. When frozen, remove them from the cookie sheet and wrap them in moisture/vapor-resistant freezer wrap. Then wrap in freezer bags or aluminum foil. Freeze. Freezer storage life is 1 to 2 months.

When you're ready to use the potatoes, remove them from the freezer and transfer them to the oven. Reheat at 375°F (190°C) for 30 to 40 minutes or until thoroughly heated.

Hash Browns

For cubes: Scrub and peel, then cut the potatoes into ½-inch (1.25m) cubes. Blanch them in boiling water for 5 minutes. Drain and cool. Package the cubes in freezer bags or freezer containers.

For shredded: Scrub and cook whole potatoes with the skins on until almost done. Cool, peel, and grate them with a vegetable grater or food processor. Package them in freezer bags or freezer containers.

Freezer storage life is 1 to 3 months.

French Fries

Scrub the potatoes, peel them, and cut them into strips. Blanch them using either the oven or oil method.

Oven method: Place the strips on a cookie sheet. Brush them with melted butter or margarine and bake them at 450°F (230°C) until the potatoes begin to brown, occasionally turning the potatoes with a spatula. Remove the potatoes from the oven and allow to cool. (You can cool them quickly in the refrigerator.) Package them in freezer bags or freezer containers.

Oil method: Blanch the strips in oil heated to 370°F (190°C) until the strips are tender but not browned. Remove them from the oil and drain. Allow to cool or cool them quickly in the refrigerator. Package them in freezer bags or freezer containers.

Freezer storage life is 1 to 3 months.

Potato Patties

This is a good use for leftover mashed potatoes. Make patties and season them with salt and pepper as desired. Place the patties on a cookie sheet and place it in the freezer. When frozen, remove the patties with a spatula and stack them in a freezer container. Place a sheet of freezer wrap between the patties to prevent sticking. Freezer storage life is 1 to 3 months.

When you're ready to use the patties, remove them from the freezer and bake them on a greased cookie sheet at 375°F (190°C) until heated through.

Canning

Canning is an economical way to store foods—from fruits and vegetables to meats and combination dishes. It's not as complicated as you might think. If you can follow a recipe, you *can* can! In this part of the book, you'll learn safe canning procedures and follow specific research-based recipes designed to please.

Canning Basics

History tends to repeat itself. We're used to having plenty of everything available in our stores, but as this book goes to press, we're dealing with less-than-full shelves at the grocery stores, supply chain delivery problems, and a realization that the lessons of the Great Depression have been largely forgotten. Since March 2020, when the COVID-19 pandemic changed our lives, we've developed a new appreciation for the thriftiness of our ancestors, and there has been a renewed interest in self-sufficiency and a desire to ensure there will always be enough food for our families.

Many people rediscovered gardening—as a remedy from the enforced isolation *and* as a means of ensuring their families would have a good supply of healthy food. However, when those thousands of folks began harvesting their crops, the demand for canning jars, rings, and lids caused massive shortages. It's not just food that we put by; it's also the supplies that allow us to preserve that food.

When the traditional brands of lids became scarce, some foreign companies were quick to capitalize on the need. Unfortunately, many of these products don't meet the standards for production set by the US government. Cheaply made products, originating in China, have flooded the market and, as evidenced by the photo on the next page, aren't safe to use. Other companies in the US have stepped up to the task and produced good-quality items. You can see the difference for yourself in the other photo. The takeaway is to know where your products are made and choose wisely when your health is at stake.

*Buckled canning lids
made of inferior material*

*Well-made canning lid
that fits properly*

The Science Behind Canning

We have the French to thank for the invention of canning—a candymaker by the name of Nicholas Appert to be precise. When Napoleon Bonaparte offered a prize of 12,000 francs to whoever could develop a system for keeping food fresh for his soldiers, Appert bit. It took him years, but he learned that if he put food in a bottle and kept out as much air as possible through a system of corks, wires, and sealing wax and then heated the foods in hot water, the food didn't spoil.

Napoleon was impressed with Appert's canned (or bottled) soups, fruits, vegetables, and gravies and awarded him the prize. The army got to eat unspoiled food and the food canning industry was born. In 1811, Appert published a book explaining his process. Since that time, much has changed, but the basic principles remain: sealing jars to keep out air and then heating the contents of the jars to destroy microorganisms that can cause the food to spoil. Appert didn't know why the process worked—that discovery was to come later.

Nicholas Appert would be quite impressed with the innovations and equipment now available to the home food preserver. We now know the science behind why his process worked and how to use heat and acidity to create a safe product.

Appert is now considered the father of canning and his birthday, October 23, is National Canned Foods Day. It's a good day to put up some canned food and honor Nicholas and his contribution to the home arts. (Incidentally, Appert is also the inventor of peppermint schnapps!)

Supplies & Equipment for Canning

Gathering the essential supplies for canning is a bit like organizing a scavenger hunt: some things you already have and some you'll need to get. If you're new to home canning, the process might seem rather overwhelming and perhaps a bit frightening. It's important to relax. Take a deep breath and approach canning with curiosity, enthusiasm, and a touch of respect. It's called a process because that's exactly what it is. Just take one step at a time, follow the directions carefully, and you'll end up with a safe, delicious product.

Boiling Water Canner

Without a doubt, this is the most versatile, handy, wonderful, and indispensable piece of equipment for the home food preserver. You can use it for blanching, making soups, and a host of other tasks—in addition to its primary function as a canner for acidic foods (discussed later in this chapter). In fact, as you get inspired by the possibilities, you might find that one isn't enough. They're reasonably priced, beginning at around $25 and going up from there. If you're heading into a marathon tomato or peach or whatever processing session, it's wonderful to have two canner loads cooking and reduce your time waiting for one pot to cool down while the jars wait anxiously for their turn.

The boiling water canner (sometimes referred to as a "water bath canner") is essentially a large pot. It's made of aluminum or porcelain-coated steel, has a lid with a handle, and comes with a removable rack that holds jars in place while the water boils and also keeps the glass from coming into direct contact with the bottom of the canner. That rack is an essential piece of equipment. Glass jars that come into direct contact with the metal while the heat is on will shatter.

Boiling water canners have either flat or ridged bottoms. If you're working with an electric range, you'll want the flat bottom. For gas ranges, the ridged one works well.

These canners come in different sizes, with the standard size able to accommodate 7 quarts or 9 pints with room for the required 1 to 2 inches (2.5 to 5cm) of water needed above the tops of the jars.

Pressure Canner

This is an essential item for canning low-acid foods. It's probably the most intimidating appliance for a novice, but it's actually simple to use. Some people fear their pressure canner will explode. The horror story in your family history probably has more to do with Aunt Mabel heading out to the garden and spending the afternoon there (forgetting she had a canner full of green beans on the stove) than any equipment malfunction. If you follow the directions and attend to business, there's no reason on this Earth for explosions. Pay attention and all will be well.

Pressure canners come in different sizes and are rated by the volume of water they can hold. The standard size pressure canner is a 16-quart model. This means it will hold 16 quarts of water. For canning purposes, it will hold 7 quart jars or 9 pint jars (just like the boiling water canner).

An older-model, dial-gauge pressure canner (left)
and a newer-model, weighted-gauge pressure canner (right)

Take some time to become familiar with your canner's features before you can your first load. Pressure canners have undergone considerable streamlining over the last few decades. They're more lightweight for sure! Older models were heavy affairs. Models made before the 1970s have thick walls with lids that either clamp or turn on. They have a dial gauge in the lid, along with a vent (either a petcock or counterweight) and a safety fuse. And yes, these veterans are still out there, working away. If you have one of these, it's important to do a yearly check on your pressure gauge. Your local Extension Service might offer a free checkup for you. You can find your local office with an online search. Newer models have thinner walls and generally have turn-on lids. The lid has a gasket, either a dial or weighted gauge, an automatic vent/cover lock, a vent port that's closed with a counterweight or weighted gauge, and a safety fuse. Compared with an older model, it has more safety features built in. Here's how those parts work:

- **Vent port, petcock, or steam vent:** These names all refer to the same thing. The vent is the escape hatch for air trapped inside the canner and it also releases steam during processing. It's part of the pressure-regulating system.

- **Weighted gauge:** This is a round piece of solid aluminum with three holes drilled into the side. Each hole corresponds to a different pressure: 5, 10, or 15. If you're processing foods at 10 pounds of pressure, you put the number 10 hole on top of the vent port. The weight jiggles back and forth during processing, releasing steam and keeping the pressure steady. The major drawback to the weighted gauge is you can't easily adjust for altitude. (See the discussion later in this section.) If you need to process at 12 pounds of pressure to adjust for altitude, you have no choice but to use the number 15 hole. This can be overkill and you might overprocess your foods. Going below to the number 5 hole isn't an option because your foods could be underprocessed and potentially unsafe.

- **Dial gauge:** More user-friendly than the weighted gauge, you can easily adjust for altitude because the gauge has 1-pound increments. You'll need to keep a close eye on a canner with a dial gauge and turn the heat up or down as necessary to maintain a constant temperature. Dial gauge canners also have a petcock but no weight to put on it. You have the petcock open (in the straight-up position) during venting and closed (flick it to the side) after venting has been completed and processing has begun. Once the air has been expelled, the petcock is closed or the weight is placed on the vent and processing begins. Dial gauges should be checked for accuracy at the beginning of each canning season and more frequently if you turn it into a workhorse. Contact your extension office for information.

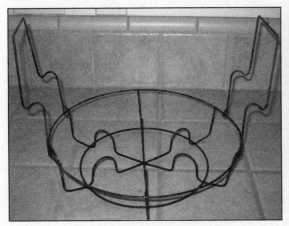

Boiling water canner rack

Pressure canner rack

- **Safety fuse, safety plug, safety release plug, or overpressure plug:** These names all refer to that little rubber plug or thin metal insert that releases pressure from the canner if the pressure gets dangerously high. You'll notice there's a red zone on the dial gauge. You want to stay out of the red zone at all costs. Think of it as the RPM gauge on your car. Red is bad. Very, very bad. Fortunately, if you're paying attention, this shouldn't ever be a problem.

- **Gasket:** This is round and made of rubber or other space-age material and is designed to fit perfectly inside grooves or slots in the lid. Not all canners use gaskets. Check the gasket at the beginning of each canning season to be sure it's still pliable, hasn't stretched, and has no cracks. If you detect any damage, purchase a new one. They're available at many hardware stores and also through the company that made your canner (another good reason to keep the instruction book handy). It's helpful to keep the instruction booklet in the canner when you're storing it for the season. That way, you'll never have to search for it and you'll be more inclined to refer to it when you should.

- **The rack.** Not a medieval torture device, this is a handy part of the canner that keeps the bottom of the glass jars from coming in contact with the hot, hot bottom of the canner. The rack for a pressure canner is constructed differently from one for use in a boiling water canner. It's a molded piece of aluminum with holes punched in it to allow water to circulate.

What About Other Types of Cookware?

In a pinch, we've all used various types of cookware for other than their intended purposes. We've boiled water in a pot when the teakettle was out of commission. We've made French toast in a skillet if the griddle was otherwise occupied. And that's just fine. However, when it comes to canning—and pressure canning in particular—substitutions aren't a good idea and can be downright dangerous.

It's just human nature to experiment, though, especially when you've gotten a new piece of kitchen equipment and you're working your way through the learning curve. And this is where listening to the experts is definitely a better choice than the self-proclaimed authority at the checkout at the hardware store.

Instant Pots are wonderful additions to the kitchen cookware arsenal. They're excellent stovetop pressure cookers, shortening the cooking time considerably. However, they're **NOT** suitable for canning.

West Virginia's Extension Service is clear on this: "Although Instant Pots and other electric pressure cookers use pressure to cook, they do not get to the proper temperature and pressure for pressure canning. Consult your user manual for recommendations on hot water bath canning or visit nchfp.uga.edu/publications/nchfp/factsheets/electric_cookers.html for more information."

Initially, the user's manual indicated these appliances were indeed safe for pressure canning. This error has since been corrected.

Glass Canning & Freezing Jars

You've probably heard these jars referred to as "Mason jars." They're named for John Mason, who invented a machine back in 1858 that was able to cut threads into zinc lids. After that, it was just one more step to make jars with threads in their necks that would receive the threaded lids for a tight fit. The third piece that completed the seal was a rubber ring that fit between the lid and the jar. Since that time, the technology has vastly improved and simplified the process.

You might not have thought about Mason jars as candidates for holding foods you'll be freezing, but modern glass canning and freezing jars work just fine. The glass is designed to withstand extremes of temperature and pressure, so they're truly double-duty items.

The two most commonly available brands of jars are Ball and Kerr, and it's the same with lids and rings. Prices differ for these two brands, but there seems to be little reason for it. Both are manufactured by the same company, Jarden, which also makes Bernardin and Golden Harvest jars!

You might be wondering about those jars you see at the grocery store that have "Mason" stamped into the glass sides. They frequently contain spaghetti sauce or fruit and you might think they'd be nifty to keep for canning. Unfortunately, these aren't true Mason jars. The glass is thinner and they're not recommended for canning and freezing.

Glass canning and freezing jars come in sizes ranging from ½ pint to ½ gallon, with pints and quarts being the ones you'll use most often. They also come in regular or wide mouth. Regular (or narrow) mouth jars work well for juices, sauces, and smaller-sized items. The wide mouth jars are better equipped to handle bigger fruits, such as pear or peach halves and bulkier vegetables. There's no difference in the carrying capacity of wide-mouth and regular-mouth jars. If your hands are small and fit inside a regular-mouth jar, you might find you prefer them. If your hands are larger, coping with narrow-mouth jars can get tiresome.

A Mason jar that isn't really a Mason jar

A range of sizes of Mason jars

Keep in mind that Mason jars are specially designed and manufactured to withstand temperature and pressure changes. However, if you have any antique canning jars, enjoy them as additions to your home décor, but don't try to freeze or can in them. Glass canning jars have a life span, as we discuss later on. Bottom line on those pretty blue or rose antique jars: They're likely to shatter and crack if you don't respect their venerable age. Fill them with buttons or dried rose petals or whatever else your heart fancies. Just don't use them for canning or freezing.

Canning Lids & Rings

Jars require lids, which rest on the rim of the jar, and rings, which screw on over the lid. It's a three-piece set: jar, lid, and ring. Jars and rings are reusable, but lids aren't unless you've purchased reusable lids. The first box of canning jars you buy will also come equipped with rings and lids. If you need additional rings and lids, they're sold together in a tall box.

Diameter of a regular-mouth jar (left) and a wide-mouth jar (right)

After that, you'll buy new lids in boxes of 12. You should buy new lids at the start of each canning season, although there's no guarantee you're getting a fresh supply. Stores can warehouse them until the following season. If lids are stored in a cool, dry location, the Extension Service notes they can last up to 5 years from the date of manufacture.

Today's lids are self-sealing, in contrast to the olden days when the home food preserver had to perform several steps to ensure the lids would seal. A modern lid is a round metal piece with a slightly raised dome in the center. You might hear them referred to as "dome lids." There's sealing compound around the edge of the lid, which is designed for one-time use only. Used lids can't be reused and must be discarded.

Also known as "screw bands," rings last a long time but might eventually rust if they're in constant contact with moisture. If they rust, toss them and buy new ones. They'll make a cleaner contact with the threads on the neck of the canning jar, ensuring a good fit, and you can avoid the frustration of trying to force them on if rust is interfering. Rusty rings can prevent your lids from sealing.

Older model canning jars used rubber gaskets and bailing wires attached to the lids. These had to be manipulated after processing, as indicated by instructions that told you to "complete the seal." Modern reusable lids are a more recent innovation, but they've been around for nearly half a century. They're a bit pricier than their nonreusable cousins, but they can pay for themselves over time. They're exactly what the name implies. They can be used over and over. They're used on modern canning jars and there's no bailing wire system to mess with. However, there's a thin rubber gasket placed under the lid and secured with a ring.

Always read and follow the manufacturer's directions. There's usually an additional step when using reusable lids. From the Extension Service: "Note, manufacturer's instruction may instruct the user to tighten the metal band immediately upon removal from the canner. If instructed, you should do so. Tightening the screw band ensures that the gasket forms a seal. The metal screw band is removed once the container is cooled and a seal has formed."

Rings (top) and lids (bottom)

Nifty Gadgets

A jar lifter is essential. Potholders become wet, and when they're wet, you can quickly get burned. Jar lifters are available at most hardware stores.

A lid wand is a fun gadget. It's not essential, but it keeps your hands out of hot water when you're reaching for a lid to place on a jar. It's a wand with a small magnet at the end that captures the lid.

A canning funnel is a must. It's wider at the base than a regular funnel and fits nicely into quart or pint jars. It keeps hot foods at a respectful distance from your hands. You'll find these at hardware stores or other stores that sell canning supplies.

Caring for Your Equipment

At the beginning of the canning season and after each load has been processed, you should carefully clean your canner. Washing the boiling water canner is a simple process. Wash it in regular dish detergent, rinse, and dry. Be especially careful with the wire rack, which loves to rust if given any opportunity to do so. When you've finished with the canner for any length of time, be sure it's completely dry before storing it. Placing a crumpled sheet of newspaper or some paper towels in the bottom of the canner will help draw any moisture away from the rack.

Washing the pressure canner is a bit trickier. If you've got a dial gauge lid, you can't submerge the lid in water. Also, be careful not to invert the lid while there's still water on it, as that water can work its way into the dial and wreak havoc.

If the vent port ever clogs, thread a needle with heavy-duty thread and draw the thread through the hole. You might find this procedure difficult to explain should a noncanning member of your family happen to pass by.

Wash the base in regular dish detergent, rinse, and dry. Avoid using scouring powder or baking soda because they'll cause the aluminum to turn dark. You can use fine steel wool if you come across some stubborn stuck-on food. Aluminum does have a tendency to pit, so don't leave food or water in the canner. Also, the canner might absorb odors from food. What this means in simple language is that you shouldn't use the pressure canner for storing food.

If the petcock is removable, you can wash it as you need to. With either model, be careful not to scrape away at the vent. The rubber material can be damaged if you get too industrious with the cleaning.

A canning funnel

Using Your Canners

Boiling water canners and pressure canners have different procedures for use.

Boiling Water Canner

Fill the canner one-half to two-thirds full of water. Raise the jar rack and secure it on the rim of the canner by hooking the handle slots on the rim. Turn the heat on high and set the lid in place. When the water has come to a boil, use a jar lifter to place jars in the rack slots. Then lift the rack handles and reposition the rack inside the canner. Replace the lid. When the water returns to a boil, begin timing. When the processing time has been completed, turn off the heat, remove the lid (being careful to turn it away from you to avoid a steam burn), and use the jar lifter to remove jars from the canner. Place them on a clean, dry dish towel. Don't touch them again until they've sealed. You might hear a distinctive "ping" as the seal sets. Leave the jars undisturbed overnight.

Rack positioned on canner rim

Pressure Canner

Place the rack in the canner. It will sit on the bottom. Put 2 to 3 inches (5 to 7.5cm) of hot water in the canner. The water will come through the holes in the rack and fill the bottom of the canner. Turn the heat on high. When the water begins to boil, use a jar lifter to position the jars on the rack inside the canner. One jar will go in the center of the rack. The rest will form a circle around the center jar. Try to keep them from touching each other. Secure the lid. Leave the petcock in the open position. When steam begins escaping through the vent in a steady stream, set the timer for 10 minutes. After the canner has vented for 10 minutes, close the petcock or place the weighted gauge on the vent.

The pressure will now begin to build inside the canner. If you're using a weighted gauge, the gauge will begin to rock and jiggle when the correct pressure has been reached. Check your owner's manual to find out how often the gauge should jiggle. You can control the frequency by controlling the heat on the stove. For example, if the weight is jiggling too often, reduce the heat. If it's not jiggling often enough, increase the heat. Once you've found the correct heat and the gauge is operating correctly, begin to time the processing.

If you're using a dial gauge, you'll see the pressure begin to climb. When the pressure has reached the correct level, turn down the heat as necessary to maintain that temperature. With an electric range, begin reducing the heat just before the needle indicator reaches the correct level. Gas ranges respond more quickly. Then begin to time the processing. It might take a little finessing to arrive at a steady pressure, but be patient. *You* control the heat. *You* control the pressure. *You* are in control!

When the processing time is up, turn off the heat and do *nothing else*! The canner will gradually lose pressure and you should do *nothing* to try to speed up the process. There are several good reasons for this:

- You could warp the canner.
- You could cause the jars to break.
- You could prevent the jars from sealing.
- You could draw liquid from the jars.
- You could get a really nasty burn.

Newer-model canners have vent locks that relax and return to the normal position when the pressure reaches zero. When the pressure has reached zero, it's time to remove the weighted gauge if your canner has one and wait 2 minutes more. Then open the lid and remove the jars. Always turn the lid away from you to prevent a steam burn. The contents will still be boiling hot even though the pressure part of the processing has been completed.

Use a jar lifter and place the jars on a flat, dry surface. A folded, dry kitchen towel works well. Allow the jars to cool and form their seal. Again, this is a process you mustn't rush. Once you've negotiated your first load of canning, celebrate! You've made the grade!

Getting the Best Products

Each load you process represents hard work and a financial investment. In addition to obtaining and caring for your equipment, there are some things to learn about the process to make sure your results come out top notch. Two of these must-know topics are acidity and heat.

Understanding Acidity

Acidity is the most important factor in determining how foods should be processed. Foods are divided into acid and low acid for purposes of canning. Their level of acidity is determined by the pH scale, which ranges from 0 to 14, with 7 being neutral. For foods to be considered acid, they must have a pH of 4.6 or lower.

Acid foods contain enough natural acidity to prevent the growth of heat-resistant bacteria or they're able to destroy them more rapidly during processing. Foods that can be safely canned using the boiling water bath are acid, have acid added to them (citric acid, lemon juice, or vinegar), or are fermented.

Over the years, new varieties of foods have been introduced and older varieties have been hybridized. In some cases, this has resulted in a change in their acidity. Tomatoes are a case in point. No longer as acidic as they used to be, it's necessary to add lemon juice to the jar before processing to ensure a safe product. Exact amounts are indicated in individual recipes.

Low-acid foods (those with a pH above 4.6) must be processed in a pressure canner to ensure a safe product. They don't have the natural acidity to prevent heat-resistant bacteria from growing. They need help. They need a heat boost—and that's delivered with pressure.

What You Need to Know About Bacteria

Bacteria are microscopic organisms that are present everywhere—in the air, in the soil, even on your skin. Some are beneficial (such as the bacteria in milk that help produce yogurt), but many are harmful, including those that cause botulism.

The common bacterium *Clostridium botulinum* is found in soil everywhere in the world. Soil in the western US is particularly high in the type of this bacterium (type A) that's especially dangerous to people.

You've no doubt read about cases of botulism, but just how rare are these occurrences? The answer is fairly rare because certain factors have to be in place for people to become sick. The bacterium has to be present in the food, the food has to be low in acid, and the food has to have been improperly processed.

The home food preserver can take measures to prevent this bacterium from contaminating home-preserved foods. The procedure is simple: Always pressure-can low-acid foods and follow research-based, approved recipes. For added safety, boil low-acid home-canned foods for 10 minutes at sea level before serving. The *botulinum* toxin is destroyed by boiling. This is why previous generations of home food preservers boiled the heck out of their vegetables before putting them out on the table for dinner. However, you don't have to cook your vegetables until they're mush for them to be safe. Just do the job right and don't take shortcuts.

Turning Up the Heat

Water boils at 212°F (100°C) at sea level. As the altitude increases, atmospheric pressure drops and the temperature at which water boils also drops. This means that no matter how long you boil the water, its temperature won't increase.

In the case of low-acid foods, this is a problem. *Clostridium botulinum* spores aren't killed at the normal temperature of boiling water. In order to kill them and prevent botulism, you must raise the temperature of the food being processed from 240°F to 250°F (115°C to 120°C). This is accomplished with pressure. As you increase the pressure, the temperature rises. Enter the pressure canner—your number one food safety insurance policy. The length of processing time depends on a variety of factors: the level of acidity of the food, the size of the jars, and how tightly you've packed those jars, for starters. That's why you'll find specific times and pressures for each food in the directions for processing that food.

Altitude Adjustments

You read in the last section that water boils at 212°F (100°C) at sea level. If you live at 4,000 feet (1.2km), water boils at 204°F (95°C), and if you're on top of the mountain at 8,000 feet (2.4km), it's a mere 197°F (92°C). To make sure your food is safe, you'll need to adjust your pressure reading to reflect your own altitude. For example, if you live at 5,000 feet (1.5km), you'll need to up the pressure from 10 to 12½ pounds (4.5 to 5.7kg). This is much more easily done if you've got a pressure canner with a dial gauge.

You'll need to determine your elevation above sea level. There are a few ways to go about this, but the easiest is probably to simply do an online search. One option is to go to www.whatismyelevation.com. Another is to use the US Geologic Service's National Map: apps.nationalmap.gov/elevation.

Consult your canner instruction book for the chart that tells you what pressure you'll need to use. The general rule is to add 1 pound of pressure for each 1,000 feet (304m) above sea level. Processing times remain the same regardless of your altitude.

Hot Pack vs. Raw Pack

These terms refer to the temperature of the foods you're putting in the jars. In hot pack, you'll heat the food in boiling water, syrup, or juice before you pack it into jars. In raw pack, you pack the food into jars without heating it and then add liquid to cover. Both hot pack and raw pack have advantages:

The advantages of hot pack:

- The food is softer and easier to fit into jars.

- More food can fit in the jar. Foods might contain up to 30% air. Cooking releases this air.

- There's less of a problem with floating food.

- Color and flavor might be better than raw pack after time in storage.

- It increases the vacuum in sealed jars.

The advantages of raw pack:

- It's better for foods that tend to lose their shape after cooking.

- It's perhaps less time-consuming than hot pack depending on the food.

Measuring Correct Headspace

The headspace is the area in a canning jar between the top of the food and the bottom of the lid. Because many foods expand during processing, it's important to leave the correct headspace for the food you're canning. Each recipe will tell you how much headspace to leave. If you don't leave enough headspace, your food is likely to erupt through your carefully prepared lid and ring, turning your canning liquid into a murky mess. Your jars will also not seal properly, so don't try to squeeze that last tablespoon of whatever into the jar when you know in your heart it's going to play havoc with your headspace (including your own).

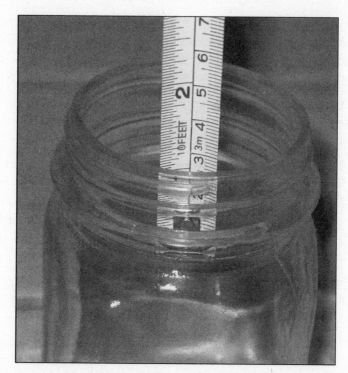

Measuring the correct headspace

Troubleshooting

Most of the time, everything turns out fine. Sometimes, though, in spite of your best efforts, weird things happen. There's always a logical reason why. Here are some of the most common problems, along with their causes and solutions.

Why Jars Break

In addition to using jars not suited for canning (such as mayonnaise jars or those grocery store jars we talked about earlier), having the bad luck to have a jar with an imperfection, or using old jars, there are three basic causes of breakage: thermal shock, pressure, and impact. Canning jars are tough, but they do have their limits. Nothing lasts forever. Canning jars have a limited life expectancy. After about 12 years, it's time to take them to the recycling bin.

Thermal shock, as the name implies, has to do with temperature extremes. The jar generally breaks into a few large sections. You might encounter this if you forget to put the rack in the bottom of the canner, if you decide to cool the jars by running cold water over them, or if you take a cold jar and dump it into boiling water.

Solution: Avoid subjecting jars to temperature extremes and do a checklist of procedures before you commit the canner to the stove. This includes checking to be sure you've put the rack in the bottom of the canner!

Pressure breaks occur when the pressure takes some wild swings during processing because you've forgotten to keep an eye on the dial gauge. This can also happen if you give in to temptation and try to hasten the depressurizing process by nudging the petcock. If you screw the jar lids on so tightly that nothing can escape—not even the air that needs to—or pack the jar to the tippy top and forget about headspace, you can also have a pressure break. These breaks can result in spidery lines, along with big cracks.

Solution: Follow procedures to the letter. Don't try to rush the process at any point and always attend to what you're doing. This means staying in the kitchen while you're processing foods with the pressure canner.

Impact breaks happen if you drop, bang, or subject the jar to some sort of insult. Using a sharp knife to remove air bubbles can also cause these kinds of breaks if the knife tip jabs into the side of the jar. These breaks have a central hole with radiating cracks.

Solution: Use a rubber spatula to remove air bubbles. And, of course, try not to drop the jars. Always inspect jars carefully for nicks, scratches, or cracks before using them. Recycle the ones that fail the test. And never, never, never bang the jar on the counter to settle the food before you consign it to the canner.

Failure to Seal

Why didn't my jar seal? This is the most plaintive cry of the home food preserver. After everything you did for it, it repays you by doing absolutely nothing. It just sits there.

Usually, after you've given it more than enough time to do the right thing, you'll unscrew the band and remove the lid to find a bit of food stuck to the adhesive compound. That's the most common culprit.

Here are some other possibilities:

- Using old lids for which the adhesive compound has degraded

- Not leaving the correct headspace

- Not following correct processing times or procedures

One other possibility is you tried to save a bit of time and used the *open kettle method* instead of opting for the good old boiling water bath. The open kettle method was an older way of putting up fruits, such as peaches. The peaches were heated in juice or water to boiling and then packed boiling hot into glass canning jars. Lids were adjusted and then left to seal on their own. Sometimes they did and sometimes they didn't. Sometimes they unsealed during storage. It's not the recommended way to ensure a good seal and can result in a whole lot of spoiled food. I know, you were told your great-great-grandmother did it this way and it was always fine. But it wasn't always, and besides, she used a button hook to fasten her shoes and wore a corset. We don't use those any longer either. So … what to do? You can either reprocess the food right then and there or put it in the refrigerator to use within a few days.

Explaining Liquid Loss

This often occurs when the pressure fluctuates during processing or if someone has opened the petcock prematurely. In the two photos on the next page, the jar of peaches on the right has the correct amount of liquid. The peaches are nestled nicely in syrup. The jar on the left has lost so much liquid that the peaches are almost certain to turn brown. Which jar would you be proud to claim as your own?

In a boiling water bath, the water must be 1 to 2 inches (2.5 to 5cm) above the tops of the jars or water will be sucked out of them during processing. In a pressure canner, you can get liquid loss by not letting the pressure canner exhaust for 10 minutes before beginning processing. What this means is that there's still air inside and you've not completely pressurized your canner. That air sucks out the liquid.

Other possibilities include the following:

- Not taking the jars out of the canner when processing has stopped but allowing them to cool down in the canner. This most often happens when you've decided to do one last load before bedtime and figure you'll just take out the jars in the morning. The solution here is to plan your day and keep to the plan.

Liquid loss from too little headspace (left) and a good amount of liquid (right)

- Not removing all the air bubbles from the jar before processing. You'd think that just pouring the liquid into the jar would fill in all the spaces between the pieces of food, but it isn't so. Air gets trapped in the smallest depressions—for example, in the hollow of peaches where you've removed the pit. When you place the peach pitted side down in the jar, you've left an air pocket. The solution here is to gently use a rubber spatula to lift the fruit to allow the liquid to fill the space. You can't see into the middle of the jar and it's likely there are also small air pockets there. Run the spatula around the edges of the jar. This will move the food that's in the center of the jar and allow the liquid to penetrate thoroughly.

- Packing the jars too tightly or too full. This often happens when you're down to your last jar to make a full canner load and you've got more food than the jar should take. You're trying to use every bit of food, so you cram it all in; however, food expands during processing and this drives out the liquid in the jar. As the jar cools down, that liquid loss becomes depressingly apparent. Always leave the necessary headspace. You have options for that extra food. You can eat it, of course, or you can refrigerate it overnight and add it to the next day's processing load.

- Starchy foods in the jar absorbed the liquid. Corn is a real culprit here. As the processing time bubbles along, the corn cooks and plumps beautifully. However, this plumping happens because the corn has availed itself of the liquid you so thoughtfully provided. Follow the directions carefully for the correct headspace for starchy vegetables.

When faced with liquid loss, what do you do? If the jar has sealed, the food is safe to eat, although you should eat it as soon as possible. The top layer is likely to darken, but you can remove this before using the rest of the contents.

When to Reprocess

The decision is up to you. If the additional processing time (and you've got to redo the whole time) won't turn the food to mush, go ahead and reprocess it. Decide then and there. You've only got about 24 hours with the food kept under refrigeration to make up your mind before the spoilage microorganisms wake up and get to work. If you don't want to spend the time or energy, just make plans to eat the food.

Food that's been sealed, stored, and then unsealed shouldn't be reprocessed. Toss it. Common sense should be your best indicator when it comes to determining whether you've got a problem or an irritation.

If you detect mold or a strange odor or if the liquid has turned cloudy in the jar, discard the food. If your food is bubbling, this is definitely not a good sign. Your food shouldn't be moving under any circumstances. Don't taste it. Destroy it.

Safe Disposal

The Centers for Disease Control (CDC) has guidelines for the proper ways of disposing foods that are suspected of harboring the *botulinum* toxin. It recommends extreme care because even a small amount of the toxin is dangerous and can be absorbed through a break in the skin or through the eyes. Their recommendations are found on their website (www.cdc.gov/botulism/botulism_faq.htm) and are as follows:

- Place any food you think is contaminated in a sealable bag, wrap another plastic bag around the sealable bag, and tape it tightly. Place the bags outside in a trash receptacle for nonrecyclable trash. Make sure they're out of reach of people and pets.

- Never discard the food down a sink, garbage disposal, or toilet.

- Avoid contact with the skin. Wear rubber or latex gloves when handling open containers of food you think might be contaminated. Wash your hands with soap and running water for at least 2 minutes after handling food or containers that might be contaminated.

- Clean up any spills using a bleach solution (use ¼ cup of bleach for every 2 cups of water). Completely cover the spill with the bleach solution, then place a thick layer of paper towels on top of the bleach solution. Let the towels sit for at least 15 minutes, then dispose of them in the trash. Wipe up any remaining liquid with new paper towels. Clean the area with liquid soap and water to remove the bleach. Wash your hands with soap and running water for at least 2 minutes.

- Discard any sponges, cloths, rags, gloves, and containers that might have come into contact with contaminated food.

Putting Canning to Work for You

Putting up food by canning is fun, thrifty, and healthful when you do it right. If you start with the freshest ingredients and follow strict guidelines for cleanliness and approved procedures for processing, you'll fill your pantry with fruits, vegetables, meats, and all manner of tasty products to last you the year.

Canning Fruits & Fruit Products

Not that long ago, canned fruits seemed to contain mostly sugar. Sugar does serve a purpose in that it helps fruit keep its color, shape, and flavor, although in old-time recipes, it sometimes seemed as if all you could taste was the sugar. These recipes called for heavy syrup and that meant about 40% sugar. Very heavy syrups were a whopping 50% sugar.

Fast forward to today. Times, tastes, and techniques have changed, and with regard to canning fruits, they've changed for the better. In fact, a very light syrup (only 10% sugar) is common and comes closest to what the sugar content of most fruit actually is. The beauty of home-canned fruits is you control the amount of sugar that's used. That's a real bonus if you or someone in your family has special dietary needs, you want to put up some baby food, or you just want to cut back on calories. You can even can fruits without sugar and still create a tasty product. More about this shortly.

The Adventure Begins

If you're new to canning, beginning with fruit and fruit products will quickly give you confidence. It's a good way to get started. Preparing food for the boiling water canner, loading the canner, monitoring the processing time, and removing jars after processing for a proper cooldown are essential skills you'll need when it's time to move on to using the pressure canner.

It might seem like there's a great deal to learn—and there is. However, as mentioned in the last chapter, it's called *processing* because it's a process. One step at a time. Make haste slowly and enjoy the experience. You'll emerge an expert!

General Procedures

Select firm, ripe fruit without blemishes or bruises. It's best to use slightly underripe fruit. Overripe fruit will break down during processing and leave you with strings and mushy places and a product that's too soft. If you wouldn't want to eat it raw, why would you want to can it anyway? Wash the fruit and remove stems, pits, and peels as necessary. Decide how you'll use the fruit because this will determine if you can it whole, halved, sliced, chopped, or made into a juice, purée, or sauce. So many choices!

Generally, it's easier to work with small batches. This means using about 3 pounds (1.4kg) of fruit per canning session. It's a manageable amount and you'll finish quickly.

A Word About Syrup

You'll need to use some type of liquid to accompany the fruit in the jars and you have options here. You can make syrups in various strengths using sugar and water (see Appendix B for measurements), you can use fruit juice, or you can use water. Sugar helps fruit stay bright and colorful, and it also helps it hang on to its texture, but it's not necessary.

However, the decrease in the amount of sugar we use today lets the flavor of the fruit come through. It cuts calories and it's cheaper to make! If you'll be making syrup, use whatever strength suits your dietary needs and tastes.

It's perfectly fine to make up a double or triple batch of syrup to save time. Refrigerate what you don't use. It will keep for several days. You can also freeze it. Pour it into rigid freezer containers, label it, date it, leave ½ inch (1.25cm) of headspace, and freeze. When you're ready to use it, remove it from the freezer and allow it to thaw.

To make the syrup following the measurements given in Appendix B, place the sugar and water in a large saucepan, turn the heat on high, and bring it to a boil. Reduce the heat to low and let it simmer while you pack fruit into jars.

You can use honey or corn syrup for part of the sugar requirement in syrup if you wish. Use 1 cup of honey, 1½ cups of sugar, and 3 cups of water to get about 5 cups of syrup. When using corn syrup, use 1 cup with 1½ cups of sugar and 3 cups of water to get about 6 cups of syrup.

Antidarkening Solutions

Light-colored fruit (such as apples, peaches, or pears) should be dipped in an antidarkening solution while they're waiting to be packed into jars. See Chapter 3 for more on how to use ascorbic acid (vitamin C) or a commercial preparation to keep the color of the fruit bright.

Estimating the Amount of Fruit to Use

Kitchen scales are useful for helping you eyeball how much fruit you'll need. Working with small amounts at a time is easiest. Think 2 to 3 pounds (1 to 1.4kg). Prepare the fruit and then work with the next 2 to 3 pounds. A rough rule is that you'll need about 10 to 12 pounds (4.5 to 5.4kg) per canner load for pints and nearly double that for quarts.

Slipping Skins

Ditch the peeler. Dip peaches or tomatoes into boiling water for about 20 seconds and then plunge them into very cold water. Their skins will slip off easily.

Canning Fruit

You've done all the following:

- The fruit is clean, slipped, cut, and dipped or peeled.

- You've run the canning jars through the dishwasher and they're keeping warm.

- The rings and lids are simmering in hot water, and the lid wand and jar lifter are at the ready.

- The syrup is made and simmering on the stove.

- There's a clean, folded dish towel on the kitchen counter ready to receive the processed jars. You've made sure it's not in a drafty location and is away from any possible contact with cold water.

- The boiling water bath is half filled with water, the lid is in place, and the heat under it is turned on. The water is starting to boil.

- You've checked the processing time for your altitude for the particular food you're canning.

Now it's time to go over the steps involved in producing a jar of canned fruit:

1. Pack the fruit into jars, using either raw pack or hot pack. (See Chapter 9.)

2. Add syrup or some other liquid to cover, leaving the appropriate headspace.

3. Insert a rubber or plastic spatula into the jar to remove any air bubbles.

4. Wipe the rim of the jar to remove any pieces of fruit.

5. Adjust the lids. (This is the phrase used for putting on the lid and screwing on the band.)

6. Using the jar lifter, pick up each jar by the neck and place it in one section of the rack in the bottom of the canner.

7. When the canner is full, place the lid on the canner. If you don't have enough jars for a full load, that's fine. Just increase the amount of water in the canner so there's 1 to 2 (2.5 to 5cm) inches of water above the tops of the jars.

8. Begin timing when the water has returned to a full boil.

9. Remove the jars from the canner with a jar lifter after time is up and place them on a clean, dry dish towel.

10. Allow the jars to cool undisturbed.

11. Listen for the sound that's music to your ears—the "ping" of lids sealing.

12. The next day, remove the rings and inspect the seals.

13. Wash the jars in warm water to remove any syrup or food residue.

14. Dry the jars and store them without rings in a cool, dark place.

Goodness in a Jar

The best peach varieties for canning include Red Haven, Red Globe, Elberta, and Fairhaven. Freestones are much easier to work with than clings. (See Chapter 4 for a discussion of the differences.)

Some varieties of fruits are widely available, but each region has its own specialties suited to canning. To find the best varieties of fruits for canning in your area, check with your Extension Service. You'll find its number online.

Removing a peach pit with a grapefruit spoon

Apricots, nectarines, and peaches can beautifully, and a large part of the appearance is the arrangement in the jar. Layer the fruit with their insides facing down and you'll get an interesting overlapping pattern. Even with slices, if you take a moment to position the fruit attractively, the result is almost art. You'll also get more fruit in each jar this way as opposed to just ladling it in haphazardly.

Apricots

Wash the fruit and leave the skins on. Apricots tend to fall apart without their skins to keep them company. Remove the pits. Apricots are usually canned as halves. You'll get quite a few in a pint jar. Raw pack is best, as they tend to break down in hot pack. Pack the jars and add syrup to cover. Leave ½ inch (1.25cm) of headspace. Remove air bubbles, wipe the rims, adjust the lids, and process in a boiling water canner. See Appendix C for the processing times. Remove the jars from the canner and allow them to cool on a flat, dry surface.

Nectarines & Peaches

These are essentially the same fruit for canning purposes. Wash the fruit. Slip skins on peaches and nectarines. Trim away any bruised portions. Slice the fruit in half and remove the pits. Use a grapefruit spoon to remove peach pits if they're stubborn. Slide the serrated tip of the spoon under the stem end and continue under the pit to loosen it. Lift the pit out. Treat the fruit with antidarkening solution.

If you'll be using this fruit for cobblers or pies, you'll want to use quart jars as opposed to pints. Use either hot pack or raw pack. Pack the jars and add syrup to cover. Leave ½ inch (1.25cm) of headspace. Remove air bubbles, wipe the rims, adjust the lids, and process in a boiling water canner. See Appendix C for the processing times. Remove the jars from the canner and allow them to cool on a flat, dry surface.

Soft Berries

Berries tend to get very soft with canning, but if you don't have room in the freezer for them, this is better than nothing. Fill the jars with berries. They'll settle with processing, so shake them down to give them the general idea of what they're supposed to do. *Never, never, never* bang the jar on the counter to force the berries down. Remember that glass jars are strong, but they're still glass and can break. (See Chapter 9 for more on pressure breaks.)

Cover the berries with syrup in the strength of your choice, leaving ½ inch (1.25cm) of headspace. Remove air bubbles with a rubber or plastic spatula, wipe the rims, adjust the lids, and process in a boiling water canner. Process 10 minutes for pints and 15 minutes for quarts. Remove the jars from the canner and allow them to cool on a flat, dry surface.

Cherries (Sweet or Pie)

To pit or not to pit, that is the question with cherries. Definitely pit cherries that are destined for pie. Unpitted cherries hold their shape better than pitted, but if you have a nifty cherry pitter and want to use it, go right ahead and pit away. If you do pit, remember to check each cherry before it goes into the jar to be sure no stray pits are trying to sneak past your vigilant eyes.

Choose either raw pack or hot pack. Pack them into jars and add syrup to cover, leaving ½ inch (1.25cm) of headspace. Remove air bubbles, wipe the rims, adjust the lids, and process in a boiling water bath. See Appendix C for the processing times.

Fruit Cocktail (Compote)

This is a great way to use up the odds and ends of fruits you accumulate at the end of a canning session. Think variety! There's no law that requires you to pack just one kind of fruit in a jar. Mix them up! Try peaches and pears together or combine several different fruits to create your own fruit cocktail. Fruit cocktail you purchase commercially is often cut into tiny cubes, but you can make your pieces any size you like.

You'll need a variety of mixed fruits (peaches, pears, grapes, cherries, and perhaps a few maraschino cherries—whatever you have) and syrup in the strength you prefer. Make the syrup and prepare the fruit. If you're feeling adventurous, try packing fruit in apple juice or white grape juice instead of syrup. It's lighter and has a delicious flavor.

Wash, sort, and cut the fruit into slices or cubes. This recipe is more easily done hot pack than raw pack because it self-mixes while it's in the syrup. Add the fruit to the syrup and cook until everything is hot all the way through. Ladle into jars, leaving ½ inch (1.25cm) of headspace. Remove air bubbles, wipe rims, and adjust lids. Process in a boiling water bath for 20 minutes for pints and 25 minutes for quarts. Remove the jars from the canner and allow them to cool on a flat, dry surface.

Figs

Figs are lower in acid than most other fruits, so they need acid added and they also require a longer processing time. Kadotas are a good variety for canning. Wash the figs. Leave the stems on and don't peel. You'll use hot pack for figs and do them whole. Pack them into jars and add syrup to cover, leaving ½ inch (1.25cm) of headspace. Add 1 tablespoon of bottled lemon juice to each pint and 2 tablespoons of lemon juice to each quart. Remove air bubbles, wipe the rims, adjust the lids, and process in a boiling water bath. See Appendix C for the processing times.

Grapefruit & Orange Sections

These are great additions to a citrus salad. You'll use raw pack for these. Wash and peel the fruit, being careful to snag all the white, spidery membrane. Use a small, sharp knife to make the first incision between sections and then pull all sections apart. Clean any extra membrane or skin and remove any seeds. Pack them into jars and add syrup to cover, leaving ½ inch (1.25cm) of headspace. Remove air bubbles, wipe the rims, adjust the lids, and process in a boiling water bath. See Appendix C for the processing times.

Grapes

Use the seedless variety please. Eating your way through an entire jar of grapes but having to spit out seeds as you go gets tedious. Thompson seedless white grapes are a good choice. Use either raw or hot pack. Pack them into jars, leaving ½ inch (1.25cm) of headspace. Remove air bubbles, wipe the rims, adjust the lids, and process in a boiling water bath. See Appendix C for the processing times.

Pears

Bartlett pears are the best choice for canning. They hold their shape well and don't tend to get mushy. Wash the fruit. Peel and cut the pears in half or in slices. Use a grapefruit spoon to remove the center strings and seeds. Hold in antidarkening solution while you prepare the batch. Use either hot pack or raw pack. Pack the jars and add syrup to cover. Leave ½ inch (1.25cm) of headspace. Remove air bubbles, wipe the rims, adjust the lids, and process in a boiling water canner. See Appendix C for the processing times. Remove the jars from the canner and allow them to cool on a flat, dry surface.

Pineapple

Pineapple might not come quickly to mind when you're thinking about canning fruit, but if you've gotten a good deal at the grocery store, it's easy to put some up. The biggest deterrent for most people is the peeling and the coring and the digging out of all those indented "eyes." However, it's actually not any more time-consuming than peeling potatoes. Approach it with enthusiasm!

Whack off the top and the bottom, and position the pineapple on a cutting board. Use a sharp knife to cut down each side, rotating the pineapple as you go along. It's rather like peeling a banana. Then you need to decide if you want rings or wedges.

For rings, slice across the diameter. Then use your apple corer to remove the core. If the core is wider than the corer, you'll need to overlap some coring or use a small, sharp knife to make an oval cut. For wedges, cut the pineapple in half lengthwise and then cut in half lengthwise again. The number of cuts will depend on the size of the pieces you want. Then cut away the core from the center pieces.

Hot pack usually gives a better result than raw pack, so simmer the pineapple in syrup until tender, about 3 to 5 minutes. Then pack into jars, leaving ½ inch (1.25cm) of headspace. Remove air bubbles, wipe the rims, adjust the lids, and process in a boiling water bath. See Appendix C for the processing times.

Plums

Choose slightly underripe plums, as the riper ones are so juicy that they'll come apart during processing. Wash the plums, remove any stems, cut them in half, and remove the pits. You can process them with the pits if you want, but make a few pricks in the skin with a table fork to keep it from bursting during processing.

Use either hot pack or raw pack. For hot pack, simmer the plums for 2 minutes in syrup. Pack them into jars and add syrup to cover, leaving ½ inch (1.25cm) of headspace. Remove air bubbles, wipe the rims, adjust the lids, and process in a boiling water bath. See Appendix C for the processing times.

Fruit Juices

Making your own fruit juices for babies or for anyone in the family is a good use of surplus fruit. There are a wide variety to choose from: apple, berry, cherry, peach, or apricot. Apple juice is best if you mix several varieties of apples in the batch. The flavor is complex and rich.

This is where you'll use your steamer/juicer—arguably one of the most ingenious labor-saving devices ever created for the home food preserver. You simply fill the bottom basin with the appropriate amount of water, put it on the burner of the stove, and turn on the heat. Place the fruit you're going to juice (blackberries or apples, for example) in the colander-type basket that fits over the bottom basin, place the lid on top, and wait for the time indicated in the instructions—usually 1 hour or so.

The juice magically appears in the plastic tube (you might have to prime it with a couple of squeezes of the metal clamp that keeps the juice from running amok across your kitchen floor) and you can begin to fill a sturdy pot with the juice.

The instructions aren't complicated. Study them carefully, and before long, you'll wonder why you waited so long to add this appliance to your canning arsenal.

Juicer/steamer (left) and boiling water canner (right)

The finished product: a canner load of blackberry juice ready for storage

The juice is also perfect for making jelly, so once you've got your juice waiting for you, prepare it as you would if you were going to be making jelly and were ready to extract the juice. See Chapter 18 for detailed instructions if you're going to use the cheesecloth-drip method. When you've prepared the juice, pour it into hot, sterilized jars, leaving ¼ inch (0.5cm) of headspace. Wipe the rims, adjust the lids, and place in the boiling water canner. Process for 5 minutes for pints or quarts and 10 minutes for half gallons.

Fruit Purées (Including Applesauce)

An excellent way to begin the process of making fruit leathers (see Chapter 20), purées are excellent foundations for fruit desserts and for baby food. Wash, stem, and pit fruit as necessary. Peeling isn't mandatory, but it will make the purée easier to manage in the food mill. Use your potato masher to crush the fruit a bit before measuring it. Then place the fruit in a large saucepan. Add 1 cup of water for each 4 cups of fruit. Turn the heat on high, bring it just to a boil, and then reduce the heat to low. Simmer until the fruit is tender. You can have at it with the masher again if you like.

Remove the saucepan from the heat and run the fruit through the food mill. The food mill is a handy food preparation tool. It's made of stainless steel and consists of two pieces. The bottom part is bowl-shaped with slots that allow you to position it securely over a medium-sized pot or bowl. However, instead of a solid bottom, it's a sieve with a small slot in the center. This slot supports a paddle you operate by a hand crank. You pour food into the bottom of the food mill and turn the hand crank. This forces cooked soft foods through the sieve.

After milling, return the purée to a clean saucepan. Sweeten it to taste if you like. Reheat the purée to boiling. If you've added sugar, be sure it's all dissolved before you remove the purée from the heat. Then pour it into hot, sterilized jars, leaving ¼ inch (0.5cm) of headspace. Wipe the rims, adjust the lids, and place in the boiling water canner. Process 15 minutes for pints or quarts.

Using a food mill

Pie Fillings

A major problem with making canned pie fillings is they tend to separate or get gummy if you use tapioca, flour, or cornstarch for thickening. A chemically modified food starch, Clear Jel, has been developed to solve this problem and it's the only thickening agent approved by the USDA for canning. However, it can be a challenge to find and you're not likely to find it at the grocery store. Contact your local extension office for sources.

If you're not willing or able to go on the hunt, you have other options. You can always can the pie filling without any starch and then thicken it with tapioca, flour, or cornstarch before putting it in the pie shell.

You can also prepare the pie filling by using your favorite recipe. Using your usual thickening agent, process quarts in a boiling water bath for 20 minutes. When you're ready to make a pie, reheat the filling and stir it to reblend the ingredients.

Tomatoes

Tomatoes are treated the same way as fruit, which they technically are. They're probably the most versatile fruit/vegetable you'll work with.

Regardless of what your intended product is, begin by sorting, removing stems, and washing the tomatoes. Then fill your boiling water canner about half full of hot water, put the lid on, and turn on the heat. When the water boils, use a slotted spoon or fried food lifter to place the tomatoes in the boiling water. Leave them about 20 to 30 seconds, then remove them from the canner and plunge them into very cold water. The skins will peel right off (just like with peaches).

If you have plenty of tomatoes, crush some of them for juice to pour over the tomatoes you'll be canning. Salt isn't necessary, so only add it if you want to. If you prefer your tomatoes unsalted, bully for you! However, you'll need to add some bottled lemon juice. Today's tomatoes aren't as acidic as in years gone by, and to make them safe for a boiling water bath, some extra acid is necessary.

Canning Wholes or Halves

Wide-mouth jars are the easier way to go for tomatoes. Choose hot pack or raw pack. Hot pack will allow you to get more tomatoes in the jars. If you're canning whole tomatoes, first put a couple of tablespoons of tomato juice or hot water in the bottom of the jar. You'll be wedging two or three tomatoes in the bottom and the liquid will help prevent a giant air bubble from forming. Add 1 tablespoon of bottled lemon juice per pint of tomatoes. Fill the jar and cover the tomatoes with juice or boiling water, leaving ½ inch (1.25cm) of headspace. Wipe the rims, adjust the lids, and process in a boiling water canner. See Appendix C for the processing times.

Tomato Sauce

Place peeled tomatoes in a large pot and use your potato masher to crush them a bit. Turn the heat on low and allow the tomatoes to simmer. Stir occasionally. As they simmer, the cells will break down, causing the tomatoes to soften and the juice to be released. When the tomatoes are cooked sufficiently, remove them from the heat and put them through the food mill.

Return the sauce to a clean pot and allow it to simmer. At this point, you can add spices according to your favorite recipe or can the sauce unseasoned after it's reached the desired consistency.

Add 1 tablespoon of bottled lemon juice per pint of tomato sauce. Then pour the sauce into jars, leaving ¼ inch (0.5cm) of headspace. Wipe the rims, adjust the lids, and process in a boiling water canner for 35 minutes for pints or 40 minutes for quarts.

Tomato Juice

Straining the tomatoes after they've simmered will give you fresh, flavorful tomato juice. Pour it into jars and add 1 tablespoon of bottled lemon juice per pint. Process in the boiling water canner for 40 minutes for pints and 45 minutes for quarts.

When the jars have cooled, you'll notice that the juice is beginning to separate. This is normal for home-canned juice. Commercial procedures are able to heat the tomatoes nearly to boiling in just seconds. This destroys enzymes that are responsible for the separation. The solution? Shake that jar before you pour!

Recipes

Cranberry sauce is a good accompaniment to all kinds of poultry, and while the whole berries freeze very well, sometimes you just want to reach for a jar of already made-up sauce. It's easy to can, so you can be ready for a last-minute change of menu! Canned fruits also make wonderful desserts. Some fruits lend themselves better to incorporating into recipes than do others. Apples, peaches, and pears are the champs. Here are some tasty desserts using canned fruits.

Cranberry Sauce

The following recipe has been slightly modified from one from Ocean Spray and has been adapted for canning. You can double this recipe.

Makes	Prep time	Cook time
2 pints	5 minutes	25 minutes

1 cup granulated sugar

1 cup water

1 (12oz) package of Ocean Spray whole cranberries, washed and sorted

1. Bring the sugar and water to a boil in a medium saucepan on the stovetop over high heat. Add the cranberries and return to a boil. Reduce the heat to medium and boil gently for 10 minutes, stirring occasionally. Remove the saucepan from the heat.

2. Ladle the sauce into jars, leaving ⅛ inch (3mm) of headspace. Remove air bubbles, wipe the rims, adjust the lids, and process the pints in a boiling water bath for 5 minutes to ensure the seal.

Pineapple Upside-Down Cake

This is an old-time favorite. Many young cooks got their start by being allowed to place the maraschino cherries in the center of the pineapple rings. Crunchy, rich, and packed with flavor, this dessert is sure to please.

Serves	Prep time	Cook time
6 to 8	25 minutes	30 minutes

½ cup butter

2 cups dark brown sugar

1 quart canned pineapple slices

maraschino cherries

4 large eggs, separated

1 cup granulated sugar

1 cup all-purpose flour

1 tsp baking powder

1. Preheat the oven to 350°F (175°C).

2. Melt the butter in a 10-inch (25cm) cast-iron skillet on the stovetop over low heat. Evenly sprinkle the brown sugar over the butter. Place one pineapple ring in the center of the skillet and arrange the other slices around it, covering the bottom of the skillet. Place a maraschino cherry in the center of each ring.

3. In a medium bowl, beat the egg whites until stiff. Set aside.

4. In a separate medium bowl, beat the egg yolks and sugar until fluffy.

5. In a small bowl, combine the flour and baking powder. Sift the mixture into another small bowl. Gently fold the flour mixture into the sugar mixture ½ cup at a time.

6. Fold in the egg whites. Pour the batter over the pineapples and spread evenly with a spatula.

7. Place the skillet in the oven and bake for 25 to 30 minutes or until a wooden skewer inserted in the middle comes out clean.

8. Use oven mitts to remove the skillet from the oven. Run a knife around the rim of the skillet and then invert the skillet onto a serving platter.

Cherry Upside-Down Cake

Not sure why there are so many upside-down recipes, but they're definitely good. This one cheats a bit in that it uses a box of cherry cake mix.

Serves	Prep time	Cook time
6 to 8	10 minutes	35 to 40 minutes

1 box of cherry cake mix

1 quart cherries, drained

½ cup granulated sugar

¼ tsp pure almond extract

1 tsp ground cinnamon

1. Preheat the oven to 350°F (175°C). Line a 12×9 inch (30.5×23cm) rimmed baking sheet with waxed paper.

2. Prepare the cake mix according to the package directions.

3. In a medium bowl, combine the cherries, sugar, almond extract, and cinnamon.

4. Spoon the cherry mixture onto the sheet and spread it evenly. Top the cherry mixture with the cake batter.

5. Place the sheet in the oven and bake 35 to 40 minutes or until a wooden skewer inserted in the middle comes out clean.

6. Remove the sheet from the oven and invert the cake on a serving platter. Remove and discard the waxed paper. Serve the cake with vanilla ice cream.

Easy Pear Salad

This is pretty—and also pretty easy to make. It uses 1 pint of canned pear halves, but the recipe can easily be doubled or tripled or whatever.

Serves	Prep time	Cook time
4 to 6	10 minutes	none

½ cup minced walnuts

½ cup diced apples

½ cup plain Greek yogurt

1 tbsp honey

1 pint canned pear halves, drained

1. In a medium bowl, combine the walnuts, apples, Greek yogurt, and honey. Spoon the mixture into the pear cavities.

2. Place the pears on a bed of mixed salad greens before serving.

Broiled Pears

When you're in a hurry and want something quick and easy, this is a good dish to rely on. As a bonus, it's also elegant!

Serves	Prep time	Cook time
4	5 minutes	5 minutes

2 pears, peeled, halved, and cored

2 tbsp light brown sugar

¼ tsp ground nutmeg

2 tsp butter

1. Preheat the oven to broil. Place the pear halves in an oven-proof casserole dish with low sides. Evenly sprinkle the brown sugar and nutmeg over the pears. Drop dots of butter over the top.

2. Place the dish in the oven and broil until the butter has bubbled and the pears are a light brown, ensuring they don't burn. Remove the dish from the oven and serve the pears with whipped cream.

Canning Vegetables

It's time to take all the knowledge you've gained and graduate to your friendly pressure canner. You'll use this for canning vegetables. If slicing and dicing and chopping don't sound like your idea of fun, take heart! There are some nifty gadgets on the market that make preparing vegetables so much easier than before. From green bean frenchers to corn slicers, canning vegetables has never been quicker and more fun. Never canned vegetables before? Once you hear those lids snapping shut, indicating a good seal, you'll be hooked. (Tomatoes are fruits and they're covered in Chapter 10.)

General Principles

Vegetables are low-acid foods, which means they have a pH value above 4.6, and that means they must be processed in the pressure canner. All the skills covered in Chapter 10 apply here—all that's different is the manner of processing.

Whether this is your first canning season or your fifteenth, reviewing safety procedures and rereading the instructions that came with your pressure canner is the smart way to begin. Most mistakes are made by veterans. It's the rookies who play by the book. Getting comfortable with the process is the goal, but being sloppy or careless and taking shortcuts aren't the way to get there. Take your time and do it right.

Taking a Test Drive

First time facing this piece of equipment? Still a little nervous? That's natural. Let's deal with the worries that might be making you nervous.

Worry #1: The pressure canner could explode.

Remember the story about Aunt Mabel in Chapter 9? You're not Aunt Mabel. You're going to stay in the kitchen and monitor the canning. You control the heat and you control the pressure. If the pressure starts to creep up, simply turn the heat down.

Worry #2: All the jars will explode inside the canner.

Place 2 to 3 inches (5 to 7.5cm) of water in the canner and monitor the heat and the temperature—and all will be fine.

Worry #3: I won't do it right and I'll kill my whole family.

You'll do it right because you're going to follow the directions and the proper procedures. You're going to give your family healthy, safe food.

Worry #4: There's too much to remember all at once.

If you've used your boiling water canner to process fruit (see Chapter 10), you have 90% of the procedures already under your belt. It's time to take a test drive:

1. Place your pressure canner on the stovetop and add 2 to 3 inches (5 to 7.5cm) of water to it.

2. Put on and secure the lid. Be sure the petcock is open. Check the diagram in the instruction manual if you need to. In fact, check the diagram even if you're absolutely, completely positive you know what to do.

3. Turn on the heat to high. When the steam starts to flow in an uninterrupted stream from the vent, set the oven timer for 10 minutes.

4. When the timer buzzes, either put on the weight or close the petcock depending on the model of your canner.

5. If you have a weight gauge canner, pull up a chair and listen for the sound of it gently rocking back and forth and releasing steam. You don't have to do anything else. When it starts rocking, set the oven timer for 5 minutes. When the timer goes off, turn off the heat under the canner and wait for all the noise to stop. Then wait 2 minutes more, remove the weight, and remove the lid.

   If you have a dial gauge canner, pull up a chair and watch the pressure gradually climb to 10 pounds. Turn down the heat as needed to keep the pressure at 10 pounds. This might take a little finessing. Don't panic if the pressure climbs a bit more while you're learning how to adjust the heat. After you've been able to hold the heat at 10 pounds of pressure for 10 minutes, turn off the canner and wait. When the pressure reaches 0, open the petcock. Wait 2 minutes more and then remove the lid.

The test drive has been successfully completed. Nothing blew up and you survived. You've tamed the beast. You're ready to go for the real thing.

About Salt

You'll come across many recipes for canning vegetables that include salt. Feel free to omit it. It's not used as a preservative, only as a flavoring agent. If you're interested in reducing your salt intake, you can start here.

About Altitude

All vegetables are processed at 10 pounds of pressure at sea level. Follow the recommendations outlined in Chapter 9 with regard to increasing the pressure at which you'll process food at your particular altitude. Processing times don't increase, but pounds of pressure do.

About Quality

Canning won't improve the quality of the vegetables you're putting up, so it's important to use the best produce you can find.

Slightly underripe vegetables are better than slightly overripe for canning purposes. You'll be cooking them hard during processing and you want them to hold up. That's difficult to do when you're past your prime, especially if you're a vegetable. Each region has varieties of vegetables suited for canning. Check with your local extension office for varieties for your area.

Getting Started

Review the directions for loading the canner, securing the canner lid, venting, and placing the weight on the vent port or closing the petcock. Set the pressure canner on the stove and add 2 to 3 inches (5 to 7.5cm) of water. Turn on the heat to high. Have the lid to the side so it doesn't get jostled while you're preparing the food. While you're monitoring the first load in the canner, review proper cooldown procedures covered in step 5 of your test drive.

Asparagus

Asparagus freezes better than it cans, but if you need to can some, it looks lovely when it's carefully arranged in a canning jar, so take the time to bring out your inner artist. Select young stalks and wash them thoroughly. Hold the stalk in one hand and grasp the bottom of the stalk with the other. Bend from the bottom to snap off the tougher bottom joint.

Measure one spear against the height of the jar minus ½ inch (1.25cm) for headspace. Use this spear as a template for cutting the other spears to the proper height. You can use either raw pack or hot pack, although raw pack is much, much easier. Processing times are the same for either method.

For raw pack, place the spears upright (tips up) in the jar. You can fill another jar with the cut pieces and use them for stews or other casserole dishes.

For hot pack, arrange a bundle of spears to stand (tips pointed up) in a wire basket and place the basket in boiling water for 3 minutes. Don't get the tips in the boiling water. It can be quite a balancing act. Then remove the spears from the boiling water and arrange the spears (tips pointed up) in the jars. They'll be hot and a bit flexible. It's sort of like trying to stack rubber bands.

Fill the jars with boiling water, leaving ½ inch (1.25cm) of headspace. Wipe the rims, adjust the lids, and process in a pressure canner. See Appendix C for the processing times.

Green Beans

Green beans and yellow wax beans can very nicely if you use varieties that hold up under processing. These include Contender, Topcrop, Tendercrop, and Kentucky Wonder. Wash them thoroughly to remove any stuck leaves or other garden debris. Remove the tips and tails, and either can them whole or cut them into pieces. If you prefer French-style beans, you can find *frenchers* through vegetable seed catalogs or at kitchen specialty shops.

A green bean frencher is a small device that clamps onto a counter or tabletop. You feed the beans into a hopper at the top and then turn a small hand crank that feeds the beans from the hopper to internal stainless steel blades that slice the beans lengthwise—a procedure called *frenching*.

As with asparagus, you can stand the beans upright in a jar. This allows you to maximize the amount you put in each jar and it also looks very appealing. You can also fill jars with cut pieces. These work well in soups, stews, and casserole dishes.

For raw pack, arrange the beans in jars and cover with boiling water, leaving ½ inch (1.25cm) of headspace. For hot pack, add the beans to boiling water and boil for 5 minutes. Then pack into jars and cover with boiling water, leaving ½ inch (1.25cm) of headspace. Wipe the rims, adjust the lids, and process in a pressure canner. See Appendix C for processing the times.

Lima Beans

Shell the beans and sort according to size. Lima beans come in different sizes, and while the smallest ones are the most desirable for canning, the larger ones also do fine. Limas tend to expand exponentially during processing, so they require considerably more headspace than other vegetables. You can use raw pack or hot pack, but hot pack will reduce the amount of headspace you need—somewhat.

For raw pack, fill the jars, but don't pack the beans too tightly. Cover with boiling water. Headspace for smaller lima beans is 1 inch (2.5cm) for pints and 1½ inches (3.75cm) for quarts. For larger lima beans, use ¾ inch (2cm) headspace for pints and 1¼ inches (3cm) for quarts.

For hot pack, add the beans to boiling water and cook for 1 minute. Drain. Fill the jars, leaving 1 inch (2.5cm) of headspace for pints and quarts.

Wipe the rims, adjust the lids, and process in a pressure canner. See Appendix C for the processing times.

Beets

Beets are accommodating vegetables. Small beets work very well canned whole and larger beets do fine as slices. Leave a portion of the top on—1 to 2 inches (2.5 to 5cm)—and also about 1 inch (2.5cm) of the root. If you don't, the beets will bleed while you're preparing them and you'll end up with a rather anemic pink ball.

Use hot pack for these because they'll be doing a bit of cooking during skin removal. Wash the beets and sort them according to size. Work with one size group at a time. Place them in boiling water and cook for about 20 minutes. Then remove them from the water and place them in cold water to slip the skins, tops, and root pieces. Don't keep them in so long that they cool down.

Pack whole beets or slices in jars and add boiling water to cover, leaving ½ inch (1.25cm) of headspace. Wipe the rims, adjust the lids, and process in a pressure canner. See Appendix C for the processing times. Beets also root-cellar if you have one (see Chapter 23) and it's the first choice for preserving them.

Carrots

Carrots do well when canned. Scrub them with a vegetable brush. That will get off the garden dirt and the skin if the carrots are young. Older carrots have thicker skins. If they're a bit older, dip them in boiling water for about 30 seconds and then plunge them into cold water. Then slip off the skins. If you prefer to leave the skins on, you can. Cut the carrots into slices (either vertical or horizontal) or cubes or leave them whole if they're tiny. Use either raw or hot pack.

For raw pack, pack the carrots into jars and leave 1 inch (2.5cm) of headspace. Then add boiling water to cover, leaving ½ inch (1.25cm) of headspace. For hot pack, add the carrots to boiling water and allow the water to return to a full boil. Remove the carrots and pack into jars, leaving ½ inch (1.25cm) of headspace. Cover with boiling water, still leaving ½ inch (1.25cm) of headspace. Wipe the rims, adjust the lids, and process in a pressure canner. See Appendix C for the processing times.

Corn

Canned corn has a crunchier texture than frozen corn and some people prefer that. It's certainly a handy item to have on hand. Husk the corn outside if you can. It's a messy process, with silk distributing itself all over the kitchen if given half a chance. This is definitely an activity suitable for everyone in the family. Wash the ears under cool, running water and run a vegetable brush over them to remove any remaining silk. Then either cut the kernels from the cob with a sharp knife or run the ears across the corn slicer, being careful to keep fingers out of the way.

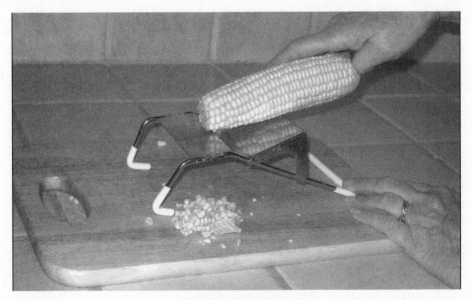

Using a corn slicer

The corn slicer is adjustable. You can set the blade to cut about two-thirds of the way through the kernels for whole kernel or about halfway through if you're planning on making creamed corn. Pay attention while you're using this device. The blade is sharp. That's the point, of course, but keep your fingers away from it.

Whole Kernel

Use either raw or hot pack. For raw pack, fill the jars loosely leaving 1 inch (2.5cm) of headspace. Then add boiling water to cover, leaving ½ inch (1.25) of headspace. For hot pack, add the corn to boiling water and allow it to return to a boil. Pack into jars and add water to cover, leaving 1 inch (2.5cm) of headspace. Wipe the rims, adjust the lids, and process in a pressure canner. See Appendix C for the processing times.

Creamed Corn

After cutting the kernels off the cob, run a table knife down each row to capture the milk. Add this to the corn. Creamed corn is quite dense and should only be processed in pint jars. Pack the jars with kernels and milk, leaving 1 inch (2.5cm) of headspace. Wipe the rims, adjust the lids, and process in a pressure canner. See Appendix C for the processing times.

Greens

Greens (such as chard and spinach) freeze beautifully, but canning tends to turn them a murky shade of greenish gray. The length of time required for processing will generally make them mush. However, you *can* can them.

Use hot pack only. Wash the greens in several changes of cool water to remove all the grit they love to harbor. Then trim the stems if you like. You can either blanch the greens for 2 minutes or steam them for about 10 minutes to get them wilted enough to be able to stuff them into jars. Pack them into jars and cover with water, leaving ½ inch (1.25) of headspace. Wipe the rims, adjust the lids, and process in a pressure canner. See Appendix C for the processing times.

Mushrooms

These freeze nicely, but if you're running out of freezer space or want some in the pantry, you can put them up in pint or half-pint jars. You'll need a great many mushrooms to make a canning load: about 14½ pounds (6.5kg) for a full load of pint jars.

Soak the mushrooms in cool water for 10 minutes to loosen any dirt or sterilized manure. Yes, that's what those dark earth-like particles are on the surface. Remove the mushrooms from the water, remove the loosened debris, inspect for spots or damage, and trim away. Wash thoroughly and then slice, dice, or leave whole. Place in a saucepan and cover with water. Boil for 5 minutes. Pack into pint or half-pint jars, leaving 1 inch (2.5cm) of headspace. To protect against discoloration, add ⅛ teaspoon of ascorbic acid powder or one 500mg vitamin C tablet to each pint jar. Wipe the rims, adjust the lids, and process either pint or half-pint jars in a pressure canner. See Appendix C for the processing times.

Okra

No Southern cook would even think of making stew without okra. You want young, tender pods without black spots. You'll be using hot pack.

Wash the okra, but leave the caps on. Add them to boiling water and boil for 2 minutes. Drain. Then cut into slices or use whole. Pack into jars, leaving ½ inch (1.25cm) of headspace. Wipe the rims, adjust the lids, and process in a pressure canner. See Appendix C for the processing times.

Peas

Select fresh pods without yellowing. Peas should fill the pods without crowding them or showing signs of sprouting. Shell the peas and pack them into jars, leaving 1 inch (2.5cm) of headspace. Peas expand as they process. Use either raw pack or hot pack. For raw pack, add boiling water but don't cover the peas. Come to ½ inch (1.25cm) of the top of the peas. For hot pack, fill the jars and cover the peas with boiling water, leaving 1 inch (2.5cm) of headspace. Wipe the rims, adjust the lids, and process in a pressure canner. See Appendix C for the processing times.

Peppers (Hot or Sweet)

You want firm peppers for canning. Avoid peppers with dark spots or other signs of damage. You can either use raw or hot pack for these. If they're small, you can process them whole. Bigger peppers can be cut into halves or quarters. Wash the peppers. If canning them whole, make several small slits in each pepper to allow air to escape. If not canning them whole, remove the seeds and pith.

Place the peppers under the broiler in the oven or arrange them on the middle rack with the oven heated to 400°F (200°C) until the skins blister. Remove them from the oven and allow them to cool. Place a damp cloth over them for a few minutes to make peeling easier. Always wear plastic gloves when working with hot peppers. Be careful not to touch your face, especially your eyes, until you've washed your hands in soap and water.

Smooshing comes next. Collapse whole peppers by pressing your palm against the side until they're flat. Pack them loosely into jars and add boiling water to cover, leaving 1 inch (2.5cm) of headspace. Wipe the rims, adjust the lids, and process in a pressure canner. See Appendix C for the processing times.

Potatoes

Uncooked white potatoes don't freeze well, but you *can* can them and have a good product. Of course, the canning cooks them, but you're starting out with raw. Scrub the potatoes, peel, and cut out any dark spots or green areas. If a potato has a great deal of greening that can't be removed, dispose of that potato. (According to the National Institutes of Health, solanine, a toxic substance, is found in green potatoes; this can cause *Solanum tuberosum* poisoning. If you or someone you know has become ill after eating green potatoes, call the National Capital Poison Center at 1-800-222-1222.)

Your potatoes are now ready for the next step. Put them in a saucepan, add hot water, and bring them to a boil. Cook whole potatoes for 10 minutes and cubes for 2 minutes. Remove the pot from the heat and drain. Pack them into jars and cover with boiling water, leaving 1 inch (2.5cm) of headspace. Wipe the rims, adjust the lids, and process in a pressure canner. See Appendix C for the processing times.

Sweet Potatoes

Scrub sweet potatoes and place them in a saucepan. Add hot water and turn the heat on high. Bring them to a boil, reduce the heat to medium, and cook for 15 to 20 minutes or until the potatoes have begun to soften. Remove the saucepan from the heat and remove the skins from the sweet potatoes.

Cut the potatoes into cubes. Don't purée or mash, as this makes them too dense to be processed safely. Pack them into jars and add boiling water to cover, leaving 1 inch (2.5cm) of headspace. Some people prefer to can these in a light syrup instead of water. See Appendix C for syrup directions. Wipe the rims, adjust the lids, and process in a pressure canner. See Appendix C for the processing times.

Winter Squash (Including Pumpkin)

Pumpkin is handy to put up in cubes for later service in pies, but early recipes that recommended mashing the pumpkin or puréeing it before canning have been replaced by a safety caution. Pumpkin is very dense and it's difficult for the heat to penetrate the entire contents of the jar to a sufficient degree to protect against spoilage and botulism. Therefore, can it in cubes and mash them when you're ready to use them.

Smaller pumpkins make better pies and are also easier to work with than bigger ones. Wash the pumpkin and then dry it so it won't be slippery when you cut it. Use a sharp knife—just as if you were going to carve a jack-o'-lantern—and grasp the pumpkin firmly while keeping a safe distance from the path of the knife. Cut a circle 2 to 3 inches (5 to 7.5cm) from the stem and remove the lid.

Now that you've got a hole to grab onto, you can make cuts down the pumpkin to cut it into sections. Remove the seeds and stringy fibers. Peel the sections and cut them into 1-inch (2.5cm) cubes. Boil the cubes for 2 minutes and then drain. Pack them into jars and add boiling water to cover, leaving 1 inch (2.5cm) of headspace. Wipe the rims, adjust the lids, and process in a pressure canner. See Appendix C for the processing times.

Mixed Vegetables

You can make up a canner-load of pints to have ready to add to soups or stews or to serve as the main vegetable for dinner. Process the load according to the longest time required for an individual vegetable. For example, for the following suggested vegetables, you'd process pints for 55 minutes and quarts for 85 minutes because corn is the vegetable requiring the longest processing time. Suggested ingredients include sliced carrots, whole kernel corn, green beans, lima beans, zucchini, and tomatoes. The USDA Extension Service notes you can substitute other vegetables or change proportions of those listed above.

Suggested amounts for a canner-load of 7 quarts include:

- 6 cups of sliced carrots
- 6 cups of cut whole kernel sweet corn
- 6 cups of cut green beans
- 6 cups of shelled lima beans
- 4 cups of whole or crushed tomatoes
- 4 cups of diced zucchini

However, don't use winter squash, creamed corn, leafy greens, dried beans, or sweet potatoes. Use vegetables with similar processing times for the best results. And remember that some vegetables with strong flavors might create an unpleasant result when you mix them with their less-potent relatives.

This concept works best if all the vegetables are approximately the same size or are cut to size. Place all the vegetables in a large saucepan and add hot water. Bring them to a boil and cook for 5 minutes. Turn off the heat and ladle the vegetables into jars, adding the boiling water from the saucepan to cover. Leave 1 inch (2.5cm) of headspace. Wipe the rims, adjust the lids, and process in a pressure canner. See Appendix C for the processing times.

Recipes

The following are some recipes that make the most of canned vegetables. These are familiar, traditional recipes with modern flavors.

Stewed Tomatoes

Commercially canned stewed tomatoes are often little more than tomatoes with a kiss of onion and a hint of green pepper. If you like stewed tomatoes with some substance—with pieces of green peppers and onions you can actually see—why not make your own? Stewed tomatoes are a good side dish for homemade mac and cheese.

Serves	Prep time	Cook time
4	20 minutes	10 minutes

1 tbsp olive oil

1 garlic clove, minced

1 medium to large white onion, sliced

1 cup sliced green or yellow peppers

1 quart canned tomatoes (whole or pieces)

1. Heat the olive oil in a medium skillet on the stovetop over medium heat. Add the garlic, onion, and peppers. Sauté for 2 to 3 minutes or until the onion is translucent.

2. Add the tomatoes, breaking them into large pieces. Mix gently and simmer for 20 minutes. Remove the skillet from the heat and serve the tomatoes immediately.

Mel's Borscht

This traditional beet soup comes to the United States via Eastern Europe and Russia.

Serves	Prep time	Cook time
4	20 minutes	none

1 quart canned beets

4 cups water

2 tsp granulated sugar (or to taste)

4 tbsp vinegar

¾ to 1 cup sour cream

1. Combine the beets, water, sugar, and vinegar in a blender. Process until smooth.

2. Gradually add the sour cream and blend again. (Don't overfill the blender! Prepare the borscht in batches and then mix the batches together in a large bowl.)

3. Transfer the borscht to an airtight container and store in the refrigerator. Shake well when ready to serve. Garnish with a dollop of sour cream before serving.

Karen's Vegetable & Beef Soup

This is a great way to use your homegrown vegetables. There's really no limit to what you can put in or leave out, so tailor this recipe to suit your family's tastes. This soup is fine the first day, better the second, and great the third. Alternatively, you can brown the meat in the olive oil first and then dump everything into the slow cooker. Cook on low for 6 to 8 hours, adding the potatoes 1 to 2 hours before serving.

Serves	Prep time	Cook time
8	25 minutes	4 to 6 hours

1lb (450g) stew meat

1 garlic clove, minced

1 tbsp olive oil

1 quart canned whole tomatoes

1 pint canned corn

1 quart canned green beans, cut into
    2-inch (5cm) slices

1 large white onion, cut into eighths

1 pint canned carrots

4 to 6 beef or vegetable stock cubes

kosher salt, to taste

freshly ground black pepper, to taste

fresh or dried herbs (parsley, sage,
    rosemary, thyme, oregano, and
    basil recommended), to taste

3 large potatoes, cut into 1-inch
    (2.5cm) cubes

1. Add the meat, garlic, and olive oil to a large pot on the stovetop over high heat. Brown the meat, turning as necessary to sear in the juices and get an even browning.

2. Reduce the heat to medium. Add the tomatoes, corn, green beans, onion, carrots, and stock cubes. Add water to cover all the ingredients. Bring to a boil, then reduce the heat to low.

3. Add the salt, pepper, and other spices to taste. Simmer for 4 to 6 hours. Add water as necessary to keep the ingredients covered and to create a rich broth. Add the potatoes 1 to 2 hours before serving.

Creamy Corn Pudding

This is a traditional Southern dish often served at Thanksgiving. This version takes a shortcut with a box of corn muffin mix.

Serves	Prep time	Cook time
8 to 10	15 minutes	45 minutes

½ cup butter

⅓ cup granulated sugar

2 large eggs

1 cup sour cream

1 pint canned corn, drained

1 pint creamed corn

1 small box of corn muffin mix

½ cup milk of choice

kosher salt, to taste

freshly ground black pepper, to taste

1. Preheat the oven to 350°F (175°C). Spray a 9×13 inch (23×33cm) rimmed baking sheet with cooking spray.

2. In a large bowl, cream the butter and sugar. Add the eggs and beat thoroughly until well mixed.

3. Fold in the sour cream. Add the muffin mix and milk a little at a time, alternating between the two until well incorporated.

4. Stir in the whole kernel corn and the creamed corn. Pour the mixture into the dish.

5. Place the dish in the oven and bake for 45 minutes or until lightly browned and a wooden skewer inserted in the middle comes out clean.

6. Remove the dish from the oven and serve the corn pudding immediately

Canning Meat, Poultry, Seafood & Game

Chapter

12

Now that you've mastered the boiling water canner and conquered the pressure canner, it's time to get serious about putting up entire meals! Preserving meats and fish you buy in bulk or harvest yourself is economical and allows you to stock up on what your family enjoys most. You can also create combination dishes to have on hand for any occasion.

A major advantage of canning meat, poultry, seafood, and game is lengthened storage life. Freezer life varies widely among these foods, but canned life is easily 1 year or more. Technically speaking, as long as the seal holds and the foods were prepared and processed properly, they'll keep almost indefinitely. True, quality might lessen over time, but it won't be anywhere near as rapidly as in the freezer.

General Procedures

Just as you preserved only the best-quality fruits and vegetables, you'll do the same with meat, poultry, seafood, and game. The same basic rules of cleanliness apply here and so do safety procedures. These are low-acid foods and must be processed in the pressure canner. Always follow approved procedures for slaughtering, chilling, and aging if you're going to harvest your own meat. Your local Extension Service has informational bulletins for beef, pork, and lamb.

Generally, you'll freeze larger cuts of meat or poultry. However, if you don't have room in the freezer or if electricity isn't reliable at the mountain cabin, you can put up pints or quarts and have plenty of healthful, good-quality food ready for use.

Keep Your Cool

This ranks right up there with keeping a clean work area. Keep everything refrigerated until you're ready to use it. If you can't get to the processing within 2 days, freeze the food until you can. Ice fish as soon as possible after catching them and cool harvested game or home-produced meat after slaughter to 40°F (4°C) or below.

Keep Trim

Lean meat is best for canning. Trim away fat from the outside of the meat and cut away any gristle. Extra fat can prevent jars from sealing. The globules work themselves loose and can lodge between the jar rim and the lid. Also, cut away any bruising you see. Remove any large bones from meat before canning. The bones take up space and you don't eat them anyway.

Keep Moving

If you're going to be canning whole meats, assemble all your supplies before you take the meat out of the refrigerator. This will help you keep your work area and your hands free and clean. Decide if you'll can the meat in pints or quarts and whether you'll raw pack or hot pack. Once you begin, you'll want to keep at it until the canner is filled so the meat doesn't sit overly long at room temperature.

Canning Beef, Pork, or Lamb

Having pint or quart jars at the ready filled with tender chunks of meat in a rich broth makes meal planning a cinch. Want to make a stew but time is short? You've got all the ingredients at hand if you're a home food preserver. How about roast beef with gravy, mashed potatoes, and canned corn for a comfort meal on a cold winter night? Again, check. You've got it covered.

Don't shy away from canning meat because it sounds tough. It's not—and neither is the meat! When you've rounded out the contents of your pantry with ready-to-use meats, you'll be sitting in the catbird seat.

You have two methods for putting up meats: raw pack or hot pack. Raw pack is definitely quicker, but hot pack eliminates shrinkage and gives a better-quality product.

Raw Pack

This method is straightforward. Wipe the meat with a clean, damp cloth. Meat shouldn't need to be washed. If canning a solid cut, cut the meat to fit the jar you'll be using. You can also use cut-up pieces, such as chunks or cubes.

Fill the jar with the meat, leaving 1 inch (2.5cm) of headspace. Add salt if you wish—½ teaspoon per pint and 1 teaspoon per quart. The salt is strictly for flavoring and doesn't work as a preservative, so feel free to leave it out. Don't add any liquid to the jar. The meat will create its own juices as it processes. Wipe the rims, adjust the lids, and process in a pressure canner. See Appendix C for the processing times.

Hot Pack

There are three steps for this method:

1. Make stock to use in filling the jars after you've packed the meat. You can also use boiling water, but stock will give the meat more flavor.

2. Precook the meat to be packed.

3. Pack the meat, add the liquid, and process.

If you've made meat stock, this is an excellent use for it. Otherwise, gather up the meat scraps and bones, and place them in a large saucepan to make broth. Add water to cover. Turn the heat on high and bring the broth to a boil. Reduce the heat and simmer for 2 to 4 hours. Then drain the broth from the saucepan and place it in the refrigerator. When the broth has cooled, remove any fat that's congealed on the surface. Return the broth to the saucepan and bring it to a boil. Alternatively, you can use your slow cooker to free up some space on the stove.

Next, cook the meat. You're aiming for rare because the meat will cook further during processing. You can boil it, broil it, or fry it. Cut the meat to fit the jars and loosely pack hot meat into the jars. Add liquid to cover, leaving 1 inch (2.5cm) of headspace. Insert a plastic or rubber spatula to remove air bubbles. Wipe the rims, adjust the lids, and process in a pressure canner. See Appendix C for the processing times.

Ground Meats

Ground beef, pork, and lamb can well. Brown the meat first, breaking up any clumps that form. You want the meat loose. Pack the meat loosely into jars and add broth or boiling water to cover. Leave 1 inch (2.5cm) of headspace. Insert a spatula to remove air bubbles. Wipe the rims, adjust the lids, and process in a pressure canner. See Appendix C for the processing times.

Lamb & Pork Sausage

Yes, you *can* can sausage. Lamb and pork sausage make wonderful patties for breakfast. If you're using bulk sausage, make the patties bigger because they'll shrink a bit as they cook. If you're planning on making your own sausage, go easy on the spices. Some get stronger or even change flavor during processing. Brown them on both sides and then transfer them to the canning jar, adding boiling hot broth to cover. Leave 1 inch (2.5cm) of headspace. Insert a spatula to remove air bubbles. Wipe the rims, adjust the lids, and process in a pressure canner. See Appendix C for the processing times.

Hard Sausages

If you find a great deal at the grocery store on hard sausages, such as salami or pepperoni, take advantage even if you don't need them for dinner. Hard sausages have been dried, but they'll spoil if not refrigerated. Even then, their shelf life is limited.

All you have to do with these is either slice them or cut larger pieces to fit in the jar. Leave 1 inch (2.5cm) of headspace. Don't add liquid. Adjust the lids and process in the pressure canner. See Appendix C for the processing times. When you want to make pizza or whip up a batch of salami and cheese sandwiches, you're ready.

Canning Poultry

Poultry refers to domesticated birds: chicken, turkey, duck, goose, guinea hens, and pigeon. Fresh chicken is available year-round and there are frequently good sales where you can stock up. Consider canning some of this, along with freezing some.

Fresh turkey is generally found around Thanksgiving; the rest of the year, you'll likely find it in the frozen meats section of the grocery store. Fresh duck or goose is difficult to find commercially and generally comes to you courtesy of a successful hunter. In addition to smoking, canning is a good way to put some up.

Cutting Up

Obviously, you're not going to be able to put the whole bird into the canning jar. You're going to need to cut it up. Fortunately, all birds are built along the same lines, so if you know how to cut one up, you can deal with them all. There are four basic cuts to turn a whole bird into parts:

1. Cut through the wing and remove the drumette. The drumette is the fleshy part of the wing and it's what you'll be served if you order wings at a restaurant. Many people discard the wings, not realizing there's some good meat there.

2. Make a cut where the leg attaches to the body. Then disjoint the leg. Hold the bird down with one hand while you take the leg in your other hand and bend the leg backward until you've exposed the joint. Cut through the joint and remove the leg.

3. Separate the thigh from the leg. Make a cut over the joint where the thigh attaches to the leg. Hold the meaty portion of the leg in one hand and the bottom portion of the leg in the other, then bend the leg backward until the joint is exposed. Then cut through the joint.

4. Cut along the breastbone—the ridge along the top of the bird. Then pull the two sections apart and cut through the bones holding the parts together.

At this point, you'll decide if you want to bone the bird or can it with bones. This decision is strictly a personal preference and will depend on your intended use later on. Removing the leg bone is probably the best choice because it's big and will take up quite a bit of room in the jar. To do this, make a cut along the length of the leg, exposing the bone. Then carefully peel the flesh from the bone.

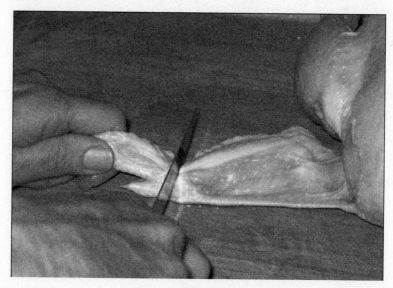

Removing the drumette

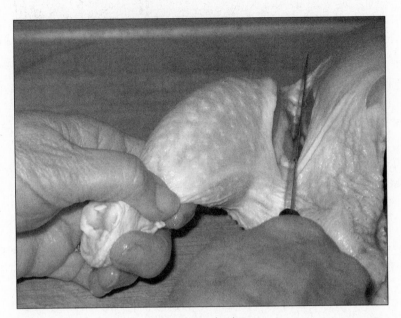

Removing the legs

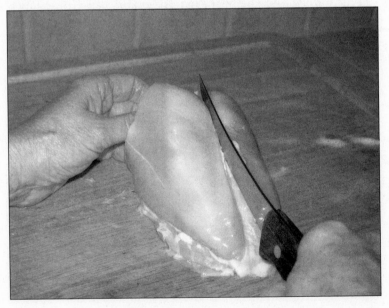

Cutting the breast in half

To debone the breasts, use a small, sharp knife to make a cut between the ribs and the flesh along the length of the breast. Then continue on, cutting and separating the ribs as you go. When you reach the bottom, the ribs will lift away and you'll have a boneless breast. Considering the cost of boneless poultry, knowing how to bone it yourself makes good sense. Now you're ready to cut the poultry into pieces that will fit in the jars.

For raw pack, pack pieces into jars, leaving 1¼ inches (3cm) of headspace. Don't add liquid. Wipe the rims, adjust the lids, and process in a pressure canner. See Appendix C for the processing times.

For hot pack, precook the poultry in stock or broth until it's medium well. Pack hot poultry loosely into jars and add boiling broth or water to cover, leaving 1¼ inches (3cm) of headspace. Wipe the rims, adjust the lids, and process in a pressure canner. See Appendix C for the processing times.

Rabbit or Squirrel: Neither Fish nor Fowl

These don't have wings, but they're handled the same as poultry for canning purposes. They can be dry, so the recommendation is to dress the rabbit or squirrel and then soak it for 1 hour in water containing 1 tablespoon of kosher salt per 1 quart of water. If you're working with wild rabbit, the saltwater helps take away some of the "gaminess." Drain and rinse. Remove all excess fat. Then treat it the same as poultry. See Appendix C for the processing times.

Canning Seafood

Fish should be fresh and iced as soon as possible after the catch. Fish are highly perishable and bruise easily. Be careful not to crush them by stacking them several deep during transport. Shellfish should be live when you begin to work with them. Keep them cool and moist.

Fish

Fatty fish, such as mackerel, trout, and bluefish (but not tuna), can best. Clean and gut the fish as soon as possible after catching. When ready to can, scale the fish and then remove the heads, tails, and fins. Wash the fish thoroughly and remove the bones. Cut the fish in half lengthwise and then cut to fit the jars. Safe processing times haven't been developed for using quart jars for fish. Use pint or half-pint jars.

You can either soak the fish in a salt brine (1 cup of kosher salt per 1 gallon of water) for 1 hour or add 1 teaspoon of kosher salt to each 1 pint. Pack raw fish tightly into pint or half-pint jars, leaving 1 inch (2.5cm) of headspace. Wipe the rims, adjust the lids, and process in a pressure canner. See Appendix C for the processing times.

You'll sometimes find crystals in home-canned salmon. These are magnesium ammonium phosphate crystals, they occur naturally, and they're not harmful. When you heat the salmon, the crystals usually dissolve. There's nothing you can do to prevent them and you don't need to worry about them.

Smoked Fish

Smoked fish have a wonderful flavor and aroma but a short shelf life. Even refrigerated, they're not going to keep longer than 7 to 14 days. To be sure you have enough on hand, try canning some. You'll keep that smoked goodness and the fish will keep much longer. The first rule is to smoke only the amount of fish you'll be able to can in a day. Because smoked fish can dry out during canning processing times, new recommendations advise you to do a light smoke with them. This means smoking the fish for up to 2 hours in a home smoker at 140°F to 160°F (60°C to 71°C). Then use pint jars, not quart jars.

The method for processing smoked fish is a bit different from that of other seafood. Pack the fish vertically into the jars, leaving 1 inch (2.5cm) of headspace. You can loose pack or tight pack. Wipe the rims and adjust the lids. Pour 4 quarts (16 cups) of cool—not hot—water into the pressure canner. Then add the jars to the canner. The water will come up to the jar rims and this is what you want. See Appendix C for the processing times.

Shellfish

It's handy having canned oysters, clams, and other types of shellfish in the cupboard. You've got the major ingredient for chowders and other dishes at your fingertips. Methods for shucking, shelling, and cleaning shellfish are covered in Chapter 6. See Appendix C for the processing times.

Here's the preparation for clams:

1. Save the juice when you cut out the meat. Heat the juice to boiling.

2. Wash the meat in a weak brine made from 1 to 3 tablespoons of salt to 1 gallon of water. (For minced clams, follow step 3 for preparing clams with a session in the meat grinder. Then continue with the remaining steps for preparing whole clams).

3. Add 2 tablespoons of vinegar or lemon juice or ½ teaspoon of citric acid to a medium saucepan. Add 1 gallon of water. Heat to a boil. Blanch the meat for 1 to 2 minutes in the boiling solution.

4. Remove the saucepan from the heat and drain. Pack the clams into jars, leaving 1 inch (2.5cm) of headspace.

5. Add the boiling juice and additional boiling water as needed to cover the clams, leaving 1 inch (2.5cm) of headspace.

6. Wipe the rims, adjust the lids, and process the jars in a pressure canner. See Appendix C for the processing times.

Here's the preparation for crabs:

1. After cleaning the crab, cook in a pot for 20 minutes in a brine made from 2 tablespoons to 1 cup of kosher salt and ¼ cup of white vinegar or lemon juice to 1 gallon of water. Remove the pot from the heat and drain. Allow the crab to cool.

2. Separate the crab meat from the shell. This can be a tedious process and you might find it easier to pull up a chair and get comfortable while you're stacking up the shells.

3. Rinse in a cool brine made from 2 tablespoons to 1 cup of kosher salt and 1 to 2 cups of white vinegar or lemon juice to 1 gallon of water.

4. Remove excess moisture from the crab by squeezing gently.

5. Pack the crab meat into pint jars, leaving 1 inch (2.5cm) of headspace.

6. Add 2 tablespoons of white vinegar or lemon juice or 1 teaspoon of citric acid to each 1 pint and add boiling water to cover, leaving 1 inch (2.5cm) of headspace.

7. Wipe the rims, adjust the lids, and process the jars in a pressure canner. See Appendix C for the processing times.

Here's the preparation for oysters:

1. After cleaning, wash the meat in a weak brine solution made from ½ cup of kosher salt to 1 gallon of water. Drain the moisture from the meat and pack it into jars, leaving 1 inch (2.5cm) of headspace.

2. Cover with a weak brine solution (1 tablespoon of kosher salt to 1 quart of water), leaving 1 inch (2.5cm) of headspace.

3. Wipe the rims, adjust the lids, and process the jars in a pressure canner. See Appendix C for the processing times.

Here's the preparation for shrimp:

1. After cleaning, cook the shrimp in a pot for 8 to 10 minutes in a boiling brine made from ¼ to 1 cup of kosher salt and 1 cup of vinegar to 1 gallon of water. Remove the pot from the heat and drain. Rinse the shrimp in cold water.

2. Pack the shrimp into jars, leaving 1 inch (2.5cm) of headspace. Cover with a boiling salt brine made from 1 to 3 tablespoons of kosher salt to 1 gallon of water.

3. Wipe the rims, adjust the lids, and process the jars in a pressure canner. See Appendix C for the processing times.

Canning Game

Wild game is different from domestic meat. That seems obvious, but it bears some explanation. What are the differences? Domestic animals live in a controlled environment. They're fenced in and fed or allowed to graze on specific pastures. They don't have to (or shouldn't have to) struggle to find sustenance. With their dietary needs more than satisfied, they put on weight. This means they have enough food to enable them to store the excess as fat. Fat makes meat tender and flavorful.

Wild game animals have a tougher life. They're constantly on the search for food. They tend to be leaner, and as a result, their meat is tougher than their domestic cousins'. Pressure canning their meat solves the toughness problem but not the gaminess that some people find distasteful. So what's that gamey taste?

Not to put too fine a point on it, but after all, it's game. It has its own particular flavor and aroma, and if you're expecting venison to taste like beef, you're going to be disappointed. But if you're expecting venison to taste like venison, you're going to be satisfied. If you're an aficionado of game, you enjoy its distinctive taste and aroma.

That said, there are a couple of factors that contribute to a gamey taste and you can do something about both of them.

First of all, be sure the game is kept properly chilled after harvesting. Once the animal becomes warm, there's not much you can do to reverse the natural processes that lead to a disagreeable taste.

Second, be sure to remove all the fat. Especially with deer meat, fat can contribute to gaminess. It might seem contradictory because the fat on domestic animals doesn't make them taste gamey, but that's just the way it works.

Some people add a teaspoon or two of white vinegar while they're cooking venison and some people insist that soaking the meat in milk before cooking it works fine. Neither of these methods will cause any harm. Salt and tomato juice are also used, and they're discussed in a moment.

Before preparing game for canning, soak it for 60 minutes in a brine made from 1 tablespoon of kosher salt to 1 quart of water. This reduces the gamey taste. Then rinse and remove the large bones. Cut the meat into strips, chunks, or cubes.

For raw pack, pack the meat into jars, leaving 1 inch (2.5cm) of headspace. Don't add liquid. You can add 1 teaspoon of kosher salt to each jar for flavor, but it's not necessary. Wipe the rims, adjust the lids, and process the jars in a pressure canner. See Appendix C for the processing times.

For hot pack, precook the meat until rare. You can stew it, roast it, or simply brown it in olive oil or fat. Then pack it into jars and cover with boiling broth, water, or tomato juice, leaving 1 inch (2.5cm) of headspace. Tomato juice is often used to deal with the gamey nature of game. Wipe the rims, adjust the lids, and process the jars in a pressure canner. See Appendix C for the processing times.

Determining Proper Processing Times

If you'd like to put up some soup, stew, or chili to have ready for a quick supper on a cold night, there are a few things to keep in mind to make sure your meal is nutritious and safe. It's as easy as 1-2-3:

1. You'll pressure process it because you're dealing with vegetables and meats.

2. The amount of time in the pressure canner will be determined by the vegetable or meat that takes the longest amount of time. It's in charge!

3. Hold off on the flour as a thickening agent until you're ready to heat the stew for serving. Flour thickens the liquid and can keep it from heating to the required temperatures necessary to ensure a safe product.

Recipes

The first recipe gives you some choices: beef, elk, or venison. You pick the meat— and then get ready for rave reviews.

Hams are generally quite big, and even if you have them cut in half, you're probably going to have more than you can use before the freezer life is up. Can some of these smaller pieces and you'll have some spectacular pea soup on short notice.

Chili con Carne

Con carne means "with meat," so there's no reason to stick to beef all the time. Expand your options and try venison or elk.

Makes	Prep time	Cook time
6 pints	25 minutes	45 minutes

3 tbsp olive oil

2 medium white onions, chopped

2 garlic cloves, minced

3lb (1.4kg) ground beef, venison, or elk

6 cups crushed tomatoes

1 tsp paprika

1 chili pepper, chopped

kosher salt, to taste

freshly ground black pepper, to taste

1. Heat the olive oil in a large pot on the stovetop over medium heat. Add the onions, garlic, and ground beef, venison, or elk. Sauté until the meat browns. Add the tomatoes, paprika, chili pepper, and salt and pepper to taste. Simmer for 30 to 45 minutes.

2. Remove the pot from the heat and ladle the meat into pint or quart canning jars.

3. Seal the jars and process in a pressure canner for 75 minutes for pints and 90 minutes for quarts. (Follow the directions for canning in chapters 10 and 11.)

4. When ready to serve, combine the meat with one or two cans (14.5oz [415g]) of red beans or kidney beans. Simmer on low heat for 30 minutes.

Split Pea & Ham Soup

"Pease porridge hot / Pease porridge cold / Pease porridge in the pot / Nine days old." Nine days might be pushing it, but this hearty soup is always best on the second and third days. Serve with crusty rolls.

Makes	**Prep time**	**Cook time**
5 to 6 pints	25 minutes	4 to 6 hours

2 cups split peas

1 ham hock

1 celery stalk, chopped

2 carrots, chopped

1 medium white onion, chopped

kosher salt, to taste

freshly ground black pepper, to taste

3 quarts cold water

1. If the peas require soaking, add them to a large pot and cover with cold water. Allow to sit overnight.

2. Place the pot on the stovetop over high heat. Add the ham hock, celery, carrots, onion, salt and pepper to taste, and cold water. Bring to a boil, then reduce the heat to low. Simmer for 4 to 6 hours.

3. If the peas don't require soaking, in a large pot on the stovetop over high heat, combine all the ingredients. Bring to a boil, then reduce the heat to low. Simmer for 4 to 6 hours.

4. Remove the pot from the heat and ladle the soup into pint or quart canning jars, leaving 1 inch (2.5cm) of headspace.

5. Seal the jars and process in a pressure canner at 10 pounds of pressure for 75 minutes for pints and 90 minutes for quarts. (Follow the directions for canning in chapters 10 and 11.)

Clam Chowder by the 4s

This recipe can be doubled or tripled to make a full canner load.

Makes	Prep time	Cook time
4 pints	25 minutes	25 minutes

4 cups clams with liquor

4 tsp butter

4-inch (10cm) salt pork square

1 medium white onion, diced

4 cups milk of choice

4 cups diced white potatoes

kosher salt, to taste

freshly ground black pepper, to taste

1. Drain the clams, reserving the liquor.

2. In a large skillet on the stovetop over medium heat, combine the butter, salt pork, and onion. Sauté until the onion is translucent, about 2 to 3 minutes.

3. Add the milk, potatoes, and clams. Season with salt and pepper to taste. Cook for 10 to 15 minutes.

4. Remove the skillet from the heat and pack the chowder into pint canning jars.

5. Seal the jars and process in a pressure canner for 100 minutes. (Follow the directions for canning in chapters 10 and 11.)

Dutch Oven (or Slow Cooker) Rabbit Dinner

Either way you choose to prepare this, the rabbit is tender and flavorful. A bonus is being able to use your canned (or frozen) peas and carrots as well as those peppers you cut up and froze at harvest time.

Serves	Prep time	Cook time
4	15 minutes	4 to 6 hours

2 tbsp olive oil

1 rabbit, jointed and cut into pieces

1 small can of tomato paste

1 cup chicken or beef stock

1 bay leaf

1 tsp fresh rosemary

1 to 2 medium white onions

kosher salt, to taste

freshly ground black pepper, to taste

1 pint canned mixed vegetables

2 to 3 medium white potatoes

1. Heat the oil in a large skillet on the stovetop over medium heat. Add the rabbit and cooked until browned.

2. In a slow cooker or Dutch oven, combine the tomato paste and stock. Add the rabbit, bay leaf, rosemary, and onion. Season with salt and pepper to taste.

3. Cook on low for 4 to 6 hours or until the rabbit tests done. There should be no pinkness to the meat.

4. Add the potatoes and mixed vegetables 2 hours before serving.

Sausage & Potato Skillet

You'll make this satisfying meal in one skillet.

Serves	Prep time	Cook time
4 to 6	15 minutes	45 minutes

2 to 3 medium Yukon Gold potatoes, cut into wedges or sliced about ½ inch (1.25cm) thick

1 yellow onion, sliced

1 garlic clove, minced

1 cup frozen sliced green peppers (mild or spicy)

1 quart canned sausage, sliced

3 tbsp olive oil, divided

½ cup freshly grated parmesan cheese

kosher salt, to taste

freshly ground black pepper, to taste

1. Heat 2 tablespoons of olive oil in a large skillet on the stovetop over medium heat. Add the potatoes and sauté until crispy and tender, about 10 minutes. Transfer the potatoes to a bowl and set aside.

2. In the same skillet, heat the remaining 1 tablespoon of olive oil. Add the sausage, onions, garlic, and peppers. Sauté for 5 minutes. The vegetables shouldn't be limp.

3. Return the potatoes to the skillet and heat thoroughly.

4. Remove the skillet from the heat and transfer everything to a serving platter. Top with freshly grated parmesan cheese.

Pickles, Relishes & Fermented Foods

Pickling, making relishes, and fermenting provide enhanced color, crunch, and flavor to foods, and their products work well as accompaniments to all kinds of main courses. The basic difference between pickles and relishes is that pickles use fruits or vegetables either whole or cut in slices, whereas relishes chop them up. With fermentation, you'll follow a simple process to preserve foods for later use. All three techniques are discussed in this part of the book.

When is a vegetable not a vegetable? When it's a pickle! Same goes for fruit, meats, and eggs. Pickles take the ordinary to the extraordinary. And jars of pickles can be pretty! It would be rather strange to give someone a gift of a plain jar of green beans, but a festively decorated bottle of dilly beans with the recipe attached is the perfect choice for someone who loves to cook. The possibilities for pickling are almost endless. In this chapter, we'll take a look at the basic ingredients and discover how they all combine to create that wonderful crunch.

The Science Behind Pickling

Also known as "fresh pack," pickling is closely tied to the fermentation process and it's an ancient way of preserving foods. In fact, just about every culture has found a way to get pickled. However, as far as food products go, early methods of pickling involved soaking in a salt brine and allowing fermentation to take place. In this process, certain types of bacterial growth are encouraged (lactic acid bacteria) and others (the ones that cause food to spoil) are discouraged. It's a selective process.

During the fermenting process, there's a delicate balance among the ingredients in the pickling crock and keeping everything in balance is the key to producing an excellent pickle. Two important players in this production are lactic acid bacteria and salt.

Lactic acid bacteria feed on the sugar contained in cucumbers. This allows the bacteria to grow and multiply, and it also imparts the familiar "bite" of fermented pickles.

Salt is very important in keeping the balance. It's like Goldilocks and the three bears. If there's too much salt, lactic acid can't survive, let alone thrive. Too little salt and the spoilage bacteria get the fighting edge. But with just the right amount of salt, your pickles will be perfect.

Oxygen is a spoiler for fermenting pickles, so making sure you're keeping out the air is essential. Keep the crock tightly covered.

Finally, the temperature needs to stay a fairly constant 70°F to 75°F (21°C to 24°C) to help the lactic acid bacteria stay alive, healthy, and on the job. By keeping the temperature at the low range of what's optimal, you'll regulate the speed of fermentation. Slow is best here for getting the best product.

The Wonderful World of Pickles

The more pickle-making you do, the more respect you'll develop for the common cabbage and cucumber. Cabbages have been cultivated for at least 4,000 years. Their scientific name is *Brassica oleracea* and they're related to broccoli, cauliflower, Brussels sprouts, and kale. Savoy cabbage, the crinkly kind with the deeply veined leaves, was developed in Germany back in the 16th century, so it's safe to say that sauerkraut has been around for a very long time.

Cucumbers (*Cucumis sativus*) are interesting in that just like tomatoes, they're a fruit used as a vegetable. They're related to watermelons, muskmelons, and squash, including pumpkins. They originated in India and have been cultivated for more than 3,000 years. They're mostly water (96%) and come in three types: slicing, pickling, and the seedless or "burpless" varieties. For pickle purposes, we use pickling cucumbers. They're smaller than slicing cukes, with warty skins that have tiny spines.

Gherkins are the smallest pickling cukes. Their name comes from the early modern Dutch word *gurken*, which simply means "small pickled cucumber." Depending on how you process them, you can make sweet or dill gherkins.

The last important plant ingredient in vegetable pickles is dill (*Anethum gravealens*). It's an herb and belongs to the celery family. It was first reported as a find in the tomb of Pharaoh Amenhotep II around 1400 BCE.

With this background knowledge, let's move on and see how to use these ingredients.

Brined or Fermented Pickles

These take the longest to make—a week or longer—but if you love pickles, they're the best. It's a curing process done in a crock. Brining and fermenting are two different processes. *Brining* uses a saltwater solution in a specific strength to cure the pickles. Afterward, acid must be added (vinegar) as a preservative. *Fermenting* causes lactic acid bacteria to grow and act as a preservative.

Kosher dill pickles have just enough garlic added to the brine to give them their characteristic texture and flavor. However, these pickles aren't necessarily kosher. It's become a commonly applied name to this particular kind of pickle. If you're buying them ready-made, you'll need to check the label to see if they were made under rabbinical supervision.

Quick-Pack Pickles

These are quick, as the name says. No crock is needed—just a large kettle or pot on the stove. You can cure these pickles for a few hours first or move directly to the cooking phase with vinegar and a mix of fresh spices. Vinegar is the pickling and preserving agent, and to ensure a safe product, it needs to contain 5% acetic acid. These pickles are finished in a boiling water bath.

To be safe, always use tested, approved recipes when making pickles. Don't alter the proportions of ingredients in the recipe and you'll help prevent the growth of harmful bacteria, such as *Clostridium botulinum,* the bacteria that causes botulism.

Relishes

Relishes are pickles gone bite-size. Fresh fruits or vegetables are chopped into small pieces, added to a spicy vinegar solution, and cooked for a short period of time on the stovetop. Relishes are finished in a boiling water bath. See Chapter 16 for complete directions and recipes.

Pickling Fruits & Vegetables

Think sweet and sour for these pickles. They can be created from one variety of fruit or vegetable or a mix of several. The right proportions of sugar and 5% vinegar are combined with fresh spices to make a safe product that's finished in a boiling water bath. See Chapter 14 for complete directions and recipes.

Equipment & Supplies

The first ingredients to consider are the fruits or vegetables you'll be pickling. If you start with firm, ripe, fresh produce, you'll be well on your way to a fine pickle. Don't be seduced by the bargain bin. Moldy, overripe, or shriveled produce isn't a good deal. If you wouldn't eat it, you shouldn't pickle it. You'll need about 14 pounds (6.4kg) of cucumbers to make a full canner load of 7 quarts of pickles.

Cucumbers come in two basic types: slicing and pickling. Choose pickling cucumbers! The slicing varieties don't hold up to the pickling process. They're meant to be eaten fresh. Pickling cucumbers are generally smaller than slicing cucumbers. They also have wartier skins—a real knobby texture. You'll probably have an easier time finding these at a pick-your-own farm or at a farmers' market. Supermarkets generally carry only slicing cukes. Also, cucumbers shouldn't be waxed because the wax is a barrier that keeps the brining solution from entering. Don't delay after you've gotten your produce picked or purchased. Pick and process the same day if you can. If you must wait until the following morning, keep the produce refrigerated.

Either lime or alum appears frequently as an ingredient in older recipes. They were used as firming agents. Just give your cucumbers a good ice water soak for 4 to 5 hours before you begin the pickling process and you'll get crisp pickles without these additives.

For fermented pickles, you'll need pickling or kosher salt, a stoneware crock, and a weight (such as a dinner plate) to keep the pickles under the brine. Be sure the crock is large enough to hold the pickles and salt, with a few inches to spare at the top to accommodate the brine that forms during the fermenting process. A general rule is 1 gallon of space for each 5 pounds (2.3kg) of fresh produce.

For quick-pack pickles, you'll need pickling or kosher salt, 5% vinegar, sugar, and spices, according to the recipe you'll be following. The salt you use is important. Kosher and pickling salt are pure, which means they have no additives (such as iodine, which can turn pickles dark and the pickling liquid cloudy) or anticaking ingredients that keep the salt free-flowing. Kosher salt tends to be coarser than pickling salt. Kosher salt can be used as a substitute for pickling salt as long as it doesn't contain any anticaking agents. Morton's does, so it's not recommended for pickling. Diamond Crystal doesn't contain anticaking agents, so it would be an acceptable substitution for pickling salt.

Kitchen scales aren't a luxury item. If the recipe specifies a certain weight of produce, you'll need to get an exact measurement. Especially in fermented pickles, guesswork is almost certainly an invitation to failure. You've got a considerable investment in produce as well as in your time and effort. Don't sabotage it!

General Procedures

Have a plan for your produce. Everything big or small has a place in pickle-making. If you'll be making gherkins, use the smallest cucumbers—about 1½ inches (3.75cm) in length. Dills use the larger-sized cukes—about 4 inches (10cm) long. Produce that's overly large can be sliced or chopped to make relishes or pickled fruits or vegetables.

Wash the produce thoroughly. You don't want any soil remaining to potentially cause softening of the pickles. For the same reason, slice off the blossom end that contains enzymes that can cause softening. Just a tiny slice will suffice.

Assemble all the ingredients before you plunge into processing. It's aggravating to have to stop and search for an ingredient when you're in the middle of something important. Preparation prevents pickle problems. Follow the recipe exactly. Don't change the amounts of salt, sugar, or vinegar. You can exchange or omit certain spices. If you don't like turmeric, leave it out. Love cinnamon? Add an extra stick to your pickled fruits.

Wash all jars in hot soapy water, rinse them thoroughly, and keep them hot until you're ready to fill them. Just because a jar looks clean doesn't mean it's clean. Be scrupulous!

Always finish with the proper time in the boiling water canner. This inactivates certain enzymes that can cause changes in color, texture, and flavor; destroys spoilage microorganisms; and ensures the seal. If you'll be processing your jars for less than 10 minutes, sterilize the jars by boiling them for 10 minutes before packing them.

Some pickle recipes call for pasteurization instead of processing in a boiling water bath. This method uses lower temperatures (180°F to 185°F [80°C to 85°C]) and can give you a higher-quality product. If your recipe indicates this method, follow this procedure:

1. Place the jars in a boiling water canner that's been filled halfway with warm water (120°F to 140°F [50°C to 60°C]). Add additional warm water to cover the jars to a level 1 inch (2.5cm) above their tops.

2. Turn on the heat under the canner to high. When the water reaches 180°F to 185°F (80°C to 85°C), begin timing. Process for 30 minutes at this temperature. Use a thermometer to ensure the water remains in this range. If the temperature increases, the pickles might soften.

3. After 30 minutes, remove the jars immediately from the canner and set them on a clean, dry surface.

Again, a reminder: This process should only be used in recipes that indicate it's safe.

Storing

The first step in storing is testing the seals within 12 to 24 hours of processing the jars. To do this, you'll remove the ring. Your jar is sealed if the lid is concave in the center. (Compare it with an unused lid and you should see a difference. The unused lid is raised in the center.) The lid shouldn't move when you press on it. One old-time way of checking a seal was to hit the lid with a spoon and listen for a pure ring (as opposed to a dull thud). However, this method isn't all that reliable.

If your lids have sealed, you're ready to move on to step two: washing the outside of the jars. Many jars are sticky after processing and rinsing them in warm water will remove that sticky residue. Wipe with a clean, dry towel.

Next, use an indelible pen to label each lid with the jar's contents and the date. Leave the ring off. Leaving the ring on can make a jar that's come unsealed appear to still have a tight seal. Also, rust can form between the ring and the jar, and that can make unscrewing the ring later quite difficult. It also looks nasty.

Finally, store the jars away from sunlight in a cool, dry location. The shelf life for home-canned pickles is about 1 year. As long as they were properly prepared, processed, and stored and the lids are still sealed, the food should be fine. However, quality decreases over time, so eat up! The best way to make sure your preserved produce stays fresh is to rotate your stock! Just as stores rotate their stock—putting older items out front and placing new items behind them—so should you. "First in, first out" is the home food preserver's motto.

Before using your pickled products, check to be sure the lid is still sealed. If it's bulging or any liquid has seeped out (indicating a poor seal) or if after opening the jar you notice an off-putting odor, mold, foam, questionable texture to the pickles, or any kind of movement of the liquid in the jar, dispose of the product without tasting it. Boil the food for 10 minutes and dispose of the contents in the garbage.

You can reuse the canning jars even if the pickles have spoiled. The Extension Service recommends cleaning them with a solution made from 1 part chlorine bleach to 5 parts water. Allow the solution to remain on the glass surfaces for 5 minutes, then rinse. You can then wash them in the regular cycle of your dishwasher.

This message bears repeating often: *Never* taste food you suspect has spoiled.

Troubleshooting

In a pickle about your pickles? When pickles go wrong, it can be frustrating. Generally, there are some simple explanations for what happened and knowing the cause gives you a chance to find a remedy for the problem. Here are some of the most common pickle problems and what to do about them.

Hollow Pickles

A hollow pickle can start out as a hollow cucumber. This can happen if the cuke didn't mature properly, was on the vine too long, or sat around on the counter or in the refrigerator waiting to become a pickle. You can usually spot these when you're giving them their initial scrub in the sink. They're floaters. That doesn't mean they're not useful in relishes, where they're cut up into small pieces, but they're definitely not whole pickle timber. If you're fermenting pickles and end up with some hollow ones, the fermenting process might have been too quick or the temperature during fermenting might have been too high.

Soft Pickles

Nobody likes soft pickles. Soft is sometimes coupled with slippery and it's just not a good thing at all. You can't turn a soft pickle crunchy again, so it's best to prevent it in the first place. Depending on what caused the softening, the pickle is either safe to eat or it's not. Did you remove the blossom at the tip? Enzymes responsible for softening are located there, so be sure to slice off the end. If this is the cause, the pickles are safe to eat but unappetizing.

If harmful bacteria got a chance to grow during the fermenting process because the salt concentration was too light, toss the pickles. They're not safe to eat. It's essential to follow the recipe exactly regarding the amount of ingredients and proper procedures. Don't cut back on the salt or the acid, and be sure the cukes remain covered with brine throughout the fermenting process. Also, skim off any scum that forms.

Finally, observe proper processing procedures. Follow the fermenting process with the correct amount of time in a boiling water bath to ensure a proper seal. If the seal fails, the pickles aren't safe to eat and must be disposed of.

Splotches & Blotches

These problems are cosmetic. The pickles are safe to eat but won't win any prizes for beauty. Too much sun can cause skin scalding and too much time on the vine can make cukes old. In that case, you're probably really dealing with age spots. Also, keeping the cucumbers in the fridge too long before processing can cause browning. Cucumbers should be fresh, firm, not overripe, and a uniform green color if they're going to make a pickle worth its salt.

Weird Colors

Pickles that turn out an alarming shade of green or garlic that becomes blue or purple usually means copper is to blame. If that's the case, the pickles should be discarded. Where does the copper come from? You might have some expensive copper cookware that works beautifully for most kinds of cooking, but it's not the right choice for making pickles—and neither is brass or iron. Also, avoid using galvanized utensils. Copper reacts with acid and salt to make copper sulfate and creates these changes. If you use stainless steel, enamelware, or stoneware, you won't have this problem.

Dark Pickles

Dark pickles might look unattractive, but the pickles are still safe to eat.

It could be a spice problem. If you've used ground spices instead of whole, used too much (didn't follow the recipe), or left the whole spices in the pickling solution when you packed the jars, you might end up with dark pickles.

Darkness could also be a salt problem. Use pickling or kosher salt—never iodized table salt—for your pickles.

Or it could be a water problem. Soft water—not hard—is best for pickling.

Shriveled Pickles

These pickles are screaming "Too much! Too much!" Follow the recipe carefully. If you use too much sugar, too much salt, or too much vinegar at the outset and then cook the pickles too much or process them too long, they'll shrivel. Be sure to follow the directions exactly! The pickles are safe to eat but won't impress the judges.

Pickling Fruits & Vegetables

Think pickles and your brain conjures up all kinds of cucumber products. What you might not know is you can pickle almost any kind of fruit and also a great many vegetables. This chapter will cover quick-pack pickles. Quick-pack pickles don't require a brining process. They're quick to make and add interest, texture, color, and flavor to every main course. You assemble the ingredients, simmer the pickling solution, add the fruit or vegetables, pack the jars, process—and you're done.

Pickling Fruits

Whether sweet and spicy or sweet and sour, fruit pickles are easy to make and are excellent gift items. Get started early because pickles take time to develop flavor. If you make a batch as each fruit comes into season, you'll have a nice selection when the holidays roll around.

Small-sized fruits are the best for pickling whole. These make a prettier product and you can usually find small fruits at roadside orchards. You can sometimes get good bargains on small fruit because it's … well, small—and people like big fruit for eating. Check out peaches, nectarines, and pears.

For other fruits, such as cantaloupe and watermelon, size doesn't matter because you'll cut cubes in uniform sizes for an attractive presentation. In the case of watermelon, you can even make a delicious pickle from the rind! More on this later in the chapter.

General Procedures & Supplies

For starters, you'll want fruit that hasn't been waxed. Waxing is a pain to deal with, and if you're working with whole fruit, wax makes it just about impossible for the pickling agents to penetrate the skin.

How do you spot a piece of waxed fruit? Easy! It's very shiny and glows about as brightly as your furniture after you've finished your spring cleaning.

Go organic when you can. The fruit isn't gassed or waxed. We've gotten so used to demanding perfect-*looking* fruit that we forget what fruit is all about: good taste!

Mixing fruits results in some wonderful combinations of pickles. Try mixing cantaloupe and peaches or pears and cherries. Or pickle a fruit salad. Don't be afraid to experiment. Fruit is acidic, so the addition of sugar and vinegar makes any experimentation on your part perfectly safe.

The process and the ingredients for making all kinds of pickled fruits are essentially the same. You'll need vinegar, sugar, water, spices, and, of course, fruit.

- Vinegar can be either white or apple cider. Some recipes call for white, some call for apple cider, and some don't specify, so you can use either kind. Keep in mind that white vinegar is clear and apple cider vinegar is brown. If color matters, use white. Vinegar is what adds the acidity to pickles and is important in producing a safe as well as tasty product. Cider vinegar is generally used more for fruits because it's milder than white vinegar.

- Sugar in fairly large amounts is necessary, although not nearly as much as is needed in jams and jellies. You can use granulated (white) or brown, although brown will darken the syrup a bit. Unless corn syrup is specifically called for, it's best to avoid it as well as honey. They can change the flavor of the pickles— and not for the better.

- You'll get a better pickle if you use soft water as opposed to hard. If you don't know if your water is hard, boil a quart of it and then let it sit for 24 hours. If there's any scum on top or sediment on the bottom, you've got hard water. If your water is hard, skim off any scum on the top and dip out the water you need without stirring up the sediment on the bottom.

- You're using fresh fruits, so your spices should also be fresh. Generally, you'll need whole cloves, cinnamon, and nutmeg. Unless a recipe specifically calls for ground spice, stick with the whole variety. Ground spices can make your pickles dark and cloudy.

You'll see that many of these recipes recommend using a spice bag to keep the spices from making the pickle too strong during storage. However, this is a matter of taste. For example, a spiced peach with a small clove embedded in it is scrumptious. If you decide to go with the spice bag, you can't reuse the spices in it.

Spice bags are easily made from materials you have around the house. You can use cheesecloth, a foot cut from a clean pair of hosiery, or any other porous fabric that will allow the spices to transmit their flavor to the syrup.

Pickling Vegetables

Vegetables are low-acid foods, which means you must add the right amount of vinegar to make them not only tangy but safe to eat. It's the single most important part of the pickle—apart from the food.

Just as with fruits, feel free to create your own combinations of vegetable pickles. Mix cauliflower florets and green bean slices or carrots and pearl onions. The sky's the limit! The vinegar makes these low-acid foods safe.

Chapter 13 gives the general procedures for making pickles, so let's get started right away with some recipes to fill your pantry and provide you with gifts galore for your friends and family.

Recipes

Never change the amount of vinegar specified in the recipes. Bottled vinegar in 5% strength is a preservative for quick-pack pickles, and in the case of vegetables, it lowers their pH below 4.0, making them safe as well as delightfully tart.

The next step is to sort the vegetables, keeping similar sizes together. If you're making pints and want the cucumbers whole, measure them against the side of the jar to get the right size. Gherkins use shorter cucumbers, while dills are traditionally longer. Always slice off the blossom end. It can contain enzymes that work to cause softening.

For each recipe, follow the general directions for canning in chapters 10 and 11.

Pickled Grapes

This is something quite fun! The flavor develops over several days and the skins will shrivel a bit, but the taste is something special.

Makes	Prep time	Cook time
4 pints	20 minutes	10 minutes

4lb (1.8kg) seedless grapes

1 tbsp broken ginger root

1½ tbsp whole cloves

2 pieces of cinnamon

1 cup granulated sugar

2 cups water

1 cup vinegar

1. Wash the grapes and remove any stems. Add the ginger root, cloves, and cinnamon pieces to a spice bag.

2. In a large saucepan on the stovetop over medium heat, combine the sugar, water, vinegar, and spice bag. Cook until the sugar dissolves.

3. Add the grapes and cook slowly until tender.

4. Remove the pot from the heat and ladle the grapes into hot, sterilized jars.

5. Seal the jars and process in a boiling water bath for 5 minutes.

Pickled Peaches, Apricots, or Pears

Seckel peaches make excellent pickles. They're firm enough to take the processing and yet just the right texture for good eating. For the following recipe, you can combine fruits for added interest.

Makes	Prep time	Cook time
8 pints	20 minutes	20 minutes

4 quarts small peaches, apricots, or pears

whole cloves

8 cups sugar (granulated or brown or a combination of the two)

1 quart vinegar

6 (3-inch [7.5cm]) pieces of cinnamon

1. If you're using peaches, remove the skins. (See Chapter 4). You can peel the pears if desired. Apricots require no special preparation. These fruits are pickled whole, so you don't remove the pits or core them.

2. Push 4 cloves into each piece of fruit.

3. In a large saucepan on the stovetop over medium heat, bring the sugar and vinegar to a boil. Cook for 2 minutes.

4. Add the fruit to the syrup and cook gently until soft.

5. Remove the saucepan from the heat and ladle the fruit into hot, sterilized jars. Add a small piece of cinnamon to each jar and enough syrup to cover, leaving ½ inch (1.25cm) of headspace.

6. Seal the jars and process in a boiling water bath for 5 minutes for pints and 10 minutes for quarts.

Pickled Watermelon Rind

Sometimes you run across a watermelon with a really thick rind. While this isn't what you want for eating purposes, it's terrific for making pickles. If you've got one of these treasures with an average rind width of ½ inch (1.25cm) or more, read on! A 16-pound (7.25kg) watermelon will give between 5 and 6 pounds (2.3 and 2.7kg) of rind—and 1 pound (450g) of rind will make about 1 pint of pickles.

Makes	Prep time	Cook time
4 to 5 pints	20 minutes	30 minutes

4 quarts watermelon rind

boiling water

2 tbsp kosher salt

1 quart vinegar

8 cups granulated sugar

¼ cup broken cinnamon sticks

1 tbsp whole cloves

1. Cut away all the green outside skin and all the pink inside flesh of the rind. (It won't crisp up.) You want pure white rind—or as pure as you can get it. Cut the rind into cubes. (The cube size will vary according to how thick the rind is.)

2. In a large saucepan on the stovetop over low heat, add the cubes and enough boiling water to cover. Add the salt. Simmer until the rind is tender. Drain the water and chill the rind in very cold water at least 1 hour or overnight.

3. In a small pot on the stovetop over high heat, bring the vinegar and sugar to a boil. Add the cinnamon sticks and whole cloves to a spice bag, then add the bag to the pot.

4. Drain the rind and add to the syrup. Reduce the heat to low and simmer until the rind becomes somewhat translucent.

5. Remove the saucepan from the heat. Remove and discard the spice bag. Pack the rind into hot, sterilized jars and add the syrup, leaving ½ inch (1.25cm) of headspace.

6. Seal the jars and process in a boiling water bath for 5 minutes.

Pickled Cantaloupe

A melon that's slightly underripe works best for pickles. You can double this recipe if you want to end up with pints instead of half-pint jars.

Makes	Prep time	Cook time
2 pints	20 minutes	1 hour

1 medium cantaloupe

2 cups water

1 quart vinegar

1 tsp whole mace

2 pieces of cinnamon

2 tbsp ground cloves

4 cups granulated sugar

1. Cut away all the outside skin and scoop out all the seeds and pulpy inner fiber from the cantaloupe. That will leave you with firm orange flesh. Cut this into cubes or scoop into balls. Aim for uniform sizes.

2. In a large saucepan on the stovetop over high heat, bring the water and vinegar to a boil. Combine the mace, cinnamon sticks, and ground cloves in a spice bag. Add the bag to the saucepan. Add the melon to a glass or ceramic bowl. Pour the boiling vinegar solution over the melon. Let stand overnight on the counter.

3. Pour the vinegar into a saucepan on the stovetop over high heat. Bring to a boil, then add the sugar and melon. Simmer until clear, about 1 hour.

4. Remove the saucepan from the heat. Remove and discard the spice bag. Pack the melon into hot, sterilized jars and add the boiling syrup.

5. Seal the jars and process in a boiling water bath for 5 minutes for pints and 10 minutes for quarts.

Wilma's Bread & Butter Pickles

These are probably the best bread and butter pickles you'll ever find. They're sweet and tart—and definitely crunchy.

Makes	Prep time	Cook time
9 pints	20 minutes	10 minutes

4 quarts thinly sliced medium cucumbers, unpared

6 medium white onions, sliced

2 green peppers

3 garlic cloves, sliced

1 small jar of pimientos

⅓ cup kosher salt

crushed ice

3½ cups granulated sugar

1½ tsp celery seeds

1½ tsp ground turmeric

2 tbsp mustard seeds

6 cups cider vinegar

1. In a large bowl, combine the cucumbers, onions, peppers, garlic, pimientos, and salt. Mix well. Cover with the crushed ice and let stand for 3 hours. Thoroughly drain and add the cucumber mixture to a large pot.

2. In a small bowl, combine the sugar, celery seeds, turmeric, mustard seeds, and vinegar. Pour this mixture over the cucumber mixture.

3. Place the pot on the stovetop over high heat. Bring the mixture to a boil.

4. Remove the pot from the heat and pack the pickles into hot, sterilized jars.

5. Seal the jars and process for 10 minutes for quarts and 5 minutes for pints.

Quick Kosher Dill Pickles

The old-fashioned kosher dills are fermented and take time to develop flavor. These are the quick-pack variety—very crunchy and very tasty.

Makes	**Prep time**	**Cook time**
6 to 7 pints	20 minutes	5 minutes

4lb (1.8kg) pickling cucumbers
(4 inches [10cm] long)

14 garlic cloves, halved

¼ cup pickling salt

2¾ cups 5% distilled white vinegar

3 cups water

14 heads of fresh dill

28 black peppercorns

1. Wash the cucumbers and cut them in half lengthwise.

2. In a small saucepan on the stovetop over high heat, bring the garlic, salt, vinegar, and water to a boil.

3. Remove the saucepan from the heat and place 4 garlic halves into each jar. Pack the cucumbers into hot, sterilized jars, adding 2 heads of dill and 4 peppercorns to each jar. Pour the hot vinegar solution over the cucumbers, leaving ½ inch (1.25cm) of headspace.

4. Seal the jars and process in a boiling water bath for 10 minutes for pints and 15 minutes for quarts.

Pickled Beets

If you're looking for easy, this is easy. All you need are beets, vinegar, sugar, and whole cloves.

Makes	Prep time	Cook time
6 pints	25 minutes	45 minutes

3 quarts small beets, peeled

4 cups vinegar

1½ cups granulated sugar

½ tsp whole cloves

1. Add the beets to a medium pot on the stovetop over medium heat. Cook for 10 to 25 minutes or until tender. Remove the pot from the heat and plunge the beets into cold water to slip off their skins.

2. In the same medium pot on the stovetop over low heat, combine the vinegar, sugar, and cloves. Simmer for 10 minutes.

3. Add the beets and simmer for 10 minutes more.

4. Remove the pot from the heat and pack the beets into hot, sterilized jars. Add the pickling solution, leaving ½ inch (1.25cm) of headspace.

5. Seal the jars and process in a boiling water bath for 20 minutes.

Reduced-Sodium Pickles

You can't reduce the amount of salt in fermented pickles, but you can with quick-pack pickles. This recipe gives you the best of both worlds.

Makes	Prep time	Cook time
4 to 5 pints	30 minutes	15 minutes

3lb (1.4kg) pickling cucumbers
(4 inches [10cm] long)

1⅔ cups plus 1 quart 5% distilled
white vinegar, divided

3½ cups granulated sugar, divided

1 tbsp whole allspice

2¼ tsp celery seeds

1 tbsp canning or pickling salt

1 tbsp mustard seeds

1. Wash the cucumbers. Cut ⅟₁₆ inch (0.20cm) off the blossom end and discard. Cut the cucumbers into ¼-inch (0.5cm) slices.

2. In a small saucepan on the stovetop over high heat, combine 1⅔ cups vinegar, 3 cups of sugar, whole allspice, and celery seeds. Bring to a boil. Keep the syrup hot until ready to use.

3. In a large kettle on the stovetop over low heat, combine the salt, mustard seeds, the remaining 1 quart of vinegar, and the remaining ½ cup of sugar. Add the cucumbers. Cover and simmer until the cucumbers change color from bright to dull green, about 5 to 7 minutes.

4. Remove the kettle from the heat and drain the cucumbers. Pack the cucumbers into hot, sterilized jars and cover with the hot syrup, leaving ½ inch of headspace.

5. Seal the jars and process in a boiling water bath for 10 minutes.

4-Day Sweet Gherkins

Four days might not seem all that quick, but it's still quicker than brining. Gherkins are distinctive little pickles. They're crooked and knobby and very tasty.

Makes	Prep time	Cook time
6 to 7 pints	20 minutes	10 minutes

7lb (3.2kg) cucumbers (1½ inch [3.75cm] in length or shorter)

boiling water

½ cup canning or pickling salt, divided

6 cups 5% distilled white vinegar, divided

8 cups granulated sugar, divided

¾ tsp ground turmeric

2 tsp celery seeds

2 tsp whole mixed pickling spice (optional)

2 cinnamon sticks

½ tsp fennel seeds (optional)

2 tsp pure vanilla extract (optional)

1. Wash the cucumbers. Cut a ¹⁄₁₆ inch (0.20cm) slice off the blossom end and discard, but leave ¼ inch (0.5cm) of the stem attached.

2. Place the cucumbers in a large container and cover with boiling water. Let the bowl sit on the counter for 6 to 8 hours.

3. Drain the water. Cover the cucumbers with 6 quarts of fresh boiling water containing ¼ cup salt. Repeat this process for a second day.

4. On the third day, drain the water. Prick the cucumbers with a table fork.

5. In a large pot on the stovetop over high heat, combine 3 cups of vinegar, 3 cups of sugar, turmeric, celery seeds, pickling spice (if using), cinnamon sticks, and fennel. Bring to a boil, then pour over the cucumbers.

6. Let sit for 6 to 8 hours, then drain, returning the pickling syrup to the pot. Add 2 cups of vinegar and 2 cups of sugar to the syrup. Heat to boiling, then pour over the pickles.

7. On the fourth day, drain and save the syrup.

8. In a medium saucepan on the stovetop over high heat, bring 2 cups of sugar and the remaining 1 cup of vinegar to a boil. Pour this mixture over the pickles. Let sit for 6 to 8 hours, then drain, returning the syrup to the pot.

9. Add 2 teaspoons of vanilla extract and the remaining 1 cup of sugar to the pot. Bring to a boil.

10. Remove the pot from the heat and pack the cucumbers into hot, sterilized jars. Cover with the hot syrup, leaving ½ inch (1.25cm) of headspace.

11. Seal the jars and process in a boiling water bath for 5 minutes.

Pickled Mixed Vegetables

This makes an attractive side dish for any meal. It's colorful and has different textures and shapes.

Makes	Prep time	Cook time
about 10 pints	20 minutes	10 minutes

4lb (1.8kg) pickling cucumbers, washed and cut into 1-inch (2.5cm) slices

2lb (1kg) small white onions, peeled and quartered

4 cups celery, cut into 1-inch (2.5cm) pieces

2 cups carrots, peeled and cut into 1-inch (1.25cm) pieces

2 cups red bell peppers, cut into 1-inch (1.25cm) pieces

2 cups cauliflower florets

cubed or crushed ice

5 cups 5% distilled white vinegar

¼ cup prepared mustard

½ cup canning or pickling salt

3½ cups granulated sugar

3 tbsp celery seeds

2 tbsp mustard seeds

½ tsp whole cloves

½ tsp ground turmeric

1. In a large bowl, combine the cucumbers, onions, celery, carrots, red bell peppers, and cauliflower. Cover with 2 inches (5cm) of cubed or crushed ice. Refrigerate for 3 to 4 hours.

2. In an 8-quart kettle on the stovetop over high heat, combine the vinegar and mustard. Mix well. Add the salt, sugar, celery seeds, mustard seeds, whole cloves, and turmeric. Bring to a boil.

3. Drain the vegetables and add to the hot pickling solution. Cover and slowly return to a boil.

4. Remove the pot from the heat and drain the vegetables again, but save pickling solution. Pack the vegetables in hot, sterilized pint or quart jars, leaving ½ inch (1.25cm) of headspace.

5. Seal the jars and process in a boiling water bath for 5 minutes for pints and 10 minutes for quarts.

Pickling Meats, Fish & Eggs

Pickling as a means of preserving was developed long before refrigeration and was a way of making sure there'd be enough meat to last through the long winter. Meats, fish, and eggs are often overlooked when it comes to pickling, but they make great pickles! Expand your food-preserving skills by trying something new. Whether you prefer sweet, hot, or spicy, there's a pickling recipe to suit your taste buds.

Pickling Meats

Older methods for pickling meats called for saltpeter (potassium nitrate). Saltpeter enhances taste, gives meat its characteristic red color, has some ability to inhibit botulism, and is also used as a preservative. Saltpeter isn't necessary, however, and you can make a very acceptable pickling solution without it. Potassium and sodium belong to the same family of elements. Potassium nitrate and potassium nitrite as well as sodium nitrate and sodium nitrite are different compounds but have similar properties. The health concern that's been raised is with nitrates and nitrites, but current research indicates that the sodium nitrate and sodium nitrite contained in pickling salts and processed meats don't pose health risks. The choice of whether to use nitrates and nitrites is up to you. You can use kosher or any other noniodized table salt instead. Table salt is sodium chloride (NaCl).

Beef

Corned beef is a type of pickled beef that's familiar to most of us. Corning is a means of preserving meat that gets its name from the large salt crystals, or *corns*, that were once used to rub into the meat to cure it. Beef lends itself quite well to pickling and the brisket (taken from the chest just ahead of the foreshank) and tongue as well as roasts (including boneless round or chuck roast) work well. The *corning* process isn't difficult, and if you'd like to try it yourself, you'll save some money over the corned beef you'll find at the grocery store.

Ingredients

You'll need salt. It's the essential ingredient. Kosher salt is excellent for pickling and brining, although you can also use noniodized table salt. For a 5-pound (2.3kg) roast, you'll need about ¾ cup of salt.

Then come the spices. Here you have considerable leeway and it's all right to experiment with different combinations and amounts of spices. If you want a sweeter corned beef, add brown sugar. If you prefer it a bit tangier, omit it. Here's a general list of ingredients:

- 1 to 2 tablespoons cracked black peppercorns
- ½ teaspoon sage
- ½ teaspoon paprika
- 1 garlic clove, diced
- ½ teaspoon ground ginger
- 1 tablespoon light brown sugar
- ¼ teaspoon ground nutmeg
- ½ teaspoon ground thyme
- 2 bay leaves

Vary these amounts and ingredients to suit your own tastes.

Method

In a medium bowl, mix together the spices, garlic, and salt. Wash and dry the cut of meat. Place it on a cookie sheet. Rub the meat on both sides with the spice mixture.

If you have a medium-sized stone crock, put the meat inside, cover it with water, and weigh it down with a plate to keep the meat under the water. The salt will work into the meat, releasing juices and creating the brine that will corn (pickle) the meat. Keep the crock in a cool location and turn the meat once a week for 4 weeks. Check to see if the brine is salty enough for your taste, and if it isn't, you can add more salt.

Another way that's definitely more modern and less messy than loose meat in the crock is to use a gallon freezer bag. Put the meat in the bag, burp out as much air as you can, zip it closed, and then put it in the crock. Weigh the bag down with a plate. Keep the crock in a cool location. Turn the freezer bag over every day for 4 weeks. Make sure the meat is totally covered with brine at all times.

When you're ready to use the corned beef, remove the meat from the crock and rinse it in cool water to remove the brine. If you find that the brine is very salty, you might want to soak the meat in cool water for about 30 minutes. Then rinse and pat it dry. It will keep for about 1 month in the fridge. To make Corned Beef & Cabbage, see page 244.

Pigs' Hocks & Pigs' Feet

These pickled products are interesting to try. The following method was taken from the Cooperative Extension Service, Bulletin 865, from the University of Georgia at Athens.

Ingredients

Your butcher should have some pigs' feet or pigs' hocks, but they're not a common item in the meat case, so you'll probably need to ask. Then you'll need the following:

- 2 quarts white vinegar
- 1 small red bell pepper
- 2 tablespoons grated horseradish
- 1 teaspoon whole black peppercorns
- 1 teaspoon whole allspice
- 1 bay leaf

Method

Use a scrub brush to scrub the feet or hocks thoroughly in cool water. Then scald, scrape, and clean them thoroughly. Place in a medium-sized bowl, sprinkle lightly with kosher salt, and let stand for 4 to 8 hours in the refrigerator. Rinse well. Then place them in a large pot, cover with water, bring to a boil, reduce the heat, and cook until tender but not until the meat is so tender that it falls off the bones.

Place the remaining ingredients in a medium-sized pot and bring to a boil.

Remove the feet from the hot water and pack them into hot glass canning jars, leaving ½ inch (1.25cm) of headspace. Fill the jars with the pickling solution, leaving ½ inch (1.25cm)of headspace. Remove air pockets by inserting a spatula into the jar and running it around the inside. Wipe the jar rims and adjust the lids.

Process for 75 minutes in a pressure canner: 10 pounds for a weighted gauge pressure canner and 11 pounds for a dial gauge pressure canner. Follow the directions for altitude adjustment, proper processing, and proper cooling. When the pressure has returned to 0, remove the lid, remove the jars, and allow them to cool on a flat, dry surface. They'll keep for at least 1 year in the pantry. Store them in a cool, dry place. Pigs' hocks or feet are served cold, so be sure to refrigerate a jar for several hours before serving.

Pickling Fish

Pickling fish isn't difficult and it's an excellent way of preserving the catch. The best product results from using fish with a high oil content, such as herring, shad, striped bass, Chinook salmon, or black cod. It's all a matter of taste, so many other varieties of fish and shellfish can be pickled. To be sure your product is safe, always follow approved, research-based recipes that have been extensively tested by experts in food safety. The recipes that pass muster consistently produce a safe product and are recommended for the home food preserver.

The pickling process uses vinegar, also known as "acetic acid." The vinegar makes the fish acid, which prevents botulism. Vinegar also adds flavor, softens the fish bones, and stops spoilage caused by certain bacteria. To kill all the bacteria present would take a vinegar with 15% acetic acid, but the vinegar you buy at the store is usually 5 to 6% acetic acid. Distilled white vinegar is preferred because apple cider vinegar can impart a "fruity" taste to the fish, which obviously wouldn't be desirable.

Pickled fish isn't a good food for people on sodium-restricted diets. About 5 ounces (140g) of pickled herring contains more than 1,200 milligrams of sodium! However, fatty fish, such as herring, is also high in omega-3 fatty acids—the good fats. It's also a good source of vitamins A and B_{12}.

Vinegar can't do it all though. Enzymes are still active and vinegar can only slow them down to a certain extent. This means you should only pickle as much fish as you're likely to use within 4 to 5 months and then be sure to keep it refrigerated.

Salting

Salting is usually an important first step in the pickling process. Salt removes water from the fish, serves to ensure good texture, deactivates certain enzymes, and kills some bacteria. If you won't be pickling the fish right away, salting cures the fish so you can store it without having to refrigerate it. With this method, the fish will keep anywhere from 2 to 3 months. If refrigeration isn't a problem, the fish will keep longer (6 to 12 months). If the recipe doesn't require salting, you should freeze the fish prior to pickling. Keep it in the freezer for 3 to 4 days to kill parasites that might be present in the fish.

The Pickling Process

The pickling process is spread out over about a week and involves four steps: preparing the fish, preparing the pickling solution, curing, and pickling.

Step 1: Preparing the Fish

Clean, scale, and gut the fish. Remove the head. Remove the backbone from large fish. This isn't necessary for small fish, such as herring, but be sure to cut away the kidney, which is next to the backbone. It can be difficult to see because it's just a darkish line.

Step 2: Preparing the Pickling Solution

There are many recipes for a pickling solution, but the Extension Service provides the following basic pickling solution for fish. It makes about 1 gallon of solution:

- 3 pints of water
- 4 pints of 5% white vinegar
- 2 cups of granulated sugar
- 4 tablespoons of kosher salt
- ¾ cup of pickling spice
- 2 small white onions (chopped or sliced)
- ¼ teaspoon of chopped dried garlic (or 1 to 2 chopped fresh cloves)

To prevent the risk of botulism, never decrease the amount of vinegar needed to make a solution that contains one or more parts of 5% vinegar to each part water. If you want a sweeter solution, add more sugar, but don't cut back on the vinegar. Bring all ingredients to a boil and allow them to cool before using.

Step 3: Curing the Fish

This involves dry salting or curing with brine for 5 to 8 days.

If you dry salt, lay down about ¼ inch (0.5cm) of kosher salt in the bottom of a container suited to the size of the fish you're curing. Alternate layers of fish and salt. Place the top fish skin side up and cover it with a layer of salt. It's best to refrigerate the curing fish, but if you don't have room, keep the fish below 50°F (10°C) during the curing process.

If you brine the fish, make up a brine mixture that's 1 part kosher salt to 3½ parts water. You'll need an equal volume of fish and brine. Pour the brine into a crock suitable for pickling and then add the fish. Be sure the brine completely covers the fish. You'll need to put a weight on the fish to keep them from rising above the brine. Again, refrigeration is best, but at least keep the fish at 50°F (10°C) or below during the curing process.

Step 4: Pickling the Fish

If you've dry salted the fish, rinse them in cool water to remove any excess salt. If you prefer, you can let the fish soak in cool water for up to 24 hours to remove additional salt. This is called *freshening*. If you've brined the fish, rinse it in cool water.

If you prefer the fish without skin, this is the time to remove it. Decide if you want strips or chunks, then cut the fish accordingly. Pack the fish into glass jars, cover with pickling solution, secure the lids, and let the curing process finish under refrigeration. It will take 1 to 2 weeks for the bones to soften.

Pickling Eggs

Pickled eggs are fun to make and recipes range from sweet and sour (see the recipe at the end of this chapter) to dilled. They're made from adding a pickling solution to peeled, hard-boiled eggs. Eggs are a nutrient-dense food, packed with vitamins and minerals, and they're also an excellent source of protein. Eggs contain all the essential amino acids and are low in fat. However, eggs—or, more specifically, egg yolks—are a significant source of cholesterol. One egg can contain 210 milligrams of cholesterol.

Better Boiling

Eggs that are a few days old before they're cooked peel more easily than fresh eggs, but fresh is always preferable to not-so-fresh.

Here's the easiest recipe for perfect hard-boiled eggs you'll ever find. Place the eggs in a single layer in a saucepan and add water to cover the eggs by 1 inch (2.5cm). Cover the saucepan and bring just to a boil, turn off the heat, and remove the saucepan from the burner to prevent further cooking. With the cover in place, allow the eggs to remain in hot water for 15 to 17 minutes.

Drain the water from the saucepan and then run cold water over the eggs or you can put the eggs in ice water until the eggs are completely cooled down. Crack the shell all around. Then beginning at the larger end of the egg, peel the shell from the egg. This is where the air cell is located; you'll have an easier time of it if you start here. It's also easier to peel an egg if you keep it under cool running water.

Ingredients

Basic ingredients for pickling eggs include vinegar, water, a mixture of spices, and onion. Water and vinegar are usually in equal proportions. You'll find recipes for two different types of pickled eggs in the Recipes section of this chapter.

Method

You'll want to use a quart glass canning jar for the next step. Fill the jar loosely with peeled eggs. The jar should hold about a dozen. Heat the pickling mixture to a near boil and then let it simmer for 5 minutes. Turn off the heat and pour the mixture over the eggs in the jars, being sure to cover the eggs completely. Set the lid and ring in place and store in the refrigerator.

It will take anywhere from 1 to 4 weeks to season the eggs depending on their size. Keep them refrigerated during this time. They'll keep for several months.

Recipes

Pickling is the first step and enjoying what you've pickled is the next and best part! The following recipes will get you started.

Sweet & Sour Eggs

Pickling eggs is fun and quite easy. There are many different recipes for safely producing this food. This recipe is courtesy of the Georgia Egg Commission's publication *Peter Piper Picked a Peck of Pickled Eggs*.

Makes	**Prep time**	**Cook time**
1 dozen eggs	20 minutes	15 minutes

1 dozen large eggs, hard-boiled and peeled

1½ cup apple cider

½ cup apple cider vinegar

1 (12oz [340g]) package of cinnamon candy

1 tbsp mixed pickling spice

2 tsp kosher salt

1 tsp garlic salt

1. Loosely fill a quart jar with the eggs. Set aside.

2. In a small saucepan on the stovetop over high heat, combine the apple cider, apple cider vinegar, cinnamon candy, pickling spice, salt, and garlic salt. Bring to a boil, then reduce the heat to low. Simmer for 5 minutes.

3. Remove the saucepan from the heat and pour the mixture over the eggs, being sure to cover them completely.

4. Seal the jar and refrigerate for anywhere from 1 to 4 weeks to season the eggs depending on their size. Keep them refrigerated during this time. They'll keep for several months.

Dark & Spicy Eggs

Here's another tasty recipe courtesy of the Georgia Egg Commission's undated publication, "Peter Piper Picked a Peck of Pickled Eggs."

Makes	Prep time	Cook time
1 dozen eggs	20 minutes	15 minutes

1 dozen large eggs, hard-boiled and peeled

1½ cup apple cider vinegar

½ cup water

1 tbsp dark brown sugar

2 tsp granulated sugar

1 tsp mixed pickling spice

¼ tsp liquid smoke or hickory smoke salt

2 tsp kosher salt

1. Loosely fill a quart jar with the eggs.

2. In a small pot on the stovetop over high heat, combine the apple cider vinegar, water, dark brown sugar, granulated sugar, pickling spice, liquid smoke, and salt. Heat to a near boil, then reduce the heat to low. Simmer for 5 minutes.

3. Remove the pot from the heat and pour the mixture over the eggs, being sure to cover them completely.

4. Set the lid and ring in place and store in the refrigerator. It will take anywhere from 1 to 4 weeks to pickle the eggs depending on their size. Keep them refrigerated during this time. They'll keep for several months.

Deviled Eggs

These are great as appetizers and a frequent guest at potlucks.

Makes	Prep time	Cook time
1 dozen	10 minutes	15 minutes

6 large eggs, hard-boiled and peeled

¼ cup mayonnaise or enough to make a creamy mixture with egg yolks

¼ tsp mustard powder

⅛ tsp curry powder

paprika, to taste

1. Slice the eggs in half lengthwise and scoop out the yolks.

2. In a small bowl, combine the yolks, mayonnaise, mustard, and curry powder. Use a fork to mix well.

3. Use a tablespoon to fill the egg cavities. Top the eggs with paprika to taste.

Pickled Egg Salad

This is a great sandwich mixture. Add a slice of deli ham and pack it all between slices of hearty bread or rolls.

Serves	Prep time	Cook time
4	10 minutes	15 minutes

6 large eggs, hard-boiled and peeled

¼ cup mayonnaise or enough to make a creamy mixture with egg yolks

2 tbsp sweet pickle relish

¼ tsp mustard powder

¼ cup diced white onion

kosher salt, to taste

freshly ground black pepper, to taste

1. Chop the eggs into bite-sized pieces or use an egg slicer.

2. In a medium bowl, combine the eggs, mayonnaise, sweet pickle relish, mustard powder, and onion. Mix well. Season with salt and pepper to taste. Store in the fridge in an airtight container for up to 5 days.

Pickled Herring in Cream Sauce

This is a traditional Scandinavian food. Serve it with scrambled eggs and toast.

Serves	Prep time	Cook time
4	10 minutes	none

2 herring fillets (about ½lb [225g] each)

⅓ cup sour cream

1 white onion, sliced thinly

1. Cut the herring fillets into bite-sized pieces.

2. In a small bowl, combine the herring, sour cream, and white onion. Mix well. Store in an airtight container in the fridge for up to 6 days.

Green Chili Fish Stew

This makes for a hearty meal on a cold winter evening. The slow cooker does all the work for this "dump everything in the pot" recipe.

Serves	Prep time	Cook time
6	10 minutes	4 to 6 hours

½lb (225g) pickled white fish or salmon, chopped into bite-sized pieces

1 (28oz [800g]) can of diced tomatoes with basil, garlic, and oregano

1 (4oz [120g]) can of diced green chilis

1 (32oz [910g]) box of seafood stock

2 garlic cloves, smashed

1 medium white onion, cubed

1 (10oz [285g]) can of whole baby clams with liquid

1 (8oz [225g]) bottle of clam juice

1 cup uncooked long grain white rice

1. Combine all the ingredients in a slow cooker. Cook on low for 4 to 6 hours.

Pickled Fish Pasta

Once you've mastered making a white sauce, the world's your oyster.

Serves	Prep time	Cook time
4 to 6	25 minutes	30 minutes

8oz (225g) fettuccine or linguine

1 tbsp butter

2 garlic cloves, smashed

12 scallops

½lb (225g) pickled white fish or salmon

asparagus or broccoli, steamed

½ cup freshly grated parmesan

for the white sauce

2 tbsp butter

2 tbsp all-purpose flour

¼ tsp kosher salt

dash of freshly ground black pepper

1 cup hot milk of choice

1. Cook the fettuccine or linguine according to the package directions. Drain, cover, and set aside.

2. In a large skillet on the stovetop over medium heat, melt the butter. Add the garlic and scallops, spacing carefully. Sear for 2 minutes, flip, and sear for 1 minute more. Don't overcook or they'll be rubbery. Add the scallops and garlic to the pasta.

3. Cut the fish into cubes. Add the fish and the asparagus or broccoli to the pasta.

4. To make the white sauce, in a medium saucepan on the stovetop over medium heat, melt the butter to begin making a roux. Add the flour, salt, and pepper. Mix well. Scald the milk and add to the roux, stirring constantly over low heat until the mixture comes to a full boil and thickens. Pour over the fish and pasta. Stir well.

5. Add the parmesan and continue stirring over low heat until the sauce is thoroughly mixed and heated through.

6. Remove the pot from the heat and transfer the fish pasta to a serving bowl.

Corned Beef Hash

This is a good use for leftover meat. Serve it with your favorite vegetable dish.

Serves	Prep time	Cook time
4	15 minutes	30 minutes

2 medium white potatoes

1 tbsp olive oil

1lb (450g) corned beef brisket, cubed

1 white onion, cubed

1. Peeling the potatoes is optional. Add the potatoes to a large pot on the stovetop over high heat. Boil until fork-tender. Remove the pot from the heat and cut the potatoes into cubes.

2. In a large bowl, combine the potatoes, corned beef, and onion.

3. Heat the olive oil in a cast-iron skillet on the stovetop over medium heat. Add the potatoes, corned beef, and onion. Press down with a spatula until flattened.

4. Cook until the bottom is nicely browned. Use a spatula to flip the meat mixture and cook for a few minutes more or until the other side is nicely browned.

5. Remove the skillet from the heat and transfer the hash to a serving platter.

Corned Beef & Cabbage

This is a dish more associated with the Irish in America than in Ireland and it's definitely part of St. Patrick's Day feasting. The ingredients are simple and the dish is satisfyingly filling.

Serves	Prep time	Cook time
6	25 minutes	2½ hours

1 corned beef brisket

carrots (one for each person)

white potatoes (one for each person)

1 medium to large head of cabbage

1. To a large pot on the stovetop over high heat, add the corned beef brisket and some of the pickling solution (if you've corned the meat in a gallon bag). The amount is a matter of taste. If you find the solution saltier than you like, just add a little water. If it's not too salty, you can add more. Add cool water to cover.

2. Bring to a boil, then reduce the heat to low. Simmer gently for 2½ hours or until the meat is tender.

3. About 1 hour before serving, peel the carrots and potatoes. Cut the carrots in half lengthwise and add to the pot. Add the potatoes whole. Quarter the cabbage and remove the core. Add the cabbage to the pot and cover with a lid. Cook for 20 minutes or until the vegetables are done and the meat is tender.

4. Remove the pot from the heat and serve immediately.

Relishes

Relishes are quite a bit like pickles, except they're in smaller pieces. They belong to the quick pickle category and they're made from chopped fruits or vegetables, assembled in any variety of combinations, and simmered in a spicy vinegar solution. Just because they're small in size doesn't mean you can take shortcuts in making them. Just as with their bigger cousins (pickles), you must have the correct ratio of vinegar (5% acidity), fresh produce, salt, and sugar to create a safe and tasty product.

General Procedures

The key word here is "fresh." Fresh vegetables and fruits are not only tastier, but they're also more attractive and easier to cut. Young, tender vegetables and fruits make the best relishes, so this isn't a place for the tired, the shriveled, and the shopworn. Choose the best ingredients and get started on your relishes without delay.

There are quite a few ways to arrive at a bowlful of nicely chopped fruits or vegetables. You can use a sharp knife and cutting board, a food processor, or a vegetable shredder. The process isn't complicated, but it can be a bit messy if you're working with juicy fruits and vegetables.

Size is a matter of personal taste and the term "bite sized" is relative. Some folks dice the vegetables and fruits to get them super small, while others like bigger chunks. There's no gold standard here. Let whatever you like to eat guide your hand. While you're working at this task, tip the cutting board every so often and pour the liquid that accumulates from cutting fresh vegetables and fruits into a small bowl. You'll want to capture that juice and not watch it spill off onto the counter.

Roma tomatoes

Making Salsas

Salsas (the Spanish word for sauces) are bright, colorful, crunchy, and essential parts of Tex-Mex cuisine. There are a wide variety of ingredients you can choose to put in your own salsas. The basics include tomatoes, peppers, and onions.

You can use bottled lemon or lime juice instead of vinegar as long as you keep the proportions the same. Bottled lemon or lime juice is more acidic than vinegar, so you can substitute them for the vinegar but not the other way around. The percentage of acidity is constant in bottled lemon or lime juice, but it can vary widely in fresh juice. For safety, always use bottled juice.

The main caveat in making salsas is to not reduce the proportions of vegetables (low-acid foods) to the tomatoes and acid components. It's the acidity that makes the salsas safe to eat.

The proportions given in the recipes at the end of this chapter follow recommendations from the Extension Service for safe products. For more salsa recipes, request the brochure *Salsa Recipes for Canning* from your local Cooperative Extension Office.

A Tomato Primer

There are many different types of tomatoes and they come in a wide range of sizes and colors. For salsas, Romas are probably your best bet and tomatillos are also excellent. Romas are red and tomatillos are green, so together, they make a fiesta!

If you're not familiar with tomatillos, they're an interesting fruit. Like tomatoes, they belong to the nightshade family, even though they look a bit strange on the outside. After you remove the dry outer skin or husk, you're looking at a nice, round, green, almost tomato-type item. Peeling and seeding aren't necessary for tomatillos.

The tomatillo (*Physalis philadelphica*) is a relative of the tomato. It originates from Central America and has been cultivated in Mexico and Guatemala since pre-Columbian times. It's also referred to as the *husk tomato*, *jamberry*, or *groundcherry*.

For salsas, you want tomatoes with thick walls and firm flesh that hold up well during chopping and processing. It's true you can use regular eating or salad tomatoes, but you're likely to end up with a watery product that lacks shape. The difference is obvious when you slice into a Roma. You'll notice a distinct lack of juice spilling off the cutting board. You'll also see less mush accumulating as you chop and slice away.

Tomatillo in the husk (left), and a husked tomatillo (right)

A Pepper Primer

Tomatoes give salsa substance and peppers give it texture and heat. Actually, not all peppers turn on the heat, and if you prefer a mild salsa, you've got plenty of varieties of peppers to choose from. Peppers run the gamut from mild to hotter than Hades. If the recipe you're using calls for long green chilis, choose a mild variety.

There's actually a rating scale for heat in peppers: It's called the Scoville Heat Unit Scale, named for Wilbur Scoville, the man who created the system back in 1912. The bell pepper, a staple of salads, salad bars, and stuffed pepper dishes, rates a mere zero on the Scoville scale. Blocky and firm, bell peppers are green but turn red when mature and also come in shades of yellow or gold. The hottest peppers score in the thousands on the Scoville scale. For the purposes of making salsa, you might want to mix some bells with an Anaheim (a bit hotter, with a Scoville index around 1,000) or a jalapeño (around 5,000 on the index!).

The shapes of hot peppers are different from the milder varieties and many are elongated and wrinkled. Anaheims can be deep green at the red end of the color spectrum, so they might appear almost burgundy. They're usually around 4 to 5 inches (10 to 13cm) long with a flattened pod. Jalapeños are most often red or green and from 2 to 3 inches (5 to 7.5cm) in length. Whatever peppers you enjoy eating will be good additions to your salsa.

Be careful when handling hot peppers. You can seriously irritate your eyes if you happen to rub them while working with the hot varieties. The seeds are also hot. Wear gloves when handling hot peppers and wash up thoroughly afterward.

If you want to peel them (and you don't need to), slice along each side of the pepper. This makes an escape vent for the steam you'll be generating. Then place the peppers on a cookie sheet and put them in an oven that's been preheated to 400°F (200°C) for 6 to 8 minutes or under the broiler until the skins blister.

Remove the peppers from the oven and cover them with a damp cloth. After they've cooled for a few minutes, you'll be able to slip the skins and they'll be ready to chop.

You can remove the seeds from the hotter varieties of peppers if you wish. Also, the white membranes that extend from the seeds to the walls of the pepper have the highest concentration of capsaicin, the substance that gives peppers their heat. Remove that membrane and the seeds—and you'll turn down the thermostat a little.

An Onion Primer

Onions are the third main ingredient in salsa. Just as with peppers, you have a choice of colors and intensity of flavors. Yellow onions have the strongest flavor and that lets them compete favorably when mixed with a slightly hot pepper, such as an Anaheim. White onions are milder and red onions are sweeter.

Onions do sometimes bring tears to your eyes and there are as many recommendations for dealing with this as there are cures for hiccups. Here are some ways to stop the tears:

- Peel onions under cool, running water. That will work, although it's tough to dice and chop that way.

- Breathe through your mouth. It's worth a try, although it's the compounds stinging your eyes that cause the watering, not your nose.

- Eat a piece of bread while you're peeling. This is probably a variation on the "breathe through your mouth" advice. Your mouth will be open while you're biting into the bread and you'll most likely also take a breath then.

- Work quickly and use a sharp knife. Be careful around sharp knives, although if the knife is well honed, your work will go faster and you'll spend less time on close terms with the onion irritant.

- Try using a small fan to blow the fumes away from you.

- Cut off the root end first and toss it in the garbage. This operates on the theory that the problem is located in this part of the onion only.

- Wear a pair of swimming goggles. This has to work, but if you chop a great many onions, a major topic of conversation at dinner will be the circles around your eyes.

Keep in mind that onions get stronger as they age, but their flavor actually decreases, so it's best to use them promptly.

Keeping Your Produce Fresh

The nice thing about ingredients for making salsa is that they all come ripe around the same time: toward the end of the garden year. Whether you've grown your own produce or have made your purchases at the farmers' market or grocery store, it's important to store these items under optimal conditions until you're ready to create your salsas. You'll need fresh produce for your salsas, but for short-term storage, each item has different requirements.

For tomatoes, this means keeping them at room temperature and out of direct sunlight until they've fully ripened. Stored in the fridge, tomatoes get soft and lose their flavor. Always store them stems up because the shoulders are the most vulnerable spots on this fruit for bruising.

Green peppers keep well in the vegetable compartment of your refrigerator. If there's a humidity regulator, take advantage of it and increase the humidity as much as possible. Take the peppers out of any plastic bag you transported them in. This helps the air circulate and keeps the peppers from softening quickly. Plan on using them within a few days.

Onions like it cool and dry. Keep them out of direct sunlight and they'll keep for months.

Spices

Here you can use whatever you like. Black pepper, oregano, cilantro, and cumin are often used. If you prefer to use fresh cilantro for its aroma and flavor, add it to the salsa just before you serve it. Otherwise, it will turn into a stringy or leafy greenish mush.

Recipes

After so much talk about salsa, it's time for recipes! There are also some fruit and vegetable relishes to round out this chapter. For each recipe, follow the general directions for canning in chapters 10 and 11.

Tomatillo Salsa

Go totally green with this classic mild salsa. You can use either green tomatoes or tomatillos. If you're looking for salsa with a bit more zip, you can replace an equal amount of mild chilis with hotter ones. Just keep the proportions the same. The following recipe is adapted from *Salsa Recipes for Canning* (PNW0395), a publication of Pacific Northwest Extension Publications.

Makes	Prep time	Cook time
4 to 5 pints	30 minutes	20 minutes

5 cups chopped tomatillos
 (or green tomatoes)

2 cups seeded and chopped
 long green chili peppers

4 cups chopped onions

1 cup bottled lemon or lime juice

6 garlic cloves, finely chopped

kosher salt, to taste

freshly ground black pepper, to taste

1. In a large pot on the stovetop over high heat, combine the tomatillos, green chilis, onions, lemon or lime juice, garlic, and salt and pepper to taste. Bring to a boil, then reduce the heat to low. Simmer for 20 minutes, stirring occasionally.

2. Remove the pot from the heat and pack the salsa into hot, sterilized glass pint canning jars, leaving ½ inch (1.25cm) of headspace.

3. Seal the jars and process in a boiling water bath for 15 minutes.

Serving suggestion: Before serving, blend in 1 tablespoon of freshly chopped cilantro leaves to each 1 pint. Chill before serving.

Roma Salsa

This is a good, chunky salsa with enough color to liven up a bowl of tortilla chips. The following recipe is adapted from *Salsa Recipes for Canning* (PNW0395), a publication of Pacific Northwest Extension Publications.

Makes	Prep time	Cook time
14 to 16 pints	30 minutes	25 minutes

7 quarts Roma tomatoes, peeled, cored, and chopped

4½ cups seeded and chopped long green chili peppers

5 cups chopped onions

½ cup seeded and finely chopped jalapeños

6 garlic cloves, finely chopped

2 cups bottled lemon or lime juice

kosher salt, to taste

freshly ground black pepper, to taste

1. In a large saucepan on the stovetop over high heat, combine the tomatoes, green chilis, onions, jalapeños, garlic, lemon or lime juice, and salt and pepper to taste. Bring to a boil, stirring frequently. Reduce the heat to low and simmer for 20 minutes more, stirring occasionally.

2. Remove the saucepan from the heat and pack the salsa into hot, sterilized glass pint canning jars, leaving ½ inch (1.25cm) of headspace.

3. Seal the jars and process in a boiling water bath for 15 minutes.

Serving suggestion: Before serving, blend in 1 tablespoon of freshly chopped cilantro leaves to each 1 pint. Chill before serving.

Cranberry, Apple & Orange Relish

Just when the winter blahs have descended and there doesn't seem to be a bit of color anywhere, along comes this vibrant, zesty relish to brighten your main course. This recipe is courtesy of Ocean Spray Cranberries.

Makes	Prep time	Cook time
about 8 cups	30 minutes	none

1 bag cranberries

4 to 5 medium apples, cored and finely chopped

2 oranges, peeled, seeded, and chopped

¼ cup orange peel

2 cups granulated sugar

1. In a large bowl, combine the cranberries, apples, oranges, orange peel, and sugar. Chill before serving.

Harvest Time Apple Relish

Be sure to wear gloves when working with hot peppers. Keep your hands away from your face. If you don't fancy wearing gloves, wash your hands thoroughly with soap and water before touching your face. Recipe credit to the University of Georgia Extension Service.

Makes	**Prep time**	**Cook time**
7 to 8 pints	45 minutes	10 minutes

8lb (3.6kg) apples (Honey Crisp, Cameo, or Pink Lady recommended)

4 tbsp (¼ cup) finely chopped red serrano peppers

1 tsp ascorbic acid

4 quarts plus 2 cups water, divided

3 cups 5% distilled white vinegar

2½ cups granulated sugar

2 tsp ground cloves

8 pieces of cinnamon (3 inches [7.5cm] each)

1 tbsp ground allspice

4 tsp ground ginger

1. Rinse the apples, peel if desired, and core. Combine the ascorbic acid and 4 quarts of water. Immerse the apples in this solution to prevent browning. Coarsely shred the apples in a food processor and return them to the acid bath.

2. Rinse the peppers and remove the stem ends. Trim to remove seeds. Finely chop.

3. In a large pot on the stovetop over high heat, combine the vinegar, sugar, cloves, cinnamon sticks, allspice, ginger, red serrano peppers, and the remaining 2 cups of water. Bring to a boil, stirring to dissolve the sugar.

4. Drain the apples and add them to the hot syrup. Bring the mixture to a boil and cook for 5 minutes or until the apples are mostly translucent, stirring occasionally.

5. Remove the pot from the heat. Remove the cinnamon sticks from the relish and place one piece in each jar. Pack the relish and syrup into the jars, leaving ½ inch (1.25cm) of headspace, making sure the fruit is completely covered with syrup.

6. Seal the jars and process in a boiling water canner for 10 minutes.

Oscar Relish

You can make this mild or with a little bit of a bite. Recipe credit to the University of Georgia Extension Service.

Makes	Prep time	Cook time
6 pints	45 minutes	1 to 2 hours

8 cups chopped fresh peaches

3 cups 5% distilled white vinegar

8 cups chopped ripe tomatoes

2 cups water

2 cups diced green bell peppers

1 tbsp ground red chili pepper

2 cups ground onions

1½ tsp canning or pickling salt

4 cups firmly packed light brown sugar

1½ tsp canning or pickling salt

2 cups 5% apple cider vinegar

4 tbsp pickling spice, tied in a spice bag

1. Rinse all the produce well. Peel and pit the peaches. Chop into small pieces. Peel and chop the tomatoes into 1-inch (1.25cm) pieces. Remove the stems and seeds from the bell peppers and dice into ¼-inch (0.5cm) pieces. Peel the onions before grinding in a food chopper (which you can also use for the red chili pepper).

2. In a 10-quart saucepan on the stovetop over medium-high heat, combine all the ingredients. Cook for 1½ to 2 hours or until the relish reaches your desired thickness, stirring often.

3. Remove the saucepan from the heat and pack the relish in hot, sterilized jars, leaving ½ inch (1.25cm) of headspace.

4. Seal the jars and process in a boiling water canner for 10 minutes.

Variation: Use two small hot peppers if you like a hotter relish. For a milder relish, substitute hot sauce to taste (½ to 1 teaspoon) for the peppers.

Beet Relish

Beet skins will slip off easily if you plunge the beets into very cold water after cooking. Always leave some root and crown attached to keep the beets from bleeding while they're cooking. You want your relish to be beet red!

Makes	Prep time	Cook time
3 pints	45 minutes	1 hour

12 medium-sized beets, cooked, skins slipped, and diced

1 medium white onion, chopped

2 cups finely chopped cabbage

1 red bell pepper, diced

1½ tsp kosher salt

¾ cup granulated sugar

1½ cups white vinegar

1. In an 8- to 12-quart saucepan on the stovetop over high heat, combine the beets, onion, cabbage, red bell pepper, salt, sugar, and vinegar. Bring to a boil, then reduce the heat to low. Simmer for 15 minutes.

2. Remove the saucepan from the heat and pack the relish into hot, sterilized glass canning jars.

3. Seal the jars and process in a boiling water bath for 5 minutes.

Corn Relish

Fresh corn on the cob is one of the true delights of summer, but as the season winds down, you might find some of the corn you're either picking or buying isn't quite as young and tender as you'd like. Enter corn relish to solve that problem. You want the kernels to be a bit chewy for this relish.

Makes	Prep time	Cook time
4 to 5 pints	1 hour	25 minutes

12 medium ears of fresh corn

1 cup diced red bell peppers

1 cup chopped celery

½ cup minced white onions

1½ cups apple cider vinegar

¾ cup granulated sugar

2 tsp kosher salt

1½ tsp ground mustard

1 tsp celery seeds

½ tsp ground turmeric

1. Husk the corn and remove all the silk.

2. Add the ears to a large pot on the stovetop over high heat and cover with water. Bring to a boil and cook for 5 minutes. Remove the pot from the heat and allow the corn to cool. Use a sharp knife or corn slicer to remove the kernels from the cobs, being careful not to scrape the cobs. (That would give your corn a "cobby" taste.)

3. In an 8- to 12-quart pot on the stovetop over high heat, combine the red bell peppers, celery, onions, apple cider vinegar, sugar, salt, ground mustard, celery seeds, and turmeric. Bring to a boil, stirring frequently.

4. Add the corn and mix well. Boil for 5 minutes more.

5. Remove the pot from the heat and pack the relish into hot, sterilized glass canning jars, leaving ½ inch (1.25cm) of headspace.

6. Seal the jars and process in a boiling water bath for 5 minutes.

Piccalilli

This is a very old favorite, dating back to the 18th century and maybe the Revolutionary War days. The origin of the term is lost in the mists of time, but you can almost see the word "pickle" in it. Maybe it means "little pickle pieces"? Hard to tell, but this is a very good relish. Piccalilli is also a good way to use up odds and ends from the garden at the end of the season and expand your home food-preserving pantry.

Makes	Prep time	Cook time
4 pints	1 hour	40 minutes

6 medium green tomatoes, coarsely chopped

6 red bell peppers, coarsely chopped

6 medium white onions, coarsely chopped

1 small cabbage, coarsely chopped

¼ cup kosher salt

2 cups white vinegar

2½ cups light brown sugar

2 tbsp pickling spices, in a spice bag

1. In a large ceramic or glass bowl, combine the tomatoes, red bell peppers, onions, and cabbage. Sprinkle the salt over the top and let stand overnight on the counter. This draws out the moisture from the cabbage. The next morning, drain off the water. Cover the vegetables with cool water and drain again.

2. Transfer everything to an 8- to 12-quart pot on the stovetop over high heat. Add the vinegar, brown sugar, and pickling spices. Bring to a boil, then reduce the heat to low. Simmer for 20 minutes.

3. Remove the pot from the heat and discard the spice bag. Pack the piccalilli into hot, sterilized glass canning jars, leaving ½ inch (1.25cm) of headspace.

4. Seal the jars and process in a boiling water bath for 5 minutes.

Summer Squash Relish

This is another great way to use all that zucchini. Credit to the University of Georgia Extension Service.

Makes	Prep time	Cook time
5 pints	30 minutes	5 minutes

4lb (1.8kg) fresh, firm yellow or zucchini summer squash

½ cup diced sweet onions

2¼ cups granulated sugar

2 cups 5% apple cider vinegar

2 tsp ground turmeric

2 tsp celery seeds or celery salt

4 tsp mustard seeds

1. Rinse the squash and remove both ends. Shred in a food processor.

2. Peel the onions and remove the root and stem ends. Rinse and dice or shred in a food processor.

3. In a large pot on the stovetop over high heat, combine the sugar, apple cider vinegar, turmeric, celery seeds, and mustard seeds. Bring to a boil, then carefully add the squash and onions. Return to a boil and cook for 5 minutes, stirring often.

4. Remove the pot from the heat and pack the relish and liquid into hot, sterilized jars, leaving ½ inch (1.25cm) of headspace. Remove air bubbles and adjust the headspace if needed. Make sure the liquid covers the top of the food pieces.

5. Seal the jars and process in a boiling water canner for 15 minutes.

Note: You can use all yellow squash, all zucchini squash, or a combination of both. You can dice the squash or shred it by hand. For recipe development, Vidalia onions were used. Any variety of onion is acceptable.

Fermenting

What do bread, beer, wine, spirits, yogurt, sourdough waffles, vinegar, kosher dill pickles, cheese, olives, and sauerkraut have in common? Yes, they're all fermented foods and they're all a result of a happy accident that occurred thousands of years ago and spread to nearly every culture on the planet. In fact, beginning with this chapter and continuing on through the end of this book, we'll see how coincidence and serendipity combined to produce some of our favorite preserved foods.

Origins of Fermentation

The discovery of fermentation was probably accidental, at least as far as food was concerned. Scientists believe that as far back as 10,000 BCE, people were drinking the fermented milk of camels, goats, sheep, and cattle in North African regions. This was probably a naturally fermented product. The microorganisms (a form of lactic acid) in the milk plus the extremely hot daytime temperatures turned the bags of goat milk tied to the camels' backs into yogurt.

Later, somebody somewhere in a more temperate climate left the grape juice out and it changed. It acidified but kept a certain tangy sweetness. It had fermented. And thus wine was born.

The next great leap forward probably happened when someone left the apple juice out. Later, it became apparent that it had also changed.

Perhaps someone dropped a piece of food, perhaps a cucumber, into a vat and left it there for someone else to fish out. When the person did, they noticed it had changed too. It hadn't spoiled and even had a nice crunch. It was the first pickle.

Regardless of its beginnings, fermentation has become a staple of food preservation.

The Science of Fermentation

Fermentation is a natural process by which fruits, milk, and grains change their chemical composition by converting sugar to carbon dioxide and alcohol in the absence of air (an anaerobic environment). Fermentation preserves foods by making them so acidic that undesirable microorganisms can't grow and spoil the food being fermented. As a science, fermentation earned the name *zymology* back in 1856, when Louis Pasteur was studying the role of yeasts in fermentation. Other scientists built on his work— and the rest, as they say, is history.

The basics of fermentation involve encouraging the good microbes to propagate and discouraging the undesirable microbes from contaminating the food. It's a delicate balance, and indeed, fermentation has been called *controlled rot*. It's not a very appetizing term, but it's correct. Fermented food isn't rotten, but it's definitely not fresh. It's an acquired taste.

There are two main avenues for fermentation:

- The first is natural fermentation, where the microorganisms are naturally present, as we find with sauerkraut and kimchi and our earlier illustration of the goat milk turned to yogurt.

- The second has the appealing name of *backslopping*. This is how we replenish a sourdough starter, for example. We add a bit of what was previously fermented to the food we wish to ferment.

One subtopic of science is health and some have made claims that the probiotics found in the fermentation process (*lactobacillus*) have benefits for digestive health. The science is still out on this and studies are ongoing.

General Procedures

If you'd like to try your hand at fermenting foods, we'll take a look at the most popular candidates. Let's start with pickles!

To make a good-quality fermented pickle, it's absolutely essential to follow a tested and approved recipe to the letter. If you don't take shortcuts with the process, you'll be well rewarded for your time and effort.

Time is a crucial ingredient with fermented pickles and they can take from 4 to 6 weeks to arrive at the proper degree of readiness. During that time, you can't ignore them or neglect them, so be sure to start them when you can supervise their progress.

During that 4- to 6-week time slot, the pickles will be immersed in brine. They're not just hanging around though. Important bacterial action is taking place just below the water line. The bacteria in question are lactic acid bacteria and they're found naturally on cucumbers. Fermentation encourages their growth as they work to preserve cucumbers by lowering their pH level to less than 4.0. This level indicates an acidic food, if you remember its importance from our section on canning. In addition to their efforts in lowering the pH level, lactic acid bacteria give fermented pickles their characteristic taste.

A stoneware crock is the traditional vessel for fermenting. Check to make sure the crock is free of chips and cracks that could allow the liquid to seep through. If you find some damage, you can line the crock with a heavy, food-grade piece of plastic and secure it around the rim.

If you don't have a crock, food-grade plastic containers work well. Many fast-food restaurants or bakeries will let you buy or beg some.

Brine Basics

Each recipe will give you specific directions as to the amounts of ingredients to use in making the brine, including water. Hard water can cause the brine to become cloudy, but if you don't have soft water, you can boil hard water and then let it sit for 24 hours. If any scum forms, skim this off. Also, as you take water from the saucepan to make the brine, don't disturb the sediment on the bottom of the saucepan.

Brine Maintenance

This includes monitoring the temperature. You want the temperature to remain constant within the ideal range of 65°F to 80°F (16°C to 27°C). If the temperature gets colder or hotter than this, pickles will either spoil or be of poor quality.

Removing the scum that forms on top of the crock during fermentation is a daily task. This scum is made up of yeasts and molds that feed on lactic acid and produce enzymes that make the pickles soft. Without sufficient lactic acid, the pickles will spoil, so keep your crock scum-free.

Brine Bubbles

It's alive! It truly is. The bubbles that rise to the surface of the brine tell you that fermentation is happening. When the process is complete, the bubbles stop. Check the pickles at this time. Take a cucumber out of the crock and slice it in half. There should be no visible rings or white spots.

You'll probably see that the brine has become cloudy. This is because of bacterial growth that occurs during the fermentation process. Carefully pour the brine through a strainer and into a large pot. Heat the brine to boiling and reserve it to use in covering the pickles after you pack them into jars.

Fermenting by the Numbers

There's a logical sequence to the fermentation process. It takes several days, but the steps are always the same. You should see the following:

- Clear brine for the first 1 to 3 days
- Cloudy brine and gas bubbles the next 2 to 3 days
- Cloudy brine and no gas bubbles for 5 to 6 days
- Finished (10 to 12 days from the beginning)

Before packing the pickles, check to be sure they're perfect. They should be firm, crisp, and have good color. If you detect any signs of spoilage—soft, slippery, stinky, a strange color—don't eat them. Dispose of them.

Fermented Dill Pickles

The following procedures are from the USDA's *Complete Guide to Home Canning*. (See Appendix F.) This is an example of using a tested and approved recipe— something the home food preserver should always do!

You'll need the following ingredients to make 4 pounds (1.8kg) of pickles:

- 4 pounds (1.8kg) of 4-inch (10cm) pickling cucumbers
- 2 tablespoons dill seed (or use 4 to 5 heads of fresh or dry dill weed)
- ½ cup kosher salt

- ¼ cup 5% distilled white vinegar

- 8 cups water

Those are the basics. You can then add one or more of the following ingredients:

- 2 garlic cloves

- 2 dried red bell peppers

- 2 teaspoons whole mixed pickling spices

Here's the general method:

1. Wash the cucumbers and cut ¹⁄₁₆ inch (0.20cm) from the blossom end and discard. (This end contains enzymes that can cause soft pickles.) Leave ¼ inch (0.5cm) of the stem attached.

2. Place half the dill and half the spices in the bottom of a stoneware crock or other suitable container. Then add the cucumbers and the rest of the dill and the spices.

3. Dissolve the salt in the vinegar and water. Pour this over the cucumbers.

4. Add a weight (such as a dinner plate weighted down with a leak-proof plastic bag filled with water and securely tied) and drape a clean cloth over the top of the crock to keep out dust or insects.

Place the crock where the temperature will remain between 70°F and 75°F (21°C to 24°C) for the 3 to 4 weeks it will take for the fermentation process to complete. Cooler temperatures will slow down the fermentation process and higher temperatures will cause the pickles to become soft.

If possible, have the crock already in the place where you'll be keeping it during fermentation. This saves wear and tear on your back trying to lift it and avoids spills.

Check on the pickles every day if you can, but be sure to check on them at least several times a week. Remove any surface scum that forms. If the pickles become soft, slimy, or begin to smell bad, dispose of them and abort the mission.

When fermentation is complete, you can continue to store the pickles in the original container in the refrigerator if it will fit. You'll still need to check in on it and remove any mold or scum that develops on the surface. If that seems less than satisfactory, canning the pickles is the way to go.

To process the pickles, pour the brine into a large saucepan on the stovetop over medium heat and slowly bring it to a boil. Reduce the heat to low and simmer for 5 minutes. Pack the pickles into jars and cover them with hot brine, leaving ½ inch (1.25cm) of headspace. Wipe the rims, adjust the lids, and process the jars in a boiling water bath for 10 minutes for pints and 15 minutes for quarts.

These pickles might also be processed by low temperature pasteurization. See Chapter 13 for specific instructions for this method. Also see Chapter 13 for troubleshooting fermented pickles.

Sauerkraut

Cabbage originated in Asia but made an early entrance into Europe. If you remember your grade school geography and the list of explorers you needed to memorize, you'll remember Jacques Cartier. His significance to the home food preserver is his introduction of cabbage to the new world.

Cabbage grows well in many climates and keeps well over the winter. It's not surprising, then, that people decided it would be a good candidate for fermenting. The result is a food that's known and loved in cultures around the world.

Although fermented cabbage has its origins in Asia, the word "sauerkraut" is German: *sauer* meaning sour and *kraut* meaning cabbage. It's a staple in most German households and a favorite of many folks of German descent. If you're of German descent, you probably consider sauerkraut to be a vegetable and you probably slap some butter on it after it's heated on the stove.

If the farmers' market has a good supply of cabbage or if you've grown your own cabbage crop and have root cellared all you'll need over the winter and still have some heads to spare, try your hand at making sauerkraut. Select firm, large heads of cabbage.

You'll need the following ingredients:

- 25 pounds (11.3kg) of cabbage

- ¾ cup pickling or kosher salt

You'll get about 9 quarts of sauerkraut from 25 pounds (11.3kg) of cabbage, but the actual amount depends on how finely you shred the cabbage and how small the core is.

Wash the cabbage and remove the outer leaves and any other damaged leaves. Cut the cabbage in half and then quarter it. Remove the core. Treat the cabbage gently. It might look like a tough vegetable, but if the leaves get bruised, the sauerkraut will suffer. This starts a chain reaction that will spoil the kraut:

- Bruised portions tend to pack together.

- This keeps the brine from being able to penetrate thoroughly.

- Unbrined cabbage spoils or doesn't ferment evenly and the sauerkraut is a bust.

How finely should you shred the cabbage? Not too coarse and not too fine. Aim for about ¼ inch (0.5cm) thick. This will usually be the coarse blade on your vegetable shredder or food processor.

The traditional vessel for making sauerkraut is a big stoneware crock. You can also use glass, enamel, or food-grade plastic containers. Garbage cans or non-food-grade plastic containers might react with the acid produced during fermentation and might make the sauerkraut unsafe to eat or give it a bad flavor.

You'll need to do some serious eyeballing to make sure the crock is deep enough to hold all the shredded cabbage and brine and still leave 4 to 5 inches (10 to 13cm) of space below the rim. Why so much space? During fermenting, gas bubbles will rise. If there's not enough room, the brine will bubble over and you'll have a major science experiment in the kitchen or wherever you've placed the crock.

The procedure for making sauerkraut is called *dry salting*. Place the shredded cabbage in the crock and add 3 tablespoons of kosher salt. Mix thoroughly with clean hands and then pack the cabbage down firmly into the container. This is your first layer. Repeat this procedure with the next 5 pounds (2.3kg) of cabbage and continue the layering until all the cabbage and salt is in the crock. A concentrated brine forms when the salt leaches moisture out of the cabbage.

The brine will form fairly quickly. If it hasn't completely covered the cabbage within 1 hour, add some prepared brine to the crock. Add 1½ tablespoons of kosher salt to 1 quart of water, heat to boiling, and cool. Make as many quarts as you need to get the job done.

Place a plate on top of the cabbage to weigh it down under the brine. Add a weight to the top of the plate if needed and cover everything with a clean, heavy cloth (a bath towel works well). Check the brine frequently—once a day is recommended—and remove any scum that forms.

You can also use a brine-filled bag to weight down the cabbage. If you go this route, don't lift the bag out of the crock until the bubbling has stopped and fermentation has completed. Place a 2-gallon food-grade plastic bag inside another. Fill with brine made from adding 1½ tablespoons of kosher salt to 1 quart of water. Tie securely. You'll need about 3 quarts of brine for a 5-gallon crock.

Now it's time to have some faith. You'll need it during the first week because the fermenting cabbage frequently produces a horrific odor. Don't despair, as this is normal and will go away as the fermentation process continues. (Although it's probably a good reason not to keep the crock in the kitchen or any other room you need to visit frequently.)

If you keep the temperature between 70°F and 75°F (21°C to 24°C), the sauerkraut will be fermented in 3 to 4 weeks. Then it's ready for eating, canning, or storage in the refrigerator. (It will keep for several months there.)

For canning, you can choose either hot pack or raw pack:

- **Hot pack:** Place the kraut and brine in a large pot, turn the heat on high, and bring to a boil. Stir frequently to be sure the entire batch is hot throughout. Then pack it firmly into jars and add brine to cover, leaving ½ inch (1.25cm) of headspace. Process in a boiling water canner for 10 minutes for pints and 15 minutes for quarts.

- **Raw pack:** Pack the kraut firmly into jars and cover with the brine, leaving ½ inch (1.25cm) of headspace. Process in a boiling water canner for 20 minutes for pints and 25 minutes for quarts.

Troubleshooting Sauerkraut

You know you did everything by the book. Well, almost everything. Surely there's some leeway in the directions? It shouldn't matter if you changed the ingredients or the temperature or took some shortcuts. Right?

Wrong, unfortunately. When you're dealing with fermentation, everything has got to be just right, and even then, it might seem the fates are conspiring against you. Here are some common problems, along with their possible causes and recommended solutions:

- **The sauerkraut is really dark:** This can have several causes: using iodized salt, not mixing the salt into the cabbage thoroughly, having the temperature too high during fermenting or storage, or not cleaning and trimming the cabbage properly as you began. The solutions are found in the causes. Follow the directions carefully.

- **The sauerkraut is soft and mushy:** Again, salt is the culprit—too little or not mixed in well enough. The temperature might also be too high. If you didn't pack the cabbage firmly into the crock, air pockets can form and play havoc with the fermentation process. Use the amount of salt called for and mix it in thoroughly as you're preparing the layers in the crock. Pack the cabbage firmly and be sure to store the crock in a location where the temperature won't soar into the danger zone.

- **There's a white scummy surface on top of the brine:** Air got in because the weight didn't weigh enough to keep it out. If the plate's not heavy enough, add bags full of brine. You can skim off the scum. The kraut should be fine.

- **There's a moldy surface on top of the brine:** The temperature got too warm during the fermentation process and/or the crock wasn't covered well enough to keep out the air. This one isn't a keeper. Discard the sauerkraut. It's potentially unsafe to eat. Next time, keep the crock in the 70°F to 75°F (21°C to 24°C) zone and covered to exclude air.

- **The kraut is rotten:** The same conditions that cause mold to grow on the surface can cause the kraut to go bad. Keep the temperature in the 70°F to 75°F (21°C to 24°C) zone and keep the crock covered to exclude air. Dispose of the kraut. It's bad.

- **The kraut is slimy:** This points to too little salt and too high a temperature during the fermenting process. Discard. Next time be scrupulous about the correct amount of salt and the proper temperature range.

As you can see, operator error is usually the culprit. Because you're only dealing with two ingredients (cabbage and salt), the right proportions are essential to get a good result. If you read the directions carefully before you begin and keep tabs on the temperature during fermenting, the sauerkraut should turn out great.

Yogurt

If you're a bit intimidated by the steps involved in making fermented pickles or sauerkraut, you can purchase a yogurt maker for around $40 or use the yogurt function on your Instant Pot. It's practically painless and you can find numerous recipes online or consult the instruction book that came with your appliances. Yogurt is one fermented food that needs the backslop—that's the starter.

Sourdough Starter

Sourdough is interesting in that it adapts to its environment. If you borrow some starter from a friend in the wilds of Montana, it's going to change to fit in to its new home in California. That's the nature of the yeast. If you've begged some starter, you're all ready to go. Just remember to replace what you've taken out each time you use it. Instructions follow. If you need to make yours from scratch, here's how.

All you'll need are equal parts all-purpose flour and water. That's it. The yeasts present in the flour will get to work as soon as they've had a drink. You'll mix an equal amount of flour and water by weight every day for 1 week and add it to the mix. After that, it will be ready to use.

Supplies:

- All-purpose flour

- Water

- A glass or food-safe plastic gallon jar

- Scales

- Measuring cups

- Spoon

Each day, combine 4oz (120g) flour and 4oz (120g) water by weight. Add to the jar and mix thoroughly. Place the lid on the jar or place plastic wrap over the top of the jar. Set the jar in a warm place in the kitchen where it won't be disturbed. Starter likes even, warm temperatures.

For the rest of the week, continue to add the same proportions of flour and water to the jar each day, stirring completely. This is called *feeding*. The mixture will begin to have bubbles and take on a ropy texture. It will also take on a sour odor. This is good. You're making sourdough starter. When it's nice and bubbly and sour and ropy, it's ready to use. Just scoop out what you need and don't let your jar get too low. Continue to replace what you've taken out the same way you built it in the first place.

Recipes

Sauerkraut is always great on hot dogs and as an accompaniment to pork chops and roasts. The first recipe is especially scrumptious on a cold winter's night. Then there are recipes for kimchi and sourdough biscuits.

Kielbasa & Sauerkraut Casserole

Polish sausage and German sauerkraut team up to make a hearty, flavorful casserole. The secret is the little bit of brown sugar that adds just a touch of sweetness. Of course, the beer adds flavor, too!

Serves	Prep time	Cook time
6	30 minutes	40 minutes

2lb smoked Polish sausage or kielbasa

1 large white onion, sliced

2lb (1kg) sauerkraut with liquid

1 can of beer

2 tbsp light brown sugar

2 tbsp brown mustard

1. Preheat the oven to 350°F (175°C). Slice the sausage into ½-inch (1.25cm) pieces.

2. In a large skillet on the stovetop over medium heat, cook the sausage until browned. Remove the sausage from the skillet and drain on paper towels. Add the onion to the sausage grease and sauté until translucent, about 2 to 3 minutes. Remove the onion from the skillet and drain on paper towels.

3. In a quart casserole dish, combine the sauerkraut and liquid, sausage, onion, beer, brown sugar, and brown mustard. Bake for 45 minutes. Remove the dish from the oven and serve the casserole immediately.

Kimchi

Kimchi is indisputably the national food of Korea, with consumption averaging around 40 pounds (18.1kg) per person per year. Common ingredients for kimchi include cabbage, ginger, green onions, radishes, garlic, and powdered red pepper. This version uses cabbage. You can substitute ginger powder (1 teaspoon) for the ginger root, but fresh ginger root gives a better flavor. If you have access to an Asian foods store, buy some kimchi sauce and add 1 tablespoon to the kimchi.

Makes	Prep time	Cook time
1½ quarts	6 hours	none

2 heads of Chinese (Napa) cabbage

3 tbsp kosher or sea salt

2 carrots, shredded

1 cucumber, diced

1 bunch of green onions (scallions), chopped

4 tbsp chili powder

3 garlic cloves, minced

2 tbsp granulated sugar

1 small piece of ginger, crushed

1. Wash the cabbage and cut off the stems. Cut the leaves horizontally into four pieces and then cut these into halves lengthwise. Your goal is to arrive at pieces about 2 inches (5cm) square.

2. Put a handful of the cabbage in a plastic bag and sprinkle with salt. Repeat the layering process, ending with a layer of salt. With clean hands, gently work the cabbage inside the bag until all the salt has been absorbed and liquid begins to form. Seal the bag and set aside for 4 to 6 hours. After 2 hours, mix the cabbage and liquid once more.

3. Remove the cabbage from the bag and rinse with cold water. Gently squeeze to remove excess water. Pack the cabbage into plastic containers and add the carrots, cucumber, green onions, chili powder, garlic, sugar, and ginger. Mix thoroughly with your hands, adding more chili powder as needed to get a rich, dark color.

4. Place lids on the containers and store in a cool location for 5 to 6 days. Then place the containers in the fridge. It's ready to eat and will keep in the fridge for months.

Sourdough Biscuits

These are really good with smoked sausage gravy.

Serves	Prep time	Cook time
6	30 minutes	25 to 30 minutes

½ cup sourdough starter

1 cup evaporated milk

1 cup plus 1½ cups unsifted
   all-purpose flour, divided

1 tbsp granulated sugar

¾ tsp kosher salt

1 tsp baking powder

½ tsp baking soda

1. In a large bowl, combine the sourdough starter, milk, and 1 cup flour. (Start this process the night before if the biscuits are for breakfast and in morning if the biscuits are for dinner.) Cover the bowl with a clean kitchen towel and keep at room temperature to rise.

2. Preheat the oven to 375°F (190°F).

3. In the morning or evening, add 1 cup of flour and stir. Add the sugar, salt, baking powder, and soda. Use your hands to mix everything into a soft dough.

4. Use the remaining ½ cup of flour to flour a breadboard. Turn the dough out onto the breadboard and knead lightly. Pat or roll out the dough to ½ inch (1.25cm) thickness. Cut the dough into biscuits with a cutter.

5. Place the biscuits close together on a 9-inch (23cm) greased baking sheet and set the sheet in a warm place to rise for about 30 minutes.

6. Place the sheet in the oven and bake for 25 to 30 minutes or until nicely browned.

7. Remove the sheet from the oven and serve the biscuits immediately.

Fruit Spreads

Whether you're partial to jams, jellies, marmalades, or other kinds of fruit spreads, making them can be an activity for the whole family to enjoy. And there's nothing more fun than tasting the product as you go! Making fruit spreads is also where you can let your creativity have some space. Just follow a few simple principles and you'll get good results.

Jams, Jellies & Marmalades

Chapter

18

Are you a seat-of-your-pants kind of cook? A pinch here and a dab there? Do you like to experiment? Jam and jelly making will give you plenty of opportunities for that. Measurements must be exact or your jam or jelly just won't come out the way you want. Advances in technology have cut out all the guesswork and even the need to do your own stirring if you'd rather purchase an automatic jam and jelly maker. These run around $100 and can be ordered online.

Just one word of caution: If you're interested in these appliances, take the time to read the product reviews before purchasing one. Some reviewers indicate that the plastic innards give off an objectionable odor when the machine is in use. It's the same issue you might have experienced with newer-model traditional coffee makers. No amount of cleaning or breaking in seems to eliminate the smell.

If you decide to go the traditional route, it's not all that hard and doesn't take all that long, and your kitchen will smell wonderful. If you've shied away from making jams or jellies because the process seems too involved or because you need to restrict your sugar intake, it's really never been easier. You can now make delicious jams without sugar. It doesn't take a whole lot of fruit and you can put up a batch of freezer jam in less time than it takes to cook a roast. In this chapter, you'll find the basics on jams, jellies, and marmalades, along with specific recipes.

The Science Behind Jam, Jellies & Marmalades

Four ingredients go into making jams and jellies: fruit, pectin, sugar, and acid. Exact measurements are essential, and for this reason, use measuring cups and spoons, and follow directions to the letter. Exact boiling times are also essential, so set a timer to help you maintain accuracy.

Fruit

Most beginning home jelly makers begin with crab apple jelly. It's high in acid and pectin, and this generally means it will set up nicely. Nothing breeds confidence like success, so if you're just starting out with jelly, this is a good first fruit. Other good fruits for first ventures include grapes, green apples, and tart plums.

You can make jam from just about any kind of fruit, but strawberries are the hands-down favorite. They make up beautifully, with a rich red syrup and plump pieces of berries. There's just something cheerful about a strawberry.

When you're ready to branch out in your jam and jelly making, you'll find there's almost an infinite number of possibilities. Just about any kind of fruit will work as long as you add pectin, sugar, and acid in the right proportions and follow the recipes scrupulously.

Pectin

Pectin is a naturally occurring substance found in fruits. It's present in all fruits but is higher in underripe ones. It's responsible for the jelling of jams and jellies. When you're shopping for pectin, you're likely to see several different brands. All will work well.

Sugar

Sugar is a very important player. In fact, it plays several parts in making sure your jams and jellies turn out the way you want. You might be surprised to see just how much sugar you'll need to follow the recipes, but if you cut back, you'll be disappointed.

That said, manufacturers have worked hard to develop recipes that use less sugar and some fruit spreads can now be made with sugar substitutes. These recipes tend to be softer than those made with sugar. Think "gelatin desserts" and you'll have an idea of how these set up.

First of all, sugar helps jams and jellies jell. Jams and jellies contain about 65 to 68% sugar. If the percentage falls below 65, the end product will be runny and weak. If it's over 68, the sugar won't dissolve and you'll have sugar crystals throughout your product, which will taste gritty. If you're making jam, sugar helps the fruit stay firm so it doesn't turn into mush. It also adds flavor.

Finally, sugar helps preserve your fruit spreads and extends their shelf life. Substituting honey, corn syrup, or artificial sweeteners on a one-to-one basis with sugar in jam and jelly recipes won't work. You'll need to use recipes developed for these products.

Acid

Just as with pectin, acid content is higher in underripe fruit, so if you're making jam and jelly with ripe fruit, you'll need to add acid to be sure your fruit product jells. Acid also adds flavor. Commercial pectin products contain acid, but you might still need to add more to get to the proper percentage. Follow the directions on the box or bottle exactly to find out if and how much additional acid you'll need.

Acid is measured by the pH scale, which ranges from 0 to 14. A pH of 7 is neutral. Numbers less than 7 are acidic, while numbers above 7 are basic. A pH between 3.0 and 3.3 is what you're shooting for—and that's pretty acidic. Below 3.0, the jelly *weeps*, or forms drops of water on the surface. Above 3.3, the jelly gets weak and runny.

Lemon juice is what's usually added to fruit to get the correct amount of acidity. If you prefer to use citric acid, you'll use ⅛ teaspoon of citric acid for each 1 tablespoon of lemon juice.

General Procedures

Even though there are three different kinds of fruit spreads—jam, jelly, and marmalade—the process for making each is essentially the same. Jam or jelly making adds one more step, as you'll see a little later in the chapter. Here are the basic steps:

1. Check the jars to be sure there are no nicks, chips, or cracks. If you find any, throw the jars into the recycle bin. Canning jars—and that includes jelly jars—have a life span of about 10 to 13 years. Over time, the glass weakens. It develops stress cracks that might not be visible to the naked eye, but these cracks can cause your jar to break and that's a lot of work, time, and money wasted.

2. Wash the jars in hot, soapy water, rinse, and invert them on a clean, dry towel. If the processing time will be more than 10 minutes, sterilize the jars. (To sterilize jars, the National Center for Home Food Preservation recommends using your boiling water canner. Place the empty jars on the rack in the canner, fill the jars with hot (not boiling) water, and then fill the canner so the water level is 1 inch (2.5cm) above the tops of the jars. Turn the heat on high. When the water comes to a boil, set the timer for 10 minutes (for sea level; for each additional 1,000 feet in elevation, add 1 minute to the boiling time). Use your jar lifter to remove each jar and immediately fill it with the food to be processed. You can save the water you used to boil the jars for processing them.

3. Prepare the lids and rings. (This means your rings and lids are simmering in hot water, waiting to be called into service.)

4. Follow the directions on the pectin box or bottle for the jam or jelly you're making.

5. After skimming off the foam, fill the jars, leaving ⅛ inch (3mm) of headspace.

6. Wipe the rim of the jar with a damp towel to remove any residue.

7. Cover with the lid and screw the ring tight. Don't overtighten. Store in a cool, dry place away from sunlight. Paraffin is no longer recommended for sealing jams and jellies. The chance of mold and spoilage occurring is too great with this old method. Scraping off mold and eating the product is also not recommended, as mold spores penetrate into the rest of the product and might make it unsafe as well as unappetizing.

8. Place the jars in a boiling water bath, making sure the water is 1 inch (2.5cm) above the tops of the jars.

9. Process in a boiling water bath. Times as well as adjustments for altitude are included on the pectin box or bottle.

10. Use a jar lifter to remove the jars one at a time from the canner.

11. Let the jars cool for at least 8 hours or overnight.

12. Remove the rings.

13. Wash the jars to remove any sticky residue. Dry. Check the seal.

Equipment & Supplies

Setting up your kitchen for a jam or jelly session might remind you of a high school or college chemistry lab. For starters, there's acid, although the acid here is usually plain old lemon juice. There are also funnels and drip mechanisms, but unlike in chemistry class, you can take some shortcuts with the equipment and still get the right result.

In addition to fruit, sugar, pectin, and lemon juice (if specified), you'll need the following:

- Kitchen scales. Fruit doesn't come in uniform sizes, so you'll need your kitchen scales to be sure you have accurate measurements.

- An 8- to 10-quart pot with a flat bottom and enough depth to contain the jelly as it boils.

- A long-handled metal spoon for stirring jelly and skimming foam.

- A small bowl to hold skimmed foam.

- A potato masher if using soft fruit.

- A jelly bag.

- A jelly bag holder.

- A jelly thermometer if you're making jelly without added pectin.

Making Jam

Jam is a fruit spread made from crushed fruits cooked with sugar. Once you measure everything for your batch of jam, you'll be surprised at how quickly everything happens. For example, suppose you're making strawberry jam. You'll follow the general procedures listed earlier in this chapter, but here's the breakdown of how to combine the fruit, acid, pectin, and sugar:

1. Measure out the exact amount of crushed strawberries called for on the pectin box or bottle and put the strawberries into the large pot, along with the exact amount of lemon juice specified.

2. Stir in 1 box of pectin. You can add ½ teaspoon of butter or margarine at this time and you'll have practically no foam to skim off.

3. Over high heat, stir the mixture constantly until it comes to a full rolling boil (a boil you can't stir down).

4. Add the sugar all at once and keep stirring while the mixture once again comes to that full rolling boil.

5. Put on the timer as soon as the mixture comes to that full rolling boil and boil hard for exactly 4 minutes—no more and no less!

Strawberry jam is easy to make. Just remember to measure exactly and use your timer to time correctly.

Supplies for freezer jam

Making Freezer Jam

Freezer jam has the freshest fruit flavor. If this is your first venture into making jam, freezer jam is a great way to begin. It's quick and it's easy. Assemble everything before you begin. Measure all ingredients and set them aside. Once you begin the process, it goes quickly. Read the directions on the pectin box or bottle carefully. The procedure is different from making cooked jam.

Suppose you want to make peach freezer jam. Wash the fruit in cool water. Remove the stems and peels. Place the fruit in a medium-sized pot and use a potato masher to crush the fruit. Measure out 3¼ cups of the fruit and place it in a large bowl. Add ¼ cup of lemon juice. Gradually stir in 1 box of pectin and set the mixture aside for 30 minutes, stirring every 5 minutes to be sure all the pectin dissolves. Add 1 cup of corn syrup and mix well. Add 4½ cups of granulated sugar. Stir well until there's no grainy texture. Then pack it into plastic freezer containers or jelly or pint glass canning jars. Leave ½ inch (1.25cm) headspace. Seal, label, and date. Let stand for 24 hours to allow to set. Then store in the freezer for up to 1 year.

Making Jelly

Jelly is made from fruit juice cooked with sugar. Perfect jelly is clear and holds its shape when you slip it out of the jar. You can use commercially bottled fruit juice or you can make your own with a juicer/steamer. We discuss this process in Chapter 10.

Preparing the Fruit

Heat is what gets the juices started—and jelly is all about fruit juice! You'll be doing some simmering to begin the process. To prepare hard fruits, such as apples, peaches, and pears, wash them thoroughly in cool water. Remove any stems and cut off the blossom ends on apples and pears. Remove the pits from peaches, apricots, or nectarines, but don't core apples or pears. Cut the fruit into quarter sections or smaller. Don't pare the fruit. The cores and pares provide pectin.

Measure the exact amount of fruit specified in the instructions on the pectin box or bottle and place it in a large pot. Add 1 cup of water for each 1 quart of prepared fruit, cover with a lid, turn on the heat to low, and simmer the fruit until soft.

To prepare soft fruits, such as berries, cherries, or grapes, wash them gently in cool water. If using frozen berries, allow them to thaw before washing, but measure them while they're still frozen to get the right amount. Add the fruit to a large pot and use a potato masher to lightly crush the fruit. Add ¼ cup of water to the crushed fruit, cover with a lid, turn on the heat, and simmer until soft.

Extracting Juices

A jelly bag and a jelly bag holder are essential for making jelly if you don't have a juicer/steamer. If you don't have a jelly bag or cheesecloth, cut off one leg from a clean or new pair of pantyhose or use a clean pillowcase, coffee filters (these don't work quite as well as the others and need to be changed frequently), or a clean white cotton sock. Run the jelly bag or substitute jelly bag under cool water and wring gently to remove excess water. This will prevent the bag from soaking up the juice.

A jelly bag holder is an apparatus with three legs, from which the jelly bag is suspended. If you don't have one, hang the jelly bag from a doorknob (protect the door surface with some plastic wrap) or hang a heavy-duty clothes hanger from a cupboard handle and attach the jelly bag with clothespins. (Again, protect the door surface with some plastic wrap and cover the floor area to catch any wayward drips)

Extracting juice

It's actually possible to use an entire pair of new pantyhose and get maximum mileage from all your prepared fruit. Just treat each leg like one jelly bag. You can drape the legs over the aforementioned clothes hangers and collect fruit juice at double speed. It will look strange, but the juice will be perfect.

Now it's time to juice. Using potholders, carefully pour the softened fruit mixture into the jelly bag. Allow it to drip at its own pace. Don't squeeze the jelly bag! You might be impatient to have it finish dripping, but if you squeeze, your jelly will be cloudy.

Once the juice has dripped out, you have some options. You can proceed with making jelly or you can freeze or can the juice for later. If you decide to freeze it, pour the juice into freezer containers, leave appropriate headspace, label, date, and freeze. If you wish to can the juice, pour it into glass canning jars, leaving appropriate headspace. Adjust the lids and process pints and quarts in a boiling water bath for 10 minutes to ensure the seal. If you want to make jelly now, it's time for the next step!

Will You Need Pectin?

The riper the fruit, the lower the pectin content. Apples are naturally high in pectin, but if the apples you're working with are too ripe, you'll need to add pectin in order to make your jelly set. The Cooperative Extension Service notes that the following fruits are usually low in pectin or acid:

Apples (ripe)	California grapes	Eastern Concord grape juice	Grapefruit
Blackberries (ripe)	Cherries (sour)	Elderberries	Oranges

The following fruits always need added pectin, acid, or both:

Apricots	Pomegranates
Figs	Prunes
Guava	Raspberries
Peaches	Strawberries
Pears	Western Concord grapes

Don't feel that somehow you're being less of a purist if you use commercially produced pectin in your jelly. It cuts down on the amount of cooking time and helps preserve the natural fruit flavor. It also increases the amount of jelly you'll get compared with not using added pectin. You also can forego the testing that making jellies without added pectin requires. If you decide to use fruit juice you've bought at the store, you'll definitely need to add pectin. The commercial processing removes the natural pectins.

Getting by Without Added Pectin

Some fruits contain enough natural pectin and are acidic enough without adding pectin or acid. The Cooperative Extension Service offers this list of those fruits:

Apples (tart)	Gooseberries
Blackberries (tart)	Lemons
Crab apples	Loganberries
Cranberries	Plums (most)
Currants	Prunes (sour)
Eastern Concord grapes	Quince

If you decide to make jelly from apples or crab apples without adding pectin, don't peel or core them before simmering. Peels and cores also contain pectin. Take advantage of every source of natural pectin you can!

This jelly will need to boil for a long time. In fact, making jelly without added pectin is sometimes referred to as the "long boil" method. It takes more time to make jelly without added pectin, so be prepared to stir and stir.

To test for doneness, turn off the heat under the jelly. Dip a long-handled metal spoon into the jelly and hold the spoon so the jelly can drip off. The jelly will be done when it sheets. This means the jelly separates from the spoon in a sheet, not as individual drops or clusters of drops. You can use a jelly thermometer to let you know when you're getting close, but you'll still need to test.

If it seems close but you're not sure, put a spoonful of jelly on a dish and allow it to cool to room temperature. You can hurry this along by putting it in the freezer for a few minutes to get it to room temperature. If the jelly sets at room temperature, it's done.

Making Jelly with Added Pectin

Having the jelly turn out perfectly depends on the accurate measuring of all ingredients. Read all the directions on the pectin box or bottle before beginning to make jelly. For example, suppose you're going to make apple jelly using commercially produced pectin. Here's the breakdown for combining the fruit juice, lemon juice (if required), sugar, and pectin:

1. Measure the correct amount of the prepared juice as stated on the pectin box or bottle. This will also include lemon juice if the apples are ripe.

2. Measure into a large bowl the exact amount of sugar that's required according to the directions. Set aside.

3. Pour the juice into an 8- to 10-quart pot. Stir in 1 box of pectin or the required amount of liquid pectin. Turn on the heat to high.

4. When the mixture comes to a full rolling boil (a boil that can't be stirred down), add the granulated sugar all at once, stirring constantly. Keep stirring until the mixture again reaches a full boil, set the timer for 1 minute, and continue to stir. After 1 minute, turn off the heat and remove the pot from the burner.

Keep that jam and jelly boiling hard! Slow cooking destroys the pectin. Rapid boiling helps ensure your jam or jelly will set up nicely.

After these steps, the rest is a cinch. Skim off the foam; ladle the jelly into clean, hot jars; wipe the rims; adjust the lids; and process in a boiling water canner for 5 minutes to ensure the seal. If you choose not to process in a boiling water bath, you can invert the jars and place them on a dry, flat surface for 5 minutes. Then turn the jars right side up and allow to cool.

Remaking Soft Jellies

Jelly sometimes just doesn't set. It happens to everyone at some point. The fruit could have been too ripe or perhaps you made a double batch trying to save time or maybe you didn't add enough acid or you cut back a little on the sugar. Maybe you overcooked the fruit during the juice extraction phase and this reduced the pectin levels.

If you don't need any more strawberry or peach syrup, you might want to remake it. However, before you plunge in, wait. It's not an emergency. Put the soft jelly aside and give it a week or so. If the jars have sealed, it's not going to go bad on you. It sometimes just takes a little time.

If you've waited and the jelly still isn't cooperating, you can remake it. If one jar hasn't set, it's likely the whole batch is the same way. Remove the lids—unless you've gotten a second mortgage on your home to purchase reusable ones—and throw them away. Lids can't be reused. Wash the rings and set them aside.

You'll find directions for remaking soft jellies on the pectin box or bottle. Read the instructions carefully. Then read them again for good measure.

Making Marmalades

Marmalades are traditionally associated with Great Britain and these fruit spreads were originally used to prevent scurvy. It's how British sailors came to be called *limeys*.

Marmalades combine the best features of jams and jellies. What sets them apart is the small pieces of peel that are suspended in a soft jelly. Orange marmalade is a familiar spread on toast, but you can also try lemon, grapefruit, or lime marmalade.

You don't need to add pectin or acid when you're whipping up a batch. All you'll need is citrus, sugar, and water. See the recipes at the end of this chapter for a basic marmalade.

Making Reduced-Sugar Fruit Spreads

Sugar helps with the jelling process, so if you use a reduced-sugar recipe, the product will be softer than jams and jellies made with sugar. Recipes for making these fruit spreads are included on the package inserts for pectin. Be sure to follow them carefully. Low-calorie sugar substitutes vary in their ability to produce a good product, so it's best to check with the manufacturer's website to find specific recipes developed for use with a particular sugar substitute. See the recipes at the end of this chapter for instructions.

Troubleshooting

Even if you've faithfully followed every direction, there are times when jams, jellies, and marmalades seem to have minds of their own. They present you with some situations that might be perplexing. Here are some of the most common vexing issues.

What's with All the Foam?

Foam is the syrup with air incorporated into it. As the jam boils, air bubbles move up through the syrup and past the fruit to the top of the pot. The foam isn't harmful, but if you don't skim it off and just pour the entire mixture into jars and seal them, the bubbles will collapse over time and increase the headspace. With all this air inside, your jam can mold and spoil. Prevent foam from developing by adding a teaspoon of butter or margarine before the liquid begins to boil. You can actually heat the foam that arises during jam and jelly making in the microwave or over low heat on the stove and watch it turn back into syrup. You can save this reconstituted jam in the refrigerator to use within a few days.

Why Is Processing in a Boiling Water Bath Necessary?

Even though the jam or jelly is hot and the jars you're going to put it in are hot, they're probably not hot enough to create a good seal. Processing in a boiling water bath ensures the seal. You can also try the inversion method: After you fill the jar and put on the lid and ring, invert the jar so the lid is resting on a flat surface. Leave it that way for 5 minutes and then return it to its normal upright position. It will probably seal, but again, it's iffy and it can be discouraging to check on your jam during the winter and find that the lids have popped and you're growing a mold farm on your jam and jelly. It's not only discouraging, but it's a waste of your time, effort, and money. You should discard any moldy jam or jelly because the mold can penetrate below the visual level.

Why Is the Top Half of the Jar Jam & the Bottom Half Jelly?

This doesn't make the jam unsafe to eat, but it does look a bit strange. You can open the jar and stir the contents before serving. Prevention is the better tack to take here.

Bigger pieces of fruit are notorious for rising, so be sure to mash or chop your fruit into small enough pieces before you begin. You don't want to turn it into a purée, but you don't want huge hunks either. Also, fruit that's too ripe has a tendency to cause this problem. It's also lower in pectin. Choose ripe fruit but not fruit that's even a shade past its prime. Follow the directions on the pectin box or bottle to the letter. Set the timer to make sure you're cooking the jam according to the recipe.

When you've finished skimming off the foam, you'll see that the fruit is floating on top of the hot sugar syrup. Let the jam cool for a few minutes and then stir it gently to get the fruit to mix in.

Ladling jelly into jars

Recipes

You'll find specific recipes for all kinds of jams and jellies on the pectin boxes, but this is an old-time favorite that's worth adding to your file. For each recipe, follow the general directions for canning in chapters 10 and 11.

Apple Peel Jelly

This recipe has been a standby in many country kitchens for decades. It's thrifty and doesn't waste an essential part of the apple—the peel! When you're cutting up apples for pie slices, don't throw away the peels, especially if you're working with apples that are a bit tart.

Makes	Prep time	Cook time
4 pints	45 minutes	45 minutes

peels from 10 to 15 apples (tart and red varieties recommended, such as Granny Smith, Braeburn, McIntosh, and Cortland)

cold water

pectin, optional

5 cups granulated sugar

1. In a medium pot on the stovetop over medium heat, add the apple peels and enough cold water to cover. Cook the peels for about 30 minutes.

2. Remove the pot from the heat and slowly pour the mixture into a jelly bag. Allow the jelly to drip out into a clean large pot, but don't squeeze the jelly bag.

3. Measure the juice in the pot. At this point, you can use a commercial pectin product and follow the directions on the box or bottle.

4. If you're making the jelly without additional pectin, measure 4 cups of the juice and return that to the pot. (You can drink the remaining juice.)

5. Place the pot on the stovetop over high heat. Add the sugar and bring the juice to a boil. Boil hard for 5 minutes or until the jelly sheets. Remove the pot from the heat, skim the foam, and pour the jelly into hot, sterilized glasses. Adjust the lids and process in a boiling water canner for 5 minutes to ensure the seal. Remove the jars with a jar lifter and allow them to cool on a flat, dry surface.

No-Cook Strawberry-Blueberry Jam

Blueberry jam has a nice texture. It's rich and thick, and it makes a colorful accompaniment as a spread for scones, biscuits, and toast. This recipe is being reprinted with permission from Equal. For other recipes, go to www.equal.com.

Makes	Prep time	Cook time
40 servings	15 minutes	none

1½ cups Equal Spoonful

1 (1.59oz) package of Ball Fruit Jell Freezer Jam Pectin

2½ cups frozen unsweetened strawberries, thawed, drained, and crushed (or use the same amount of fresh)

1½ cups frozen unsweetened blueberries, thawed, drained, and crushed (or use the same amount of fresh)

1. Combine the Equal Spoonful and Ball Jam Pectin in a large bowl until well blended.

2. Add the fruit and stir for 3 minutes.

3. Ladle the fruit mixture into 5 clean 8-ounce (225g) jars, leaving ½ inch (1.25cm) of headspace. Cover with lids. Let stand at room temperature until thickened, about 30 minutes. Store in the fridge for up to 3 weeks or in the freezer for up to 1 year.

Strawberry Jam

This recipe is being reprinted with permission from Equal. For other recipes, go to www.equal.com.

Makes	Prep time	Cook time
40 servings	15 minutes	none

1½ cups Equal Spoonful

1 (1.59oz) package of Ball Fruit Jell Freezer Jam Pectin

4 cups frozen unsweetened strawberries, thawed, drained, and crushed (or use the same amount of fresh)

1. Combine the Equal Spoonful and Ball Jam Pectin in a large bowl until well blended.

2. Add the fruit and stir for 3 minutes.

3. Ladle the fruit mixture into 5 clean 8-ounce (225g) jars, leaving ½ inch (1.25cm) of headspace. Cover with lids. Let stand at room temperature until thickened, about 30 minutes. Store in the fridge for up to 3 weeks or in the freezer for up to 1 year.

Orange Marmalade

Here's a golden opportunity! Capture the sunny color and disposition of fresh oranges and lemons to enjoy the spicy tang of marmalade in the morning.

Makes	Prep time	Cook time
4 half-pints	25 minutes	30 minutes

4 oranges

1 lemon

water

granulated sugar

1. Wash the oranges and lemon. Cut the fruit in half and remove the seeds and stem end. Slice thinly.

2. In a large pot, combine 1½ cups of water for each 1 cup of fruit. Let stand for 8 hours or overnight.

3. Place the pot on the stovetop over medium heat. Cook for 30 minutes or until the fruit is tender. Remove the pot from the heat.

4. Measure the cooked fruit and liquid. Add 1 cup of sugar to each 1 cup of fruit and liquid. Return the fruit, liquid, and sugar to the pot. Cook over high heat until mixture sheets from a metal spoon. This can take about 30 minutes. You can also use a jelly thermometer to be sure the mixture has reached the gel stage.

5. Remove the pot from the heat and skim off any foam. Ladle the marmalade into clean, hot jars, leaving ½ inch (1.25cm) of headspace. Wipe the rims, seal the jars, and process in a boiling water bath for 5 minutes to ensure the seal.

Rose Hips Jam

Now that you're familiar with the basics, here's an old-time recipe that's fun to make. Rose hips are those little balls that form on rose bushes after the blossoms have fallen off. They're orangey-red and hard. If you think they look like tiny crab apples, you've got a good eye: Roses and apples are in the same family! Harvest rose hips in autumn after the first frost. Don't wait too long after, though, because you don't want them to freeze—just get a little chilly. Be sure to take the rose hips from plants that haven't been treated with insecticides or fungicides. And don't forget the garden gloves. Thorns are sharp regardless of the time of year.

Makes	Prep time	Cook time
4 half-pints	30 minutes	30 to 40 minutes

1lb (450g) rose hips   granulated sugar

water

1. Snip off the tops and bottoms (the stem and blossom ends) from the rose hips. Cut the hips in half and remove the seeds.

2. Add the rose hips to a pot on the stovetop over low heat. For each 1 cup of hips, add 1 cup of water. Simmer the hips until tender, about 30 minutes.

3. Drain the water from the pot and rub the rose hips through a fine sieve. Weigh the pulp and return to the pot.

4. Add an equal amount of sugar by weight and simmer until thick, about 30 minutes.

5. Remove the pot from the heat. Ladle the jam into hot, sterilized jars and seal.

Butters, Conserves & Chutneys

Here's where you'll find a rich celebration of textures, flavors, and aromas. From the simple to the exotic, these fruit products make excellent accompaniments to any main course. They're also stellar gift items. And what's even better, you can make them for a fraction of what you'd pay for them in a specialty store.

Getting to Know You

Jams, jellies, and marmalades (see Chapter 18) are the Type A personalities of fruit spreads. Everything must be measured accurately and timed correctly. But butters, conserves, and chutneys are the more laid-back members of the fruit spread family. "Take your time" is their motto—and you can do just that. Get a batch started today— finish it tomorrow. No problem. Just keep everything refrigerated and it will be perfect and ready to go when you are. Of course, there are reasonable limits and you'll want to finish up within a few days.

Making Fruit Butters

What's in a name? Actually, fruit butters don't contain butter at all and you'd never mistake them for butter by their appearance. But they have a smooth, spreadable consistency like butter and they're great on toast, scones, and muffins—also like butter. As the name implies, they're made from fruit and also can contain flavorings and sugar. Rich in color, the finished product is much deeper in hue than the raw fruit. For example, apple butter is a deep golden amber.

It might seem like it takes forever for certain fruits to begin the ripening process, but once it gets underway, there's no stopping it. You can slow it down by refrigeration, but as the fruit begins to soften, you'd best have a plan in place for using it.

Fruit butters are easy to make and a good use for fruit that might be a tad too ripe for eating or making jam or jelly. Of course, we're definitely not talking about spoiled fruit here. There's only one place for that—and that's the compost pile. We're talking about soft fruit that's peaked and will definitely spoil if you don't do something with it quickly.

Apple butter is the most familiar type, but you can make butters from other fruits, such as apricots, peaches, pears, cherries, blueberries, and plums.

Equipment & Supplies

You don't need much in the way of supplies, but you'll need a slow cooker or an 8- to 10-quart pot with a bottom that doesn't scorch easily. It's maddening to have to deal with a pot that insists on burning what you're trying to cook and the scorch will flavor whatever you're cooking—and not in a good way.

The other essential item is a food mill, arguably one of the handiest kitchen inventions ever. It's perfect for making smooth applesauce and other fruit purées. Forcing the purée through a sieve helps ensure you remove any bits of seeds, peels, or stems. A food processor has a purée function, but it tends to incorporate a large volume of air. The old standby, the Foley Food Mill, works like a dream. It's not terribly expensive either: You can have puréeing perfection for around $50. You'll find food mills at hardware stores or you can order one online.

Apart from those two items, you'll need fruit (of course) and sugar if your fruit is on the tart side. You'll also need wooden or metal spoons, a peeler, a corer, knives, and a grapefruit spoon for removing the pits from peaches.

Method

Work with 2 to 3 pounds (1 to 1.4kg) of fruit at a time. It's easier to stir smaller amounts and keep them from burning or sticking to the pot.

Wash the fruit in cool water. Peeling is optional, but some people prefer to peel peaches, apples, and pears before cooking. Cut the fruit into halves and then quarters. Remove pits and core the fruit. If you're working with cherries or blueberries, you can mash them lightly with the potato masher to help them break down more quickly while they're cooking.

Combine fruits to make your own personalized fruit butters. Try apple with pear or cherry with peach. Almost any combination will work well. Mix up a batch and make it your signature gift. Visit www.thebakersalmanac.com/fruit-flavor-pairing-chart for the most complete guide in existence to mixing and matching fruits, nuts, herbs and spices, and spirits. Leslie Jeon's blog also contains a wealth of good recipes and information for the home food preserver.

Once you've found the combinations you want to use, place the cut/mashed fruit in a large pot with just enough water to prevent the fruit from sticking on the bottom of the pot. Turn the heat on low and cook until the fruit is quite soft. When the fruit is mushy, turn off the heat and process the fruit in the food mill. This will give you a nice purée. You can now decide to proceed with making the fruit butter or transfer the purée to labeled and dated gallon freezer bags and pop them into the freezer for later use.

If you're forging ahead, return the purée to the pot and simmer over low heat until the fruit is thick and a spreadable consistency. This second cooking concentrates the juice and gives fruit butters their intense fruit flavor. You can add sugar to taste at this time or flavoring agents, such as vanilla or almond extract, if you wish. There are no cut-and-dried measurements here—it's all a matter of taste.

To test for doneness, take a spoonful of fruit butter from the pot and drop the fruit on a saucer. If no liquid separates out from the butter, it's done.

When you're satisfied with the consistency of the fruit butter, remove it from the heat and spoon it into hot, sterilized pint or half-pint glass canning and freezing jars. Leave ¼ inch (0.5cm) of headspace. Process in a boiling water bath for 10 minutes to ensure the seal. Remove the jars from the canner and allow them to cool on a flat, dry surface. Store them in the pantry, away from direct light and heat. They'll keep nicely for 1 year or longer.

Making Conserves

Conserves are a kind of jam that's usually made from two or more kinds of fruits, with nuts and raisins added for flavor and texture. They're not designed to be spread on bread but to be served as accompaniments to main courses instead. Fruit pieces are bigger in conserves than in jams, and while some recipes call for pectin, many don't.

If you don't use pectin, cooking times are a bit longer than if you do. If you do use pectin, follow the directions on the pectin box or bottle regarding procedures for adding additional ingredients.

Plums, peaches, apricots, and pears cook up nicely as conserves and their flavors blend beautifully with each other. Again, don't be afraid to experiment or hesitate to visit Leslie's blog for suggestions. Add blueberries, cranberries, or grapes. Whatever your favorite fruit is, there's a place for it in your conserves.

The method for making conserves is similar to that of fruit butter and working with 2 to 3 pounds (1 to 1.4kg) of fruit at a time is easiest. Peel the fruit, remove the pits, and core the fruit. Then chop or mash it coarsely. You want pieces big enough to fit on a teaspoon. They'll cook down considerably.

Place the fruit in an 8- to 10-quart pot or slow cooker, then add the raisins and spices. Simmer on low until thick. Add the nuts during the final 5 minutes of cooking. The amounts of spices and other additions to your conserves are largely a matter of personal taste, so don't be afraid to experiment.

Remove the pot from the heat and ladle the conserve into pint or half-pint glass canning and freezing jars. Process in a boiling water bath for 10 minutes to ensure the seal. Remove the jars from the canner and allow them to cool on a flat, dry surface. Store them in the pantry, away from direct light and heat. They'll keep nicely for 1 year or longer. Just as with butters, conserves make excellent gifts.

Making Chutneys

Chutneys are made with fruits or vegetables, spices, and herbs. They're richer and have a more mellow—some would say exotic—flavor than other fruit spreads. Chutneys have something of the consistency of jam. They use bigger pieces of fruit than conserves and they have substance to go with their robust flavor.

Like conserves, chutneys are used as accompaniments to main courses. They trace their history back to India and the days when the British Empire extended nearly around the world. The English took to chutneys, which soon became known throughout Europe and the New World. Usually served with curry, Indian chutneys tend to be rather thin and frequently hot. Chutneys have evolved over time and the ones we make today are sweeter and thicker.

Fruits that lend themselves to chutney include the following:

Apples	Green tomatoes	Peaches
Apricots	Mangoes	Pineapple
Dates	Papaya	Plums

You can mix and match from this list. Raisins and nuts are often added for texture. Try walnuts, especially black walnuts if you can find some. They can be difficult to locate but are well worth the effort. There are all kinds of ingredients you can incorporate into chutneys, including garlic, onions, and chilies. Seasonings often include ginger, allspice, cinnamon, cloves, and nutmeg.

The procedure for making chutneys is basically the same as for making conserves. You'll need fruit, sugar, and sometimes vinegar, which increases the acidity and gives a bit of a "bite" to the sweetness. Chop the fruit coarsely and place it in an 8- to 10-quart pot. Add spices and other ingredients, bring to a boil, and then simmer until the chutney is thick and the fruit is soft. Add nuts and continue simmering for an additional 5 minutes. Ladle into sterilized pint or half-pint glass canning and freezing jars. Seal. Process in a boiling water bath for 10 minutes to ensure the seal. Remove the jars from the canner and allow them to cool on a flat, dry surface. Store them in the pantry, away from direct light and heat. They'll keep nicely for 1 year or longer. They make excellent gifts.

The National Center for Home Food Preservation has a delicious mango chutney recipe that's research based and approved: nchfp.uga.edu/how/can_06/mango_chutney.html.

Getting Spirited

Brandied fruit (*rumtopf*) is a traditional German holiday dessert. The name means *rum pot* and refers to the stoneware jar on the kitchen counter that's filled with brandied fruit. Making rumtopf is a lengthy process, but once you've gotten the mix started, you simply add fruit as it comes into season. The goal is to have a bit of everything thoroughly soused with brandy by Christmastide.

Ingredients

All you need to get started is a large stoneware crock or jar with a tight-fitting lid, fruit, sugar, and your choice of rum or brandy. You want the fruit to be ripe but not overripe. Strawberries are the traditional first fruit to go into the rumtopf. Here are other fruits to add as they come into season:

Apricots	Nectarines	Pears	Plums
Grapes	Peaches	Pineapple	Red currants

Method

You'll want about 3 pounds (1.4kg) of strawberries to begin. Pull the caps off, but don't wash the strawberries. Wet strawberries get mushy superfast. You don't want them saturated with water but with rum! Place them in a large bowl and cover them with 3 pounds (1.4kg) of granulated sugar. Let the fruit rest for 1 hour. Then pour the entire mixture into the rumtopf and add brandy or rum to just cover the fruit. Keep the fruit beneath the brandy or rum by weighing it down with a plate. Cover the jar with plastic wrap and put on the lid. (Otherwise, you can secure plastic wrap around the top with an elastic band.) Store the rumtopf in a cool, dark place.

Additional Layers

A good rumtopf isn't fast-food. It can't be rushed. Traditionally, each new layer was set down as each fruit came into season. That meant a few weeks between layers, for the most part. Today, we can buy almost any fruit at any time of the year if we're willing to pay a premium price. However, this isn't the way to construct the rumtopf. Slow and easy does the trick. Think strawberries today and apricots in a few weeks. Pace yourself and you'll reap the rewards at holiday time.

You're constructing a vertical, spirited fruit salad. That means to prepare the fruit for eating. Pit, core, and remove the stems as necessary.

The first layer has equal amounts of fruit and sugar, but each additional layer will use half that amount of sugar. For example, all the remaining layers will have 3 pounds (1.4kg) of fruit and 1½ pounds (680g) of sugar. To prepare the second layer, measure 3 pounds (1.4kg) of fruit into a large bowl and add 1½ pounds (680g) of sugar. Allow the mixture to rest for 1 hour. Then pour into the rumtopf. Don't mix this layer with the first one. Add brandy or rum to cover the fruit. Cover the jar again and store it in a cool, dry place.

Throughout the spring and summer, add to the rumtopf until the jar is full. Then let the rumtopf rest for 4 to 6 weeks. Depending on when you start, the rumtopf will be ready just in time for the holiday season.

Using the Rumtopf

The brandied fruit can be served with whipped cream or as a topping for ice cream or cake. You can also try some on cheesecake. Try using the brandied fruit as an accompaniment to roast duckling or goose. It also goes well with roast beef.

You can also drink the brandy or rum—and for many folks, this is what they've been waiting for. The liquid is flavored with all kinds of good fruit juices. Strain and serve it as an after-dinner cordial.

Recipes

With so many combinations of fruits possible, the recipes you can create are nearly endless. The recipes on the following pages are some traditional favorites for butters, conserves, and chutneys. For each recipe, follow the general directions for canning in chapters 10 and 11.

Apple Butter

Nothing says autumn more clearly than apples simmering on the stove and filling the kitchen with their scrumptious aroma.

Makes	Prep time	Cook time
5 pints	20 minutes	2 to 3 hours

5 to 6lb (2.3 to 2.7kg) apples (Fuji, Golden Delicious, and McIntosh recommended)

1 quart apple cider

granulated sugar, to taste

ground cinnamon, to taste

1. Wash and quarter the apples, retaining their skins and cores.

2. Add the apples and just enough water to cover them to an 8- to 10-quart pot. Place the pot on the stovetop over low heat and cook for about 30 minutes or until the apples are quite soft. Remove the pot from heat and process the apples in a food mill.

3. Return the apple purée to the pot and add the apple cider. Return the pot to the heat and cook until the apple butter is to your desired consistency, stirring often to prevent scorching. Add the sugar and cinnamon to taste.

4. Remove the pot from the heat and ladle the apple butter into sterilized pint or half-pint jars, leaving ¼ inch (0.5cm) of headspace.

5. Seal the jars and process in a boiling water bath for 10 minutes to ensure the seal.

Pumpkin Butter

The plant world is always teasing us with blurred definitions of what's a fruit and what's a vegetable. Pumpkins are fruit (sort of), even though they belong to the squash family and are treated like vegetables in canning. With that in mind, here's an interesting variation on fruit butter made with pumpkin. You can cheat on this recipe by buying a can of pumpkin at the store, but it's easy enough to make your own.

Makes	Prep time	Cook time
5 pints	See note.	1 to 2 hours

1 small- to medium-sized pumpkin (or 28oz [800g] pumpkin purée)

¾ cup apple juice

1½ cups granulated sugar

1½ tsp pumpkin pie spice

1. If you're using whole pumpkin, remove the seeds and rind, then cut the pumpkin into pieces.

2. Add the pumpkin pieces and just enough water to cover them to an 8- to 10-quart pot. Place the pot on the stovetop over medium-high heat and cook for about 20 minutes or until tender. Remove the pot from heat and process the pumpkin in a food mill.

3. Return the purée to the pot and add the apple juice, sugar, and pumpkin pie spice. Return the pot to the stovetop over low heat and simmer for 1 to 2 hours or until thick, stirring frequently to prevent scorching.

4. Remove the pot from the heat and ladle the pumpkin butter into sterilized pint or half-pint jars, leaving ¼ inch (0.5cm) of headspace.

5. Seal the jars and process in a boiling water bath for 10 minutes to ensure the seal.

Note: If you're using canned pumpkin purée, the prep time for this recipe is 15 minutes. If you're using homemade pumpkin purée, the prep time is 45 minutes. The Cooperative Extension Service doesn't recommend canning pumpkin purée because its density doesn't allow the product to reach sufficiently high interior temperatures to be safe. However, pumpkin butter processed with sugar and apple juice in pint or half-pint containers is a safe product.

Peach Conserve

This is a good use for peaches that might be a bit bruised and that you don't want to use for canning. Cut out the bruises, throw them away, and use the trimmed fruit for making a conserve.

Makes	Prep time	Cook time
4 to 5 pints	45 minutes	1 to 2 hours

8 cups peaches

1 cup dried plums or prunes, coarsely chopped

½ cup raisins

4 cups orange juice (with pulp)

2 cups light brown sugar

½ tsp ground ginger

¼ tsp ground cloves

½ cup walnuts, coarsely chopped

½ cup pecans, coarsely chopped

1. Remove the skins from the peaches. Add the peaches to a large bowl and use a potato masher to coarsely mash.

2. In an 8- to 10-quart pot on the stovetop over high heat, combine the peaches, dried plums or prunes, raisins, orange juice, brown sugar, ginger, and cloves. Bring to a boil, then reduce the heat to low. Simmer for 1 to 2 hours or until thick.

3. Add the walnuts and pecans. Continue to simmer for 5 minutes more.

4. Remove the pot from the heat and ladle the conserve into hot, sterilized pint or half-pint glass canning and freezing jars, leaving ¼ inch (0.5cm) of headspace.

5. Seal the jars and process in a boiling water bath for 10 minutes to ensure the seal. Remove the jars from the canner and allow to cool on a flat, dry surface.

Pear Chutney

Windfalls are a great source of pears for making chutneys. Orchards and farmers' markets often have good buys on fruit that's blown down in a windstorm before it could be picked. Even if they've got some bruises, you can cut them out and use the good parts. Pears are also readily available at farmers' markets and local grocery stores during the late fall.

Makes	Prep time	Cook time
4 to 5 pints	45 minutes	1 to 2 hours

8 cups pears

2 cups dates, coarsely chopped

1 white onion, coarsely chopped

4 celery stalks, coarsely chopped

1 cup crystallized ginger, finely chopped

2 cups light brown sugar

1 quart apple cider vinegar

2 tsp ground mustard

½ tsp ground cinnamon

¼ tsp ground cloves

kosher salt, to taste

1. Wash and peel the pears. Remove and discard the cores. Chop the pears into teaspoon-sized pieces

2. In an 8- to 10-quart pot on the stovetop over high heat, combine the pears, dates, onion, celery, crystallized ginger, brown sugar, vinegar, mustard, cinnamon, and cloves. Bring to a boil, then reduce the heat to low. Simmer for 1 to 2 hours or until thickened. Add salt to taste.

3. Remove the pot from the heat and ladle the pear chutney into pint or half-pint glass canning and freezing jars, leaving ¼ inch (0.5cm) of headspace.

4. Seal the jars and process in a boiling water bath for 10 minutes to ensure the seal. Remove the jars from the canner and allow them to cool on a flat, dry surface.

Sweet-Hot Chutney

This is tangy, just a bit hot, and oh so delicious! Mangoes give it a subtle, exotic flavor.

Makes	Prep time	Cook time
4 to 5 pints	45 minutes	45 minutes

2 small hot chili peppers,
   cut lengthwise

1 tsp whole black peppercorns

1 tsp whole allspice

1 tsp mustard seeds

1 tsp whole cloves

1 tsp celery seeds

1 orange

3 medium apples

2 peaches, nectarines, or mangoes

1 lemon

1 white onion

2¼ cups granulated sugar

1 cup white vinegar

1 cup water

⅓ cup sliced blanched almonds
   (about 50)

1. In a spice bag, combine the chili peppers, black peppercorns, whole allspice, mustard seeds, whole cloves, and celery seeds. Tie the bag closed and set aside.

2. Peel, core, and remove the seeds from the fruits and onion. Chop the fruits and onion into small pieces and add them to an 8- to 10-quart pot on the stovetop over medium heat.

3. In a medium bowl, combine the sugar, vinegar, and water. Add this mixture to the fruits and onion. Add the spice bag. Cook for 20 minutes.

4. Add the almonds and cook for 10 minutes more or until the chutney reaches your desired consistency. Remove the pot from the heat. Remove and discard the spice bag. Ladle the chutney into hot, sterilized pint or half-pint glass canning and freezing jars, leaving ¼ inch (0.5cm) of headspace.

5. Seal the jars and process in a boiling water bath for 10 minutes to ensure seal. Remove the jars from the canner and allow them to cool on a flat, dry surface.

Drying, Salting, Smoking & Root Cellaring

Part 6

These are the oldest methods of food preserving, although some of them have become new again thanks to modern technology. Smoking adds a wonderful layer of aroma and flavor to meat and fish, but it's just the first step in the preserving process. With smoking and salting especially, it's vital you adhere to strict safety guidelines and research-based practices in order to get a good, safe product. You'll learn more about all these techniques in this part of the book.

Drying

Early humans were constantly on the move seeking food and whatever they picked or killed had to be consumed quickly before spoilage set in. At some point, however, one observant hunter/gatherer must have noticed that when the heat from the sun and the breeze from air currents caused the moisture to quickly evaporate from a plant or animal that had been harvested, the food didn't spoil. They didn't know why this happened, but they did understand that now they could keep that food for later use. The ramifications of this were staggering. People could now stay in one place and branch out for the hunt or the gathering expedition and bring the bounty home and let the sun and wind do the work. This was the earliest form of food preservation and the beginning of civilization.

While technology has vastly changed the way we dry food, the principles have remained the same throughout time. Plants and animals contain moisture, and after the plant or animal has been harvested, this moisture allows the growth of bacteria, molds, and yeasts, which cause spoilage. Removing that moisture, a process called *dehydration*, stops the process of decomposition and allows the food to retain its nutritive value—in some cases, for a very long time.

We still hunt and gather, and if you'd like to try your hand at drying the blackberries you've picked, meat from your successful hunt, the bananas that were on sale, the pinto beans you grew, or the herbs from your windowsill garden, you can. You can dry almost anything. It's easy and you'll save a considerable amount of money compared with what you'd pay for dried foods at the store. Ready to begin? Here we go.

Different Methods of Drying

There are so many different ways to dry foods that you're almost certain to find the right one for what you want to do. Foods can be dried outdoors and indoors. Outdoors, you can take advantage of air movement and the heat of the sun; indoors, you can use a dehydrator, microwave, oven, and even the air itself. It might seem truly odd, but people have tried to dry food in the clothes dryer. Don't! The idea of tumble-drying jerky makes the head spin. Also, if you have forced-air heat, resist the impulse to spread your apple slices on an air vent. It might work for drying socks, but the dust and other contaminants in the air aren't good for food.

Air Drying

In warm climates with low humidity, outdoor air drying works quite well for certain foods, including herbs, mushrooms, green beans, onions, and garlic. These foods are hung away from the sun in a place with good air circulation. Moisture is the enemy and it's essential to bring drying foods indoors overnight if there's any chance of dew or increased humidity, as this can cause the foods to turn moldy and spoil.

To prepare green beans and mushrooms for outside air drying, string them together. It's the same procedure you'd use to string popcorn on a Christmas tree. Use a sturdy needle and strong thread. When you've got a string completed, hang it from a hook out of the sun and in a place with good air circulation.

Onions and garlic can be braided before hanging. Just remember to leave the long stems attached so you'll have something to braid.

Air drying also works indoors and you don't have to worry about a nocturnal rainstorm or sudden jump in the humidity. Herbs, garlic, and onions are good candidates for this type of home food preservation.

Herbs are an essential part of the home food preserver's pantry. Air drying works well for herbs, which shouldn't be dried in the sun. You'll need scissors, small paper bags (lunch size), large paper clips or Christmas ornament hangers, and yarn or twine.

Herbs need to be completely dry before you begin the drying process (which is sort of a paradox!) because the slightest bit of mold will ruin them. Cut a stem about 6 inches (15cm) long and remove the lower leaves. If the herbs are dusty, rinse them off, but be sure they're completely dry before you work with them. You can set a hair dryer on low and wave it around the herbs to make sure.

Use the twine or yarn to bundle several stems together and then insert the bundle into a paper bag. Tie the bag around the stems and be sure the herbs aren't touching the sides of the bag. If they do, they might adhere to the bag during the drying process and refuse to separate.

Bend a large paper clip into a hook or use a Christmas ornament hanger to snag the twine around the paper bag. Hang the bag away from light in an airy location. You can run a string across a doorway in a seldom-used room and hang the bags from the string. The bags will protect the herbs from sunlight and dust, and they'll also catch any stray leaves that decide to jump ship. It will take about 2 weeks for the herbs to air dry.

When they're dry, you can separate the leaves from the stems and store them away from direct heat or sunlight in a glass jar with a secure lid. They'll keep for about 1 year.

Vine-drying is another form of air drying. Numerous varieties of beans, including kidney, pinto, navy, Great Northern (white), and soy, and even lentils can simply be left alone until their vines have died a natural death and the pods have dried. Use the *shake, rattle, and roll* test. When you shake the pod and it rattles, you're ready to roll. The vines can then be pulled and the beans shelled.

Sun Drying

Sun drying uses the sun's heat and air movement, and it's the most inexpensive method for drying foods. Because of their high sugar and acid content, fruits are recommended for sun drying. Vegetables and meat products are low-acid and low-sugar foods and they're not recommended for this process. They can easily become reservoirs for harmful bacteria and spoilage.

Apricots and peaches set out to dry on wooden, slatted trays used to be a common sight in California orchards at picking time. Today, the orchards are fewer and outdoor drying is rarer, but if you venture out into the country, you might be lucky enough to spot some.

Drying outdoors requires several consecutive days of high temperatures—from the mid-90s to 100°F (35°C to 40°C)—accompanied by low humidity (below 60%) and brisk winds. If your climate lends itself to outdoor drying and the air is clean where you live, you might want to give it a try.

You'll need drying trays, which are wood frames with wood slats far enough apart to allow the air to circulate but close enough together to keep the food from falling through the cracks. Stay away from redwood or other evergreen woods. These can cause the fruit to have an off-putting flavor and can also stain the fruit. Stainless steel, plastic, and Teflon-coated fiberglass trays can also be used, but avoid *hardware cloth*, which is a galvanized metal cloth covered with cadmium or zinc that can leave harmful residues on your food. Additionally, copper or aluminum aren't recommended. Copper destroys Vitamin C and increases oxidation, while aluminum discolors and corrodes.

You'll need bird netting or cheesecloth to keep dust and insects from the food. If you'll be drying light-colored fruits—such as peaches, pears, or apples, the best candidates for outdoor drying—you'll need ascorbic acid (vitamin C) or a commercial antidiscoloration preparation and pans for holding the antidiscoloration agent.

Light-colored fruits dried outdoors used to be dusted with sulfur to keep them from darkening during the drying process. While the product was visually appealing, keeping apricots and peaches a deep orange, this process is no longer recommended, as sulfur can have serious health consequences in individuals with a sensitivity to sulfites. Instead, you can pretreat light-colored fruits with a commercial antidiscoloring preparation, ascorbic acid, or vitamin C. However, the dried fruit will be darker than sulfured fruit.

Solar Drying

This is one step up from sun drying. A solar dryer is a structure that uses reflectors to intensify the sun's heat and a ventilation system that increases airflow to speed up the drying process. This is useful if your area tends to be more humid or if temperatures aren't optimal for sun drying, although it's still iffy as a solution. Foods that are suitable for sun drying, such as fruits, are good choices for solar drying. Even though solar drying speeds up the process, it's not reliable enough to ensure that vegetables won't become contaminated by bacterial growth and spoil. If you're handy with materials, you can make your own solar dryer using found materials. For example, gardeners who like to get a head start on the season are likely to use a cold frame. A *cold frame* is simply a wooden box minus the top and bottom. It's set outdoors on the ground and plants are set inside it for shelter. The top is usually an old window that's attached with a hinge and propped up with a piece of wood during the day and closed down at night. It provides protection from wind and cold.

Lining this with aluminum foil and propping the glass open to allow air circulation will serve as a makeshift solar dryer. See Appendix F for further information.

Oven Drying

This takes the drying process indoors where climate doesn't matter. It also expands your options because you can dry vegetables, fish, and herbs as well as make fruit leather and jerky by this method. The major drawbacks to drying foods in the oven are limited space and the cost of energy. You can generally dry about 5 pounds (2.3kg) of food at a time and the only other items you'll need are a wooden spoon or an oven mitt to prop the door open a smidge while the foods are drying and a thermometer to check the internal temperature. You want to keep that at 140°F (60°C). You'll also want to check to be sure you can set your oven to this temperature. Air circulation is essential, thus the slightly open door. Be sure there are at least 3 inches (7.5cm) of free space all around your trays to let the air circulate freely. Heat is required, thus the thermometer. You'll need to keep an eye on the temperature and turn it up or down accordingly to maintain an even flow.

The temperature is warmest closest to the heating element. If you have a gas oven with a pilot light, that might be enough to give you the temperature you need. The way to check is to put a thermometer on the top rack and close the door. Check in 1 hour and see what the reading is. If it's not high enough, you'll need to turn the oven on warm. Check the temperature again after 30 minutes.

Oven drying isn't difficult, but it requires some finessing to settle at the proper temperature. You might need to do some fiddling with the temperature control until you hit on just the right setting. Do this part of the preparation work before you commit food to the oven. You can't rush the process. If you try to speed it up by increasing the temperature, you'll end up cooking your food rather than drying it. There's also something called *case hardening*, which occurs when the outside of the food cooks, thus preventing the moisture inside from escaping. This will cause your food to mold. Increasing the airflow to move moisture away from the food is the only option if you're growing old sitting by the oven waiting for things to dry, and if you have a convection oven, using this feature can help. Regardless, it takes as long as it takes.

Trays

Air circulation is essential to getting a good product, so you'll need trays made with wood slats or stainless steel screening. Most ovens have two or three racks, and if you use all three, you'll have pretty close to a full load without rigging an additional rack. Cookie sheets and other solid trays aren't suitable because they block the airflow. Be careful about the materials you use when making your trays. Keep to stainless steel or wood to prevent harmful chemicals from coming in contact with your food. Aluminum, copper, vinyl, fiberglass, and galvanized metal should be avoided.

Method

As you'll see shortly, oven drying is best begun early in the day. Place the cut food in a single layer on each tray and place each tray on an oven rack. Be sure there's room for the air to circulate around each piece of food. Prop the door open so the air can circulate, but keep an eye on the thermometer so the temperature remains between 140°F and 160°F (60°C and 70°C).

You can speed up the process a bit if you have a small electric fan to set up so the stream of air blows into the oven. Once you've got everything nicely settled, set the timer for 30 minutes.

When the timer buzzes, it's time to rotate the racks. Move each rack down one space and put the bottom rack on the top. Reset the timer. Each time you check, repeat this process so every rack will have equal time at every position. This will correct for any temperature differences inside the oven.

You can also take this opportunity to turn the food over so it dries more evenly. You can expect the process to take several hours and vegetables can take up to 12 hours. This is why it's best to get an early start. You don't want to be rotating racks and flipping food late at night.

Fruit Leather

Get out those cookie sheets again! (Be sure they're rimmed.) Smooth a piece of plastic wrap across the inside of the cookie sheet, making sure it comes up the sides. Don't use waxed paper or aluminum foil. They'll stick to the leather and you'll end up with pieces of foil or paper in your teeth.

Spread a fruit purée on top to a depth of ¼ inch (0.5cm). For each 2 cups of light-colored fruit (such as peaches, apples, or pears), add 2 teaspoons of lemon juice or ⅛ teaspoon of ascorbic acid (vitamin C) to keep the purée from darkening. You can combine different fruits, such as blackberries and peaches, or just stick to one variety.

Place the cookie sheets on the oven racks and follow the general procedures for oven drying discussed earlier. The edges of the leather will dry first, so check for doneness by touching a finger to the middle of the cookie sheet. The fruit leather will be done when it isn't sticky in the middle, but don't overdry it. You don't want it to crack when you try to roll it up.

When the fruit leather is ready, remove the tray from the oven, peel the fruit away from the plastic, and roll it up. After it has cooled, you can re-roll it in plastic for storage. Fruit leather will keep up to a month unrefrigerated or up to 1 year in the freezer.

Drying Herbs in the Oven

Just about any herb you can grow will dry well in the oven. Harvest the herbs when mature but before they've begun to flower, as the flowering takes strength from the leaves. The most potent leaves are found at the ends of the stems and they decrease in strength as you get closer to the stem.

Throw away any discolored or dead leaves. Remove the leaves from the stems and place the leaves on a drying rack, allowing space for the air to circulate. Follow the general procedures for oven drying as outlined in the preceding section. Herbs will dry in 2 to 4 hours in the oven.

The microwave isn't recommended for drying most foods because of their density, but you can use it to dry herbs. One thing to be aware of is that the microwave has a strong tendency to cook the leaves instead of drying them. If you want to try it, place a few stems on a paper towel and cover them with another paper towel. Cook on high for 2 to 3 minutes and then check them. If you're working with mint, parsley, thyme, or any other tender leaves, check them more frequently and flip them every 30 seconds or so. They're done when they crumble. If you need to nuke them a bit more, try 15-second intervals so you don't end up scorching them.

Dehydrators

These appliances are the most popular for drying food—and for good reason. They're easy to use, take up little space in storage, and produce excellent results. These units are freestanding, electric, have automatic temperature selection, are programmable, and come in a variety of sizes and price ranges. They're available at hardware stores, retail outlets that sell small appliances, natural food stores, catalogues, and online.

The bigger the dehydrator, the more trays it can hold. Smaller units will have 4 shelves, while the larger models can accommodate up to 12. If your unit has stackable trays, check to see if you have the option of ordering additional trays from the manufacturer.

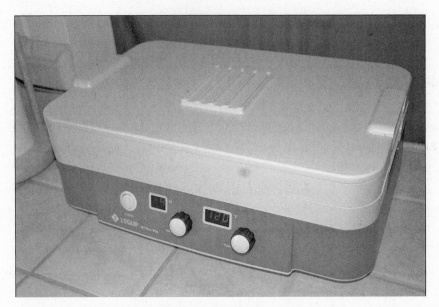

Dehydrator with stackable trays

The unit pictured here has vertical airflow. That means the heating element and fan are in the base of the unit. The one drawback to this arrangement is that foods can drip or fall into the fan vents. This can potentially be a problem if you're making fruit leather and accidentally dump purée into the heating element and fan. If this does happen, turn off the unit and use a damp cloth to soak up the spill. Be careful not to get water into the heating element.

The other option is a unit with the heating unit and fan built into the side. This creates horizontal airflow. With this design, you don't have to worry about the spills and all the foods get the same amount of heat and airflow. It might be the better choice, especially if you want to dry different types of foods at the same time or are seriously into making fruit leathers. A dehydrator is more economical to operate than an electric oven, but it's slightly less economical than gas.

Regardless of what you're drying, you'll need to keep tabs on the temperature. It needs to be high enough to cause moisture to evaporate but not so high as to cook the food.

If the temperature is too high at the beginning of the drying process, the outer layer of what you're drying will develop a hard shell, while moisture will be trapped inside the inner layers with no way out. This is case hardening, as we noted previously, and it's not good. Success is all about striking a balance and understanding how the process works.

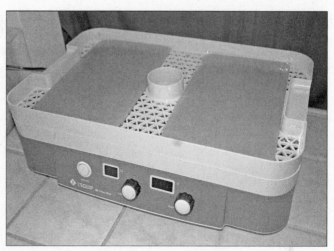

*Pouring peach purée into
the dehydrator tray (left)*

Fruit leather (right)

Preheat the dehydrator to 125°F (50°C). Then add the food to the trays and stack them in the dehydrator. After 1 hour or so, when you can see that the exterior of the food has begun to dry, increase the temperature to 140°F (60°C) and hold it there until the food is done. The drying process can take from 4 to 12 hours. Read the instruction book that comes with your dehydrator. It will save you a lot of time and guesswork. It should also include approximate drying times for various foods.

General Procedures

Fruits, vegetables, and meats are all handled differently, but a few basic principles apply to whatever you're planning on drying. First, start with the best. That means fruits and vegetables should be ripe but not overripe and should be free from bruising and other blemishes. The exception here is fruit leathers, which are an excellent use of bruised or slightly overripe fruit. Fish should be handled gently and as quickly as possible after being reeled in. Meat and poultry products should be lean and fresh.

As with other methods of preserving foods, assemble everything you'll need before you get started and arrange it in the order in which you'll use it. You'll save time and also discover if you're missing something you were sure you had but turns out you didn't.

Once you begin the drying process, keep at it until you're finished. Food that's only partially dried is a breeding ground for bacteria and molds and can spoil very quickly. If you don't have time to finish, don't start until you do.

Fruit

Fruits that dry well include the following:

Apples	Cranberries	Pears
Apricots	Figs	Plums
Bananas	Grapes	Prunes
Blueberries	Huckleberries	Strawberries
Cherries	Peaches	Tomatoes

Wash and sort the fruit. Larger fruit should be sliced or halved so it dries evenly. The thinner the slice, the quicker the drying time.

- Apples: Peel, core, and slice them ¼ inch (0.5cm) thick.

- Peaches, apricots, plums, and prunes: Cut them in half and remove the pits

- Cherries, blueberries, cranberries, and huckleberries: Remove the stems and pits.

- Pears: Cut them in half and scoop out the stringy centers with a grapefruit spoon.

- Bananas: Slice them into coins or spears.

- Tomatoes: Slice them.

If you're working with light-colored fruit, you'll want to treat it to prevent it from darkening. You can use a commercial antidiscoloration product (follow the directions on the label), ascorbic acid, or vitamin C. If you're using ascorbic acid, use ½ teaspoon of ascorbic acid crystals or 3 crushed 500mg vitamin C tablets in 1 quart of water. You'll find the crystals at the grocery store.

Plums, cherries, grapes, and blueberries are usually dried whole, but their skins are tough and keep moisture trapped inside. They need to be cracked or checked. *Cracking* means dipping them in boiling water for about 30 seconds and then plunging them into ice water. Remove them from the ice water and allow them to dry. This method works well with smaller fruits. *Checking* means scoring them with a paring knife in several places to give the inner moisture an outlet. This method is more easily used on larger fruits.

Dehydrators are a fairly painless way to make fruit leathers.

Vegetables

Vegetables that dry well include the following:

Beets	Corn	Parsnips
Broccoli	Green beans	Peas
Cabbage	Green peppers	Potatoes
Carrots	Mushrooms*	Squashes (winter and summer)
Cauliflower	Okra	Turnips
Celery	Onions	

* Use only commercially purchased mushrooms to avoid accidental poisoning.

Wash vegetables thoroughly, using a brush if needed to remove dirt.

- Beets, potatoes, and turnips: Peel and slice them.

- Cabbage: Core them.

- Carrots: Peel them if desired.

- Corn: Remove the kernels from the cobs.

- Peas: Shell them.

- Peppers: Remove the seeds and white membranes. Slice them.

Chop or slice vegetables into uniform sizes. If a vegetable needs to be blanched before being frozen, it should be blanched before being dried. Drying doesn't stop enzymes from causing flavor and color changes in vegetables. See Chapter 5 for recommended blanching times for vegetables. Peppers, onions, and mushrooms don't need blanching.

Meats & Poultry

Select fresh or frozen lean meats and poultry. Partially frozen meats and poultry are easier to slice and give more uniform results.

For beef, the leaner grades, such as standard and select, have less fat and are more suitable for drying. Rump, flank, round, and sirloin cuts are good choices.

Game meats make excellent jerky. Most people are familiar with venison and elk jerky, but the possibilities are almost limitless. Depending on where you live, you might find alligator, emu, buffalo, antelope, or bear.

Meats and poultry should be cut into long slices and shouldn't be thicker than ¼ inch (0.5cm). Cutting with the grain makes a chewier jerky, while cutting against the grain makes a more tender product. Remove all fat.

Fish

Most fish are first dry salted or brine salted and then either smoked or canned. (See Chapters 22 and 12, respectively). Air drying is an old method for preserving fish.

Herbs

Clip herbs for drying before they flower and early in the morning right after the dew is off. The exception is dill, which should be harvested after the seeds have developed.

Making Jerky

This is the backpacker's staple food, along with granola and dried fruit. You can make jerky from a wide variety of meats, including game meats, poultry, and fish. Lean meats are best, and the leaner the meat, the better the finished product. This means that for beef, you'll be looking at standard and select grades as opposed to choice or prime grade, which have more marbling.

One of the difficulties of rediscovering the old ways of preserving foods is that we often approach them without the knowledge gained over the long run by those who perfected the process. We don't have a healthy respect for the need to do the job right and want to take some shortcuts. Here are two cases in point:

Case #1

Game meats pose their own special considerations. The length of time the animal is held at ambient temperatures before getting to the cooler can allow harmful bacteria to grow and multiply. Additionally, there's the possibility of fecal contamination of the meat when the animal is being field dressed. Bottom line: Get the game to the cooler as quickly as possible and observe strict cleanliness during field dressing.

Case #2

We want to reduce the amount of salt in our diets and don't understand that that principle can't always be applied across the board. Making low-salt or no-salt jerky isn't a recommended practice. Salt binds moisture in the meat and this kills any bacteria present more quickly if water isn't available for them to grow and multiply. Salt is just one consideration though. There have been cases of illness associated with homemade jerky. The USDA recommends that to destroy harmful microorganisms, meat should be heated to 160°F (70°C) before the dehydrating process begins. Bottom line: Follow approved safety practices and approved methods for making jerky.

The following method is approved by Oregon State University and will give you an excellent product. To begin, you'll find it easier to work with meat that's been slightly frozen. If you slice the meat with the grain (along the muscle), you'll get longer strips that are chewy. If you slice against the grain (at right angles to the long muscles), the strips will be shorter and more brittle. It's strictly a matter of personal preference.

Follow these steps to make jerky:

1. Remove all visible fat and tendons. Fat that's left on the meat can turn rancid and spoil the jerky.

2. Cut the meat into long, thin strips—⅛ to ¼ inch (0.35 to 0.5cm) thick and about 1 to 1½ inches (1.25 to 3.75cm) wide. Longer strips are easier to work with.

3. Prepare the marinade of your choice in a large saucepan and bring it to a full rolling boil. You'll need 2 to 3 cups.

4. Add a few meat strips, making sure they're covered with the marinade. Let the marinade return to a full boil. Dipping the meat pieces into the boiling marinade keeps any bacteria present on the meat from contaminating the marinade. This precooking process helps ensure a safe product.

5. Turn off the heat and use tongs to remove the meat strips from the marinade. Immediately place them on drying racks in single, nonoverlapping rows.

6. Continue the process until all meat strips have been precooked in the marinade.

7. Process them in the dehydrator at 140°F to 150°F (60°C to 65°C) until done.

8. Test for doneness: Remove one piece from the dehydrator and allow it to cool. It should crack but not break when you bend it and there should be no moist or underdone portions.

9. Refrigerate the jerky overnight. In the morning, test for doneness again. If required, return the strips to the dehydrator to complete the drying process.

Testing for Dryness

You can follow a recipe or the manufacturer's instructions on your dehydrator to the letter, but many factors play a role in determining when your foods are dry:

- The kind of food being dried
- The thickness of the food
- Humidity
- The amount of air circulation
- The amount of food on the tray, in the oven, or in the dehydrator

Whatever you're drying will follow a basic pattern: The edges will dry before the middle. This also means that foods on the outside edge of each tray might dry more quickly than foods crowded into the middle. To even this out, it's important to move the food around to even out the process.

Each batch will be different. Just because the last 4 batches of dried pears took 2 hours to reach perfection doesn't mean this batch won't need 3 hours or the following batch will be done in 90 minutes. You need to check. That means taking a few pieces out of the dehydrator and allowing them to cool. If the food is warm, it will feel soft. Only after it has cooled down will you be able to determine if it's dry.

Fruit will be pliable when it's dried. You can put a pear half or another large piece of fruit in your hand and squeeze. The fruit should bend when your hand bends and open back up when you open your hand. It shouldn't feel or look wet at all.

Testing vegetables for dryness is fun and also therapeutic. Hit a test piece with a hammer and the vegetable should shatter. A word of caution here: Don't use your kitchen counter for a test surface. Take the veggie outside or use a wooden block. Note: Mushrooms, peppers, and squash don't test this way. They'll be softer.

The Final Step: Conditioning

Think of conditioning as the great evening-out process. Even if a couple of pieces in a batch are too dry and a couple of others aren't dry enough, you can fix it!

When everything has cooled, put the pieces in large freezer bags or a glass jar with a snug-fitting lid. Put the container in a warm, dry place and check it every day. Stir or shake it to redistribute the pieces of food. It will take about 1 week or so for the conditioning process to be complete. During this time, the moisture from the underdone pieces is absorbed by the overdone pieces.

If you notice sweating on the glass or moisture forming on the inside of the plastic freezer bag during the conditioning process, you'll need to send the whole batch back to the dryer to finish drying; otherwise, you'll start growing mold.

The Importance of Pasteurizing

If you dried your food outdoors, there's a good chance a stray insect decided to use it for a nursery. Destroying any insect eggs is important to keep your food safe. It needs to be pasteurized. Also, if you're worried about the possibility of mold, you can pop your dried foods into the oven or the freezer and pasteurize them.

For the oven: Preheat to 175°F (80°C). Arrange the dried food in a single layer on a tray. Close the oven door and leave the food in the oven for 15 minutes. Remove and allow it to cool before packaging.

For the freezer: Place food in freezer containers and leave in the freezer for 1 to 2 weeks.

Storage Options

Moisture/vapor-proof containers are good choices for storing dried foods. Air isn't the culprit. It's the moisture in the air that is. You also want to store food away from light in a cool, dry location. Fruits are generally good for 1 year at 60°F (15°C) or 6 months at 80°F (25°C). Vegetables vary according to their type. Usually, they're good for at least half a year, and in the case of dried beans, you might consider leaving them to your children in your will. Shrink-wrapping adds another level of protection and you can also keep dried foods in the freezer for extra insurance.

Choose smaller containers over big ones. Each time you open the container, moisture can creep in—and with moisture comes the possibility of mold taking hold. If you spot any mold on the food, toss the entire batch. Eating anything with mold on it isn't smart and can make you very, very sick.

Depending on where you plan on storing your dried foods, plastic containers might or might not be a good option. Rodents can easily gnaw through plastic and these critters have all the time in the world when a good meal is concerned. If you'll be storing your containers in the garage or basement, check in on them periodically just to be sure they're okay. Glass is always the best choice and canning jars with new rings and lids screwed on tightly are just about perfect. Second best are metal containers, also with tight-fitting lids.

Properly stored, dried foods keep up to 1 year, with jerky maxing out at about 6 months. As with other preserved foods, remember that the goal isn't to stockpile forever but to put foods aside for use when you want them. Have a plan for what you preserve and then use your dried foods—don't let them pine away on the pantry shelf.

Rehydrating

Rehydrating means exactly what it says. You replace the water that you took out when drying your food when it comes time to use it. The general rule is that dried food is about half the measure of reconstituted or fresh foods. That means ½ cup of dried carrots is equivalent to 1 cup of reconstituted or fresh carrots and so forth.

Dried fruits can be chopped into bite-sized pieces for sprinkling over cooked or cold cereals or for use in muffins and coffee cakes. Mix up a batch of chopped cherries, apricots, peaches, and other dried fruits and nuts, then store them in glass jars that can be placed on the breakfast table.

Dried vegetables are excellent in casseroles, soups, stews, and foods prepared in a slow cooker. Just be sure to add the necessary liquid to allow for rehydrating while your food cooks.

Recipes

In the following recipes, 1 teaspoon of dried herbs is equivalent to 1 tablespoon of fresh herbs. If reconstituting is required, it's noted in the recipe.

Dried Apple Coffee Cake

You can use any sliced dried fruit in this coffee cake. This is the traditional Jiffy baking mix recipe, printed with permission.

Serves	Prep time	Cook time
8	20 minutes	25 to 30 minutes

1½ cups dried apple slices

2 cups Jiffy baking mix

3 tsp granulated sugar

¾ cup milk of choice

1 large egg

2 tbsp melted shortening

for the streusel topping

¼ cup granulated sugar

1 tbsp Jiffy baking mix

2 tsp ground cinnamon

2 tbsp soft butter

½ cup chopped walnuts or pecans

1. In a large bowl, cover the apple slices with 3 to 4 inches (7.5 to 10cm) of warm water or apple juice. Allow 1 hour for the slices to rehydrate. Remove the slices from the water and drain on paper towels. Pat excess moisture with paper towels.

2. Preheat the oven to 350°F (175°C). Spray an 8-inch (20cm) baking dish with cooking spray.

3. In a small bowl, make the streusel topping by combining the sugar, baking mix, cinnamon, butter, and nuts. Mix well with a fork and set aside.

4. In a medium bowl, combine the baking mix, sugar, milk, egg, and shortening. Spoon this mixture into the dish.

5. Randomly insert the apple slices into the batter.

6. Cover the batter with the streusel topping.

7. Place the dish in the oven and bake for 25 to 30 minutes or until a wooden skewer inserted into the middle of the cake comes out clean.

8. Remove the dish from the oven and serve the coffee cake immediately.

Old-Fashioned Muffins

There are many variations you can make from this basic recipe. Add nuts and any combination of chopped dried fruits. Rehydrating isn't necessary.

Serves	Prep time	Cook time
6	20 minutes	20 minutes

2 cups all-purpose flour

½ cup (total) chopped dried fruit (use just one or a combination of apples, peaches, apricots, pears, cherries, etc.)

½ tsp kosher salt

1 tbsp baking powder

⅓ cup granulated sugar

1 cup milk of choice

1 large egg

3 tbsp melted butter

for the streusel topping

¼ cup granulated sugar

¼ cup all-purpose flour

2 tbsp butter

⅛ tsp ground cinnamon

1. Preheat the oven to 400°F (200°C). Spray a muffin tray with cooking spray or line the baking tray with paper baking cups.

2. In a small bowl, make the streusel topping by combining the sugar, flour, butter, and cinnamon. Mix well and set aside.

3. In a large bowl, combine the flour, dried fruit, salt, baking powder, and sugar. Mix well and set aside.

4. In a medium bowl, combine the milk, egg, and sugar.

5. In a separate large bowl, alternate mixing the dry and wet ingredients. The batter will be slightly lumpy.

6. Pour the mixture into the muffin tray or paper baking cups until two-thirds full. Cover the batter with the streusel topping.

7. Place the tray in the oven and bake for 20 minutes or until a wooden skewer inserted into the middle of a muffin comes out clean.

8. Remove the tray from the oven and serve the muffins immediately.

Corn Chowder

This is a cheerful chowder—golden and hearty. The salt pork gives it a nice smoky flavor and the onion adds some crunch.

Serves	Prep time	Cook time
6	30 minutes	1 hour

½ cup dried corn

3½ cups water, divided

½ cup diced salt pork

1 medium white onion, chopped

1 medium white potato, diced

2 cups milk of choice

2½ tbsp all-purpose flour

kosher salt, to taste

freshly ground black pepper, to taste

¼ tsp paprika

1. In a medium bowl, combine the corn and 1½ cups of water. Allow 30 minutes for corn to rehydrate.

2. In a medium skillet on the stovetop over medium heat, cook the salt pork until browned. Add the onions and sauté until translucent, about 2 to 3 minutes.

3. Transfer the salt pork and onions to a large soup pot on the stovetop over high heat. Add the corn and any remaining liquid. Add the potatoes and the remaining 2 cups water. Bring to a boil, then reduce the heat to low. Simmer for about 45 minutes or until the potatoes are tender.

4. In a small bowl, combine the milk, flour, and salt and pepper to taste. Mix well. Add this mixture to the soup pot. Return the chowder to a simmer, stirring occasionally.

5. Remove the soup pot from the heat and ladle the chowder into individual serving bowls. Sprinkle paprika over the top before serving. Serve with crackers or homemade bread.

Corn Pudding

Corn pudding is a traditional New England dish and it's also claimed by Southern cooks. Often served at Thanksgiving dinner, it's a good dish for any time of the year.

Serves	Prep time	Cook time
6	30 minutes	1 hour

¾ cup dried corn

3 cups water

3 large eggs, beaten

2 tbsp butter, melted

2 cups milk of choice or light cream

2 tbsp granulated sugar

1 tsp kosher salt

1. In a medium pot on the stovetop, combine the corn and water. Allow 30 minutes for the corn to rehydrate.

2. Turn the heat to medium and simmer until tender, about 1 hour. Drain the corn.

3. Preheat the oven to 350°F (175°C). Spray a quart casserole dish with cooking spray.

4. In a large bowl, combine the corn, eggs, butter, milk, sugar, and salt. Pour the mixture into the casserole dish.

5. Place the dish in the oven and bake for 45 to 60 minutes or until a table knife inserted in the center of the pudding comes out clean.

6. Remove the dish from the oven and serve the pudding immediately.

Minestrone with Italian Sausage

This is a hearty traditional Italian soup made in the slow cooker.

Serves	Prep time	Cook time
6	20 minutes	6 to 8 hours

1½ cups mixed dried beans

2 tbsp olive oil

½lb (225g) Italian sausage links, sliced

½ cup dried celery

½ cup dried white onions

½ cup dried carrots

½ cup dried zucchini

½ cup dried crookneck squash

2 to 3 garlic cloves, minced

1 quart beef broth or stock, plus more

1 (28oz [800g]) can of diced tomatoes with basil, garlic, and oregano

1 cup uncooked large elbow macaroni

1½ cups wilted spinach or other greens

kosher salt, to taste

freshly ground black pepper, to taste

1. In a large bowl, cover the beans with 3 to 4 inches (7.5 to 10cm) of water. Allow the beans to rehydrate overnight, then drain the beans.

2. Heat the olive oil in a medium skillet on the stovetop over medium heat. Add the sausages and sauté until lightly browned.

3. Add the celery and onions. Sauté until soft, about 3 to 5 minutes.

4. Transfer the mixture to a slow cooker. Add the carrots, onions, zucchini, crookneck squash, broth, and tomatoes. Cook on low for 6 to 8 hours, checking after 3 hours and adding more stock as necessary.

5. Prepare the elbow macaroni according to the package instructions. Drain and add to the slow cooker.

6. Add the spinach and cook for 15 for 20 minutes or until wilted.

7. Turn off the slow cooker and ladle the minestrone into individual serving bowls.

Shepherd's Pie

This was originally made with ground lamb, but ground beef works just fine too.

Serves	Prep time	Cook time
8	20 minutes	30 minutes

1 to 2 cups mixed dried vegetables (carrots, onions, mushrooms, and peas recommended)

1lb (450g) ground lamb or beef

2 tbsp olive oil

1 tsp Worcestershire sauce

½ cup beef broth or stock, plus more

2 cups mashed potatoes (or use reconstituted potato flakes)

1. Add the dried mixed vegetables to a medium bowl and cover with warm water. Allow 1 hour for the vegetables to rehydrate. Add water as necessary to keep the vegetables covered. Drain and set aside.

2. Preheat the oven to 350°F (175°C).

3. Heat the olive oil in a medium skillet on the stovetop over medium heat. Add the ground lamb and sauté until browned. Drain the excess fat.

4. In a large bowl, combine the lamb, vegetables, Worcestershire sauce, and broth. Stir until thoroughly moistened. Add additional broth if necessary.

5. Transfer the mixture to a medium casserole dish. Spread the mashed potatoes over the top of the lamb mixture.

6. Place the dish in the oven and bake until the potatoes are browned and the lamb mixture is bubbly, about 30 minutes.

7. Remove the dish from the oven and serve the shepherd's pie immediately.

Chicken Pot Pie

Use either chicken or turkey for this comfort food.

Serves	Prep time	Cook time
6	30 to 40 minutes	6 to 8 hours

4 cups cubed chicken or turkey

½ cup dried carrots

½ cup dried onions

½ cup dried peas

½ cup dried corn

½ cup dried mushrooms

½ tsp poultry seasoning

kosher salt, to taste

freshly ground black pepper, to taste

1 refrigerated pie crust

for the white sauce

2 tbsp butter

2 tbsp all-purpose flour

1 cup hot milk of choice

1 chicken bouillon cube

¼ tsp kosher salt

⅛ tsp freshly ground black pepper

1. In a medium bowl, cover the carrots, onions, peas, corn, and mushrooms with 3 to 4 inches (7.5 to 10cm) of warm water. Allow 1 hour for the vegetables to rehydrate. Drain and set aside.

2. Preheat the oven to 350°F (175°C).

3. To make the white sauce, make a roux by melting the butter in a small saucepan on the stovetop over low heat. Add the flour and whisk until well mixed.

4. Add the milk, bouillon cube, salt, and pepper. Use a spoon or whisk to stir constantly until thickened.

5. In a large bowl, combine the chicken, vegetables, and white sauce. Transfer the mixture to a medium casserole dish. Place the pie crust over the top of the dish according to the package instructions.

6. Place the dish in the oven and bake until the crust is brown and the mixture is bubbly, about 30 minutes.

7. Remove the dish from the oven and serve the chicken pot pie immediately.

Barbara's Boston Baked Beans

Get out the bean crock for this delicious dish. Great Northern white beans are quite good for this recipe. Start this in the morning so it's ready at dinnertime.

Serves	Prep time	Cook time
8	60 minutes	6 to 8 hours

1lb (450kg) dried white beans

1 tsp baking soda

½ to ¾ cup light brown sugar

½ cup dried white onions

1 small piece of salt pork or bacon

1 tsp mustard

kosher salt, to taste

1. Wash and sort the beans. Soak overnight in cold water.

2. In a large pot on the stovetop over high heat, combine the beans and baking soda. Boil for 10 minutes, then drain the beans. Add enough cold water to just cover the beans. Boil until soft, about 30 to 45 minutes.

3. Preheat the oven to 200°F (95°C).

4. Transfer the beans and liquid to a bean crock. Add the brown sugar, salt pork, and mustard. Stir until well mixed.

5. Place the crock in the oven and bake for 6 to 8 hours or until the beans are done. Add water while baking the if beans look dry. Check each hour until done.

6. Remove the crock from the oven and serve the baked beans immediately.

Salting

As noted in the previous chapter, food preservation quite possibly began by accident when someone noticed that the sun and wind removed enough moisture from a food to keep it from spoiling. This process took some time, and because people have been looking for shortcuts since the beginning, someone else probably wondered what would happen if some salt got tossed onto the food being dried. The answer, of course, is the salt hastened the drying process. In a way, this was the creation of the first recipe.

Salt is a naturally occurring mineral and it's necessary for life—human and animal. We seek it instinctually and animals will travel miles to find a salt lick. In fact, salt is one of our five tastes, along with sweet, sour, bitter, and savory.

Historical Perspective on Salting

Every culture has found a source for salt. The exact moment when salting food became a common practice is lost in the mists of history, but we do know that the Chinese and Egyptians were among the earliest users of this product of the earth and sea. A salt lake in northern China, Lake Yuncheng, supplied the Chinese with salt at least as early as about 6000 BCE. The ancient Egyptians were also salt consumers. They probably deduced that if salt was good for preserving mummies, then it might work equally well on meat they were planning to eat at some later date.

At any rate, in addition to personal consumption, salting food to preserve it caught on and salt mining became a major trade. Salt became so important that the money the Romans paid their military so they could purchase salt was known as *salarium*, from which we get the word *salary*.

Salt also played an important role in the Age of Exploration. Once it was discovered that salt could be used to preserve fish and that the salted fish kept almost indefinitely, it became a staple for sailors' diets and allowed long ocean voyages to get underway.

Salt was expensive because it wasn't easily obtained. It had to be evaporated from seawater or mined from salt beds, so if a meat were to be "worth its salt," it would have to be worth the trouble of salting in the first place. It would need to be meaty and fatty.

Today, salting is more of a decision point in food preservation than a goal. It's the fork in the road at the intersection of pickling and smoking. It's a useful emergency measure if you've no other way to put up food, but it leaches nutrients out of foods that then require *freshening* to remove as much salt as possible before the food is usable. Freshening is the process of rinsing and soaking meats, vegetables, or fruit in cold water to remove as much salt as possible before cooking. As we shall see, a great deal of salt is necessary for food preservation. As far as fruits and vegetables are concerned, salting is more of a curiosity than a standard practice, and for meat, it's usually just one step in the preservation process.

You might run across the term *curing*. This is just another term for salting.

A Little Science

All salt, except that created in the laboratory, comes from the sea. It's either processed in evaporation facilities by the ocean or mined from deposits deep in the earth, left behind when ancient seas dried up when the Earth was young.

Salt dries things out. That's not exactly a news flash, but it's important when it comes to preserving foods. Because certain types of harmful bacteria, yeasts, molds, and other spoilage microorganisms thrive in moist environments, salt can be used to wick away this moisture through the process of osmosis. However, there are some microorganisms that love salt and these are called *halophiles*—literally, *salt lovers*.

As mentioned earlier, we're talking about a lot of salt. A salt concentration of more than 10% inhibits the growth of most bacteria, but molds simply laugh at this. It takes concentrations of salt up to 20% to either kill these microorganisms or cause them to go dormant. To give you an idea of how much salt this is, the ocean is only about 3% salt. And probably the saltiest item in your pantry, soy sauce, can range from 12 to 18%. That's why your brining solution—the mixture of salt and water you'll use with vegetables—will be generally 1 part salt to 4 parts water, a solution of 25% salt.

When salt dissolves, it breaks down into its elements of sodium and chloride. Our nerves and muscles require sodium for proper functioning and this element also plays a role in regulating our blood pressure. Chloride is also involved in regulating our blood pressure and helps with the production of stomach acid (HCl). It's a delicate balance to consume the right amount of salt, as either too little or too much can create health problems. This knowledge has implications in the use of salt for food preservation, an issue we'll discuss later on in this chapter.

In these times, everyone with a phone seems to have become an instant expert on just about any topic. Unfortunately, what people refer to as *research* isn't. True research involves laboratories, double-blind studies, and that most precious commodity: time. We're inundated with information, but separating what's true from what's false is beyond the capabilities of a quick internet scan. Case in point: We've become aware that too much salt in our diet can contribute to a host of medical issues, ranging from hypertension to heart attack to stroke. As a result, conscientious people are reducing their salt intake for their health—and that's to the good. However, it's to the bad when we decide to reduce the amount of salt we use when we're preserving food by this method. The results can be dire.

Not following scientifically approved recipes or procedures for salt when preserving food can lead to an increased risk of *listeriosis*—one of the most serious foodborne illnesses—as well as toxin formation by *Clostridium botulinium*, the organism that causes botulism and other foodborne pathogens. You really, really, really don't want to mess with these—and you won't if you follow the established regimens to the letter and develop a healthy respect for nature in all her forms. Be educated, be aware, and be safe. Words to live by.

A Few Notes About Salt

There are three general varieties of salt: table, pickling, and kosher. Each has its specific uses. Table salt has been refined to be, well, fine. It sprinkles easily and contains additives, such as an anticlumping ingredient. It might or might not contain iodine It's not suitable for drying foods, as the iodine can make pickles dark and unattractive and the anti-clumping additive can make pickling solutions cloudy. Pickling salt is also a fine-grained salt but contains no additives.

Kosher salt is coarser-grained and might or might not contain additives. If using kosher salt, be sure it's additive-free. Keep in mind that 1½ cups of kosher salt is usually equivalent to 1 cup of pickling salt.

General Principles & Procedures for Vegetables

There are two main ways to go about salting vegetables: brine salting or dry salting. Actually, to be more precise, there are also two subgroups that involve using either a lot of salt or using less salt. Dry salting works with vegetables that contain quite a bit of moisture or that have been cut into small pieces. Brining is used for vegetables that don't have sufficient moisture in them to make enough liquid during curing. Brining is the process of preserving foods by immersing them in a saltwater solution.

When brining involves vinegar in addition to salt, it causes fermentation. It's the way corned beef and pastrami are made. (The corning process is discussed in Chapter 15.) If you don't want fermented vegetables, then you'll forego the vinegar and pack in the salt—lots of salt.

Dry salting is the process of combining salt with the juices from the food being salted to form a concentrated brine. The stronger the salt solution, the greater its ability to reduce or destroy spoilage microorganisms. The weaker the salt solution, the greater the tendency for the vegetables to ferment. This is desirable if you're making sauerkraut; it's not desirable if you're trying to preserve your green beans.

Equipment & Supplies

In addition to regular kitchen utensils, you'll need your kitchen scales, a crock, and something to weigh down the top layer of vegetables. You can use a glass or wood container if you don't have a crock, but don't use anything metal because it will react with the acid created during brining. A plate works well. So does a plastic bag filled with water and securely tied.

Dry Salting Vegetables

Wash the vegetables and discard any that aren't in great shape. Just as with other forms of preserving food, you're not going to improve on what you start with, so always start with the best. Weigh the vegetables. You'll be working with a ratio of 4:1. That means for every 4 pounds (1.8kg) of vegetables, you'll use 1 pound (450g) of salt. As noted previously, use medium-coarse pickling salt or kosher salt without additives for curing.

These have larger-sized crystals than other salts and their greater surface area absorbs moisture quickly. Don't use iodized or regular table salt. Iodized salt can turn foods dark and regular salt will cake. You need to have the salt dissolve quickly and evenly to achieve a good brine.

Next, prepare the vegetables as follows:

- Shred cabbage.

- Cut celery and okra into pieces.

- Cut corn from the cob.

- Shell and blanch peas and lima beans.

- Snip the tips and tails off green beans, cut them into pieces, and blanch.

- Peel and shred turnips and rutabagas.

Place a layer of vegetables on the bottom of a crock. Cover this with a layer of salt. Repeat the layers until you've used up all the vegetables and all the salt, ending with a layer of salt. Cover with a clean cloth or dish towel and weigh it down with a plate. Set the crock in a cool location and let it rest overnight. The next morning, check to be sure that brine has formed and is covering the top layer of vegetables. This brine comes from the moisture in the vegetables being drawn out by the salt. The vegetables need to be covered with the brine to prevent mold from forming.

If you need to add more brine to make sure the vegetables are covered, dissolve 1 pound (450g) of salt in 2 quarts of water and pour it into the crock. You might notice some bubbling. Any bubbling will stop within a few days. This bubbling isn't an indicator of fermentation. It's gas and air escaping from the vegetables. Do skim off any scum that forms early on in the salting process.

Store the crock in a cool location away from direct sunlight until you're ready to use the vegetables. Their storage life varies according to many factors. Many will keep for 1 year or more, while others need to be used up within a few months. As with all methods of home food preservation, it's good sense to have a plan for your produce in mind as you put it up. Nothing is meant to keep forever.

When it's time to dip into the crock, you'll notice that the vegetables have shrunk. That's because the salt drew out the moisture they contained. When you soak them in cool water they'll plump out again, so take about one-third the amount you'll need. For example, if you ultimately want 1 cup of vegetables, take ⅓ cup out of the crock. To use them, rinse them in cool water. If they're saltier than you like, you can soak them in cool water briefly and then drain and use. Never taste vegetables that have been preserved by salting without first boiling them for 10 minutes to be sure they're safe to eat.

Brining Vegetables

"As a method of emergency preservation, requiring a minimum amount of labor and critical materials, and offering the possibility of storing large quantities of vegetable material in bulk until further processing can be brought about, brine preservation justly deserves adequate consideration in our war program." Thus were the conclusions of J.L. Etchells, I.D. Jones, and M.A. Hoffman as reported in the 1943 Proceedings of Institute of Food Technologists and reprinted online at www.ars.usda.gov/ARSUserFiles/60701000/Pickle%20Pubs/p22.pdf.

World War II brought all kinds of challenges to the food industry and the home food preserver. Preserving vegetables by brining was one solution to the problem and the information contained in this report hasn't altered much in the intervening years. If you're interested in trying your hand at this technique, you'll begin by making your brining solution.

Prepare the brining solution by combining ½ pound (225g) of salt and 1 cup of 5% strength vinegar for each gallon of water. Then prepare the vegetables as follows:

- Leave beets, carrots, okra, and onions whole.
- Cut cauliflower into pieces or leave it whole.
- Wash greens.
- Leave lima beans and peas in their pods.
- Peel and slice or cube turnips and rutabagas.
- Leave green beans and blanch them.

Place the vegetables in the container and cover with the brine solution. Place a weight on top of the vegetables and cover this with the brine solution. As liquid is drawn out of the vegetables by the brine, the brine strength will become diluted. Add 2 pounds (1kg) of salt to the plate serving as the weight for each 10 pounds (4.5kg) of vegetables in the crock. By keeping the plate under the crock, the salt will slowly dissolve over time.

Remove any scum as it forms. Fermentation will take several weeks to be complete. When the bubbles stop rising to the surface, fermentation is complete. Many variables affect the length of time these vegetables will keep, and even if you've followed recommended procedures, you might find that some of the produce will spoil.

To use salted vegetables, remove them from the crock and freshen them by rinsing in several changes of cool water. Then cook as usual.

General Principles & Procedures for Salting Meats

Salting in this case is sometimes called *curing*. To get the best product, meat must be handled quickly and carefully after slaughter, and strict cleanliness must be observed to avoid contamination. Chilling the carcass as soon after slaughter as possible is also an essential step because warm meat will begin to spoil before the salting process can take effect.

Certain cuts of meat lend themselves more readily to salting than others. For example, in beef, the brisket, round, chuck, and plate cuts are the most common. In pork, the ham, shoulders, and belly are good candidates.

Historically, salted meats have traveled with Native Americans and polar explorers. As a source of protein, these meats were all that was available. Native Americans improved on the basic recipe and made pemmican from dried meats by pounding in grease and berries. Kept dry, the pemmican didn't spoil.

Today, the process has been adapted somewhat and you'll find recipes that call for brined meats. This kind of brining isn't done for preserving but rather more as a marinade, allowing moisture and flavorings to penetrate deep into the tissues of the meat or poultry to make it moister during cooking.

If you're interested in the traditional salting of meat, this is more easily done outside if the weather is cool. The process can be messy and take up considerable room. Salting is usually the step before smoking.

The purpose is to draw out as much moisture as possible from the meat to prevent spoilage. To accomplish this, you'll dry salt the meat, packing in as much salt as necessary to create your own version of the Gobi Desert.

Equipment & Supplies

You won't need much in the way of supplies: meat, salt, sugar in some cases, and a salting box. If you've got a small shed or workroom, that's to the good.

Salting Meats

The Oklahoma Cooperative Extension Service Bulletin ANSI-3994, "Meat Curing," gives straightforward directions for curing meat by the salting process. The first order of business is to prepare the dry-cure rub, which consists of 8 pounds (3.6kg) of salt and 3 pounds (1.4kg) of sugar. These recommendations include 2 ounces (30g) of sodium nitrate and ½ ounce (15g) of sodium nitrite. These latter two ingredients aren't essential to the cure.

For pork, use 1 ounce (30g) of the cure mixture per 1 pound (450g) of meat. Divide this amount by the number of times the meat needs to be rubbed with it. Rub this into the meat at 3- to 5-day intervals. Hams should get the rub three times, picnic and butt roasts need two rubs, and the belly gets just one. The cure takes 1 week for each 1 inch (2.5cm) of thickness of the meat.

The process is simple: Lay down a layer of salt in a wooden box, barrel, or crate. Then rub salt into the pieces of meat and place them on top of the salt layer in the salting box. Add a layer of salt on top of the meat. Then rub salt and whatever spices you want into the meat that's going into the next layer, add it to the salting box, and add a layer of salt to that.

Continue the layering process until all the meat has been salted and boxed, ending with a layer of salt. Be careful that the pieces of meat don't touch each other. Keep the meat between 32°F to 40°F (0°C to 5°C) during the curing process.

You can also dissolve the dry-cure mix in water to make a brine or pickling solution. Place the meat in a watertight container or vat and cover it with the brine. Change the brine every 7 days to prevent spoilage. This process takes longer than dry curing—a minimum of 28 days. You can expect it take about 4 days for 1 pound (450g) of meat.

When you're ready to use the meat, check each piece carefully to be sure it hasn't spoiled. If the meat is bone-in, pierce the meat along the bone and check for a fresh smell. If you detect any off-putting odor, dispose of the meat. If the meat is good, rinse it thoroughly and check it again. Look for soft spots, an off-putting odor, or other signs of spoilage. If you detect any, throw the meat away.

After the cure is completed, the meat should be either eaten, frozen, or smoked.

General Principles & Procedures for Salting Fish

It's important to begin with fresh fish. Catch it, ice it, and salt it quickly. Fish can spoil either because they break down organically or because bacteria get involved. Salting can stop both of these processes, and the more quickly the fish can absorb the salt, the better the quality will be. You can choose two types of cures.

Heavy Cure

This is the preferred method for working with fatty fish, such as mackerel, trout, and bluefish. Scale, gut, and remove the heads if you're working with small- to medium-sized fish. Split each fish down the backbone and flatten it out.

Now it's time for a thorough cleaning. Wash the fish in cool, running water and follow this with a 60-minute soak in a brine of 1 quart of salt per 1 gallon of water. This takes care of any slime that's stubbornly hanging around the skin and it also ensures that any residual blood has been washed away. Remove the fish from the brine and pat it dry with paper towels. It's time to salt.

Generally, you'll work with a ratio of 1 pound (450g) of salt to 4 pounds (1.8kg) of fish. That means you'll need to weigh the fish you have and then do the math. A kitchen scale works well here. Once you've determined how many pounds of fish you have, dredge each piece of fish in salt. Then place a layer of salt in the bottom of a crock and add a layer of fish skin side down on top of the salt. Add another layer of salt, another layer of fish, and so on, until all fish have been placed in the crock. Finish with a layer of salt.

While you're layering, try to keep the fish from touching each other. It's also helpful if you stagger the position of the fish from layer to layer so the levels even out.

Place a plate on top of the crock to weigh down the fish. The weight will also help push the moisture out of the fish. Small fish should be sufficiently brined in 2 days, while it can take up to 2 weeks for large fish to be *struck through*. When the brining process is finished, remove the fish and wash them in a brine solution made of 1 quart of salt to 1 gallon of water.

Use a stiff brush to thoroughly clean the fish. Then repack them in the crock as before, alternating layers of salt and fish, beginning and ending with a layer of salt. Then fill the crock with a fresh brine solution of 1 quart of salt per 1 gallon of water.

Store the crock in a cool location away from light. Fish should keep for up to 9 months. Check periodically to be sure the brine is covering the fish. If you detect any signs of fermentation, remove the fish, wash them, refill the crock with a fresh brine solution, and then repack.

Light Cure

If you're working with freshly caught lean fish, such as bass, haddock, mahi-mahi, cod, perch, or sole, you can use a light cure. You'll follow the same procedures as for a heavy cure, except the salt is used in a ratio of 1:10 (1 pound (450g) of salt to 10 pounds (4.5kg) of fish). Fish cured by this method will keep several months.

Curing Herring

Herring spoil so quickly that they almost seem to want to go bad the moment they're hauled in. Take them from the hook to the brine. Of course, pause a moment to clean, gut, and scale them first. You can scale herring in the brine solution, which also gets rid of any residual blood. Drain, pat dry with paper towels, and then begin the layering process. Put them in backs down for each layer except the top one, which should be backs up. Cover with the brine and change the brine solution every 2 months.

Using Salted Fish

Freshen the fish by soaking them in cool, fresh water until they're the right texture for their intended use. This can take from 90 minutes to most of the day depending on the size of the fish and the amount of salt you want to remove. After freshening, they're ready to be used in many recipes calling for fish.

Preserved Lemons

Fruit probably isn't the first food that comes to mind when you think of preservation by salting, but lemons have traditionally been preserved in this manner and used in North African and Indian cuisine. To try your hand at this, you'll need sterilized quart canning jars and two-piece lids, about 8 lemons per jar, and 1 cup of kosher salt without additives for each jar.

Scrub the lemons and then cut them in half lengthwise, being careful not to cut all the way through. Then slice them again, making 8 pieces that are still attached at the base. Your lemon should look like a rosette.

Put about 2 tablespoons of salt in the bottom of each jar. Spread the lemons open and fill with salt.

Pack the lemons into the jars, being a bit ruthless. You want the juices to start flowing and help fill the jar. Top off with another 2 tablespoons of salt. Put the lids on the jars and set them on the kitchen counter or another accessible surface. Turn the jars over each day for 1 week. Then store the jars in the refrigerator. The rinds will continue to soften. After a few weeks, the lemons will be ready to use in cooking.

Because of the acidity of the lemons, the instructions give you a bit of leeway that you won't find when working with vegetables.

Recipes

You shouldn't have to add any salt to these recipes. Indeed, removing salt by freshening is the first step in preparation.

Preserved Lemon Sauce

This is easy to make and it's a wonderful accompaniment to grilled salmon.

Yields	Prep time	Cook time
½ cup	5 minutes	none

2 preserved lemons, rinsed

¼ cup lemon juice

¼ cup honey

2 tbsp extra virgin olive oil

chopped fresh cilantro

1. In a blender, combine the lemons, lemon juice, honey, and olive oil. Blend on medium until smooth.

2. Transfer the sauce to a serving bowl and sprinkle the cilantro over the top.

Succotash

This recipe makes use of two easily salted vegetables, lima beans and corn.

Serves	Prep time	Cook time
6	5 minutes	10 minutes

1½ cups salted lima beans, rinsed

1½ cups salted corn, rinsed

⅓ cup chopped scallions

2 tbsp butter

½ cup half-and-half or light cream

1. In a medium saucepan on the stovetop over low heat, combine the lima beans, corn, scallions, butter, and half-and-half. Simmer until thoroughly heated, about 20 minutes.

2. Remove the saucepan from the heat and transfer the succotash to a large bowl.

Cabbage & Salt Pork

Cabbage is usually reserved for sauerkraut, cole slaw, or as a bland vegetable side dish. This is a hearty meal that's simple to fix and just right for a cold night.

Serves	Prep time	Cook time
4	10 minutes	25 to 30 minutes

1 tbsp olive oil

½lb (225g) salt pork, rinsed and cut into small pieces

1 medium white onion, chopped

1 medium head of cabbage, cored and loosely shredded

1. Heat the olive oil in a cast-iron skillet on the stovetop over medium heat. Add the onion and sauté until translucent, about 2 to 3 minutes.

2. Add the salt pork and cabbage. Cook until cabbage has wilted, about 10 minutes.

3. Remove the skillet from the heat and transfer the salt pork, onion, and cabbage to a serving bowl. Serve immediately with warm rolls.

Sillgratin (Herring & Potato Casserole)

The name is Scandinavian—and that's fitting because this is a traditional herring dish and herring is to Scandinavia what apple pie is to the United States.

Serves	Prep time	Cook time
4	45 minutes	1 hour

4 medium potatoes, peeled and sliced into ¼-inch (0.5cm) rounds

2 large salt herring (about ½lb [225g] each)

4 tbsp butter, divided

1 large yellow onion, sliced into ¼-inch (0.5cm) slices

kosher salt, to taste

freshly ground black pepper, to taste

⅓ cup light cream

2 tbsp breadcrumbs

1. Preheat the oven to 350°F (175°C). Spray a quart baking dish with cooking spray. Place the sliced potatoes in small saucepan filled with cool water to prevent them from darkening.

2. Soak the salt herring overnight in cool water. In the morning, rinse and drain. Make a slice along the backbone and spread the herring apart. Remove the skin and all bones. Slice the herring diagonally into 1-inch (1.25cm) pieces.

4. In a separate small saucepan on the stovetop over medium heat, melt 2 tablespoons of butter and add the onion slices. Sauté until softened.

5. Drain the potatoes and remove excess moisture with paper towels. Place a layer of potatoes in the bottom of the casserole, then add a layer of herring and a layer of onions. Season each layer with salt and pepper to taste. Repeat the layers, ending with a potato layer.

6. Add the cream. Sprinkle the breadcrumbs over the top and dot the breadcrumbs with the remaining 2 tablespoons of butter.

7. Place the dish in the oven and bake for 1 hour or until the potatoes are fork-tender.

8. Remove the dish from the oven and serve the sillgratin immediately.

Mackerel Run Down

Not every recipe using salted fish comes from Scandinavia. Here's a sensational taste treat from Jamaica, courtesy of JamaicaTravelandCulture.com.

Serves	Prep time	Cook time
4	45 minutes	40 minutes

2lb (1kg) salted mackerel

1 can of coconut milk

1 cup water

1 white onion, chopped

3 scallions, chopped

2 tomatoes, chopped

3 garlic cloves, chopped

4 to 5 sprigs of fresh thyme

1 to 2 tsp vinegar

1 to 2 tsp kosher salt

1 to 2 tsp freshly ground black pepper

1. Soak the mackerel overnight in cool water. In the morning, drain the mackerel.

2. In a large saucepan on the stovetop over high heat, add the mackerel and cover with water. Boil for 15 minutes. Remove the saucepan from the heat and allow the mackerel to cool. Remove the heads (optional) and bones, then cut the fish into small pieces.

3. In a medium saucepan on the stovetop over high heat, combine the coconut milk and water. Bring to a boil, then reduce the heat to low.

4. Add the mackerel and simmer for 15 minutes.

5. Add the onion, scallions, tomato, garlic, and thyme. Cook for 10 minutes more.

6. Add the vinegar, salt, and pepper. If you need to thicken the sauce, combine 1 tablespoon of all-purpose flour and ¼ cup of water. Stir this mixture into the mackerel pan.

7. Remove the saucepan from the heat and serve the mackerel immediately with boiled green bananas and dumplings.

Smoking

Along with drying and salting, smoking is another old form of food preservation. Not so long ago, the smokehouse was a familiar sight on farms and ranches. The size of a small shed, it was generally constructed of wood. The earthen floor held a firepit and in the roof was a vent that provided air circulation. A fire was kept smoldering in the pit, occasionally fed with hickory to keep the smoke coming.

This was the final step in preserving food for families who raised their own poultry, beef, and pork. If fishing went exceptionally well, the surplus also found its way to the smokehouse. Smoking served two functions: to be a preservative and to impart flavor to foods. The smoking was finished by the holidays, providing smoked ham, turkey, or goose for Christmas dinner.

Smoking has gone totally modern and you no longer need to live on a farm or have an outbuilding dedicated to this method of food preservation. You can choose from electric, gas, hybrid, or charcoal smokers you can fire up on your back deck or patio. Obviously, the amount of food able to be smoked in these smaller units doesn't come close to what the old smokehouse could handle, but if don't need to feed an army, these new appliances might be just what you're looking for. These compact models have built-in thermostats and wireless technology that allows you to monitor your smoker from anywhere in the house, and if you have a combination smoker/grill function, you can smoke and cook with the same appliance. Additionally, indoor models that fit on your countertop are also available. We'll discuss the pros and cons of these various types later in this chapter.

The Science Behind Smoking

Smoking is another method of drying foods that helps prevent insects from contaminating the meats being preserved in this way. Smoking generally follows salting, which is covered in Chapter 21. Once foods have been salted, they're ready for the finishing touch of the smokehouse. As we've noted in previous chapters, moisture, molds, yeasts, and bacteria are the enemies we must conquer in our quest to preserve foods. Each method touched on in this book addresses those issues. Smoking imparts flavor, and in the case of hot smoking, it also preserves foods. There are two general categories of smoking: cold and hot. In the Resources section at the end of this book, you'll find links to approved, research-based instructions for safe home smoking. Meat, poultry, and even some cheeses are good candidates for cold smoking. Fish falls into a different category and is only recommended for hot smoking.

So what's the difference between cold and hot smoking? Time and temperature, with temperature the most important part of the equation. In the traditional smokehouse, a cold-smoking process is used. The meat is smoked over a smoldering fire for anywhere from 2 days to 1 week or more. The temperature of that fire is somewhere in the vicinity of 85°F (30°C) and that means the foods being smoked are being processed in the danger zone of temperatures—between 40°F to 140°F (5°C to 60°C), the place where rapid growth of bacteria could occur. Because of this, only meat products that have been fermented, salted, or cured should be handled in this fashion. Most cold-smoked foods should be cooked to an internal temperature of 160°F (70°C) before being consumed. Cold smoking shouldn't be considered a preservative but rather a flavor enhancer.

If you're interested in hot smoking, you'll probably purchase a portable smoker. Hot smoking is a method of food preservation, and with the assistance of rubs, marinades, and liquid smoke products, it also imparts flavor. Modern smokers (gas, electric, hybrid, charcoal) are designed as hot smokers. They process meat well above the danger zone, at temperatures above 150°F (65°C) and often in the 215°F to 225°F (105°C to 110°C) range. Meats processed in this manner are considered safe to eat.

Both cold-smoked and hot-smoked foods should be refrigerated after smoking.

Supplies

Whether you go the smokehouse or the back deck/patio smoker route, you'll need some basic supplies to get the job done. Here's a list to get you started:

- Long-handled spatula and tongs
- Racks and grill brush
- Heat-resistant gloves
- Sturdy cutting board
- Set of good knives
- Workstation
- Wireless thermometer and probe
- Heavy-duty aluminum foil

Building Your Own Smokehouse

If you plan to do quite a bit of smoking, you might consider building your own smokehouse. A simple internet search will acquaint you with a good variety of plans to choose from.

Before you begin, check to see what your local ordinances require so you'll be in compliance. These requirements might include permits and inspections. Generally, the smokehouse must be made of noncombustible materials and must be located at a safe distance from other structures. Your local fire marshal is the one who makes those determinations.

The smokehouse will need a roof vent and a firepit in the center of the floor. Generally, the pit is about 2 feet (60cm) deep and 2 feet (60cm) wide. You're not going to have a raging fire in the pit—the process is to make a cold smoke. That means a bed of coals that smoke and smolder while the meat is being smoked.

Cold smoking in the smokehouse needs to be done during cool but not freezing weather. Late autumn and early spring usually provide the best chances for temperatures to hover in the 30s and 40s Fahrenheit (between -1°C and 10°C).

It's best not to interrupt the smoking process, but if you must, refrigerate the meat until you can resume. After smoking is complete (and the process generally takes several days), the meat is wrapped for storing in a cool, dry place or is placed in the freezer (the better choice). If your winter climate is severe, you want to avoid having your smoked meat freeze, thaw, refreeze, etc. This causes the quality to deteriorate, so it's best to either use the meat or freeze it.

Line is strung across the inside of the smokehouse and the meat gets hung from that. Each piece of meat should hang freely and not touch another piece. Keeping the meat separate helps prevent spoiling. Meat usually hangs 4 to 5 feet (120 to 150cm) above the pit. When the smoking has been completed, the smokehouse can serve as a storage facility.

Let the Chips Fall Where They May

The most commonly used woods for smoking are apple, hickory, and maple. Evergreen woods, such as pine, spruce, and fir, are high in resins and aren't suitable as smoking materials. During the smoking process, creosote and other resinous products could deposit themselves on the food. Not good—or good for you!

If you don't cut and split your own wood, you can purchase chips, flakes, or pellets at the hardware store. Before using these products, soak them in water to prevent them from burning up the minute you set them on the fire. You add these to the charcoal in small amounts—about ½ cup—to get that good aroma going.

Charcoal is also useful for smoking, but be selective in the kind of charcoal you use. Cheaper charcoal can be made from compressed sawdust and other wood waste products that are glued together and then burned to achieve the charcoal appearance. Following the firing process, they're saturated with lighter fluid—these are the "quick start" briquettes. Avoid them.

You might need to search a bit more diligently to find real charcoal and it might cost a bit more, but the search is worth it. Real charcoal is simply wood that's been cooked in a metal kiln or metal barrel by indirect heat so the gases are driven out.

Smoking Beef in the Smokehouse

Select the cut of meat you want to smoke and then cut out the joints and other large bones to keep the meat from turning sour while it's smoking. Trim as much fat as you can from the outside of the meat to help prevent it from turning the meat rancid.

Cut the meat into sections. Always cut across the grain. This will give you more tender meat and will hasten the smoking process. Pierce the meat with a hook and insert a piece of heavy twine. Be sure you've allowed enough space so the twine doesn't rip through the meat and dump the meat into the pit. String the meat up on the line.

Smoking Pork in the Smokehouse

Pork is handled a bit differently from beef in that you don't remove the fat or the bone, except for ball and socket joints. Pierce the meat with a hook and insert a piece of heavy twine. Hang the meat from the line. During the smoking process, fat will render from the carcass and this shouldn't be disturbed.

Smoking Poultry in the Smokehouse

Think beyond chicken and turkey when you're envisioning smoked poultry. Goose and duck are excellent when smoked, and they're no more trouble than a chicken. Again, fresh is best. If you're butchering your own chicken, had a successful bird season, or are using commercially raised poultry, keep the birds refrigerated until you're ready to brine—and get to the brining within a couple of days to get the best results.

You can purchase special poultry bags for hanging poultry from farm or hunting supply stores or you can wrap the birds in cheesecloth. This keeps them from drying out during smoking. Hang them tail up and with enough room between them for the air to circulate. You'll be using a hot-smoke method and the poultry will be ready to eat when you're finished.

Set the temperature to 170°F (75°C) for 6 to 10 hours to allow the skin to turn a light brown. Then raise the temperature to 185°F to 200°F (85°C to 95°C) and hold it at this level until the interior of the bird is 165°F (75°C), as determined by a meat thermometer inserted into the thickest portion of the breast.

After smoking, the poultry is ready to eat. It will keep in the refrigerator for several days, but if you aren't going to be eating it by then, it's best to freeze it.

Thawing

If you'll be working with meat that's frozen, it's important to thaw it first. The safest way to do this is in the refrigerator. Smaller cuts will thaw overnight, but larger cuts might take a day or two to thaw. Planning ahead becomes an important part of smoking.

Why thaw first? If you're cold smoking, frozen meat will linger too long in the danger zone of 40°F to 140°F (5°C to 60°C) and that encourages harmful bacteria to grow.

Marinades & Rubs

Some people prefer their meats without fancy marinades and rubs, while others prefer the zest a little extra treatment can give. Check out www.beefitswhatsfordinner.com for a good list of marinades and rubs to try.

Rubs are dry mixtures of spices. You can find a wide variety at any specialty store or mix up your own. Most include brown sugar, cumin, paprika, garlic—the possibilities are endless. They do more than intensify the flavor though. They form a light crust around the meat, sealing in the good juices while your meat is in the hot smoker.

Marinades are a mix of spices along with an acidic base made either from vinegar or even wine. Their principal function is to tenderize the meat before cooking. Italian salad dressing, barbecue sauces, and balsamic vinegar with Dijon mustard are just a few options. Mix up your concoction and put it in a food-safe plastic storage bag with a zip closure, add the meat, and turn the bag frequently to keep the marinade soaking all the meat. If your recipe calls for marinating the meat for a period of time, be sure to do that marinating in the refrigerator. Again, you want to keep meat in the temperature safety zone. And always boil any leftover marinade that's been used for meat and poultry before you serve it at the table. Make sure you bring it to a rolling boil for a full minute before transferring it to a serving container.

Portable Smokers

With the various types, sizes, and price points of these appliances, you should be able to find a smoker that's the perfect fit for what you want to do. Here's a look at some of the pros and cons of each type.

Gas Smokers

These come in two types: natural gas and propane. If you choose a natural gas model, you'll have it professionally hooked it up to your home's supply system. If you go with propane, you'll need a tank. These are easy to find and generally come in a 20-pound (9.1kg) size. There will be a place over the heat source for the chips, flakes, or pellets you'll use to flavor your meats.

Gas smokers have dials for regulating gas flow and, thus, temperature, but instruction manuals will guide you through the learning curve. One advantage of gas is that when it's on, it's on and when it's off, it's off—instantly.

Electric Smokers

Just plug these in and you're ready to go. The pricier models have wireless technology, which is a nice feature, and with their built-in thermostats, they're very easy to use. If you go lower on the price range, you'll be adjusting the dials until you get the correct temperature for what you're smoking.

Electric smokers take a bit of time to heat up and turn off, unlike the gas types, which are immediate on and off. But for convenience, electric wins. However, purists feel that gas smokers produce a more flavorful product than electric models.

Other Smokers

Charcoal smokers require a bit more hands-on activity, so be prepared to settle in for the long haul while you keep an eye on the temperature and airflow. This isn't the type of smoker where price doesn't matter. It does, so if you want charcoal, be prepared to spend what it takes to get a really good one.

Offset smokers are also an option, but again, don't take the cheap route. Cheap means flimsy—and flimsy means uneven heating and smoked meat that can be overdone in one part of the smoker and underdone in another. Also, when you think about it, smoke rises—it doesn't prefer to go sideways. Just some things to chew on when you're considering your purchase. Take the time to do your research. There are many online sites that discuss the pros and cons of specific brands and it's well worth your time to check these out before you invest in a unit.

Common Sense & Safety

Common sense sometimes isn't all that common. Whether you're using a commercially manufactured portable smoker or have improvised one on your own, don't be tempted to cut corners or take shortcuts when you're smoking meats. Where there's smoke, there's fire. Heed these general cautions:

- Don't use galvanized steel cans or garbage cans as improvised smokers. Chemicals released by them during smoking can contaminate your foods.

- Use approved fire starters. Don't use gasoline or paint thinner to get the fire going. And never squirt a shot of lighter fluid onto a smoldering charcoal bed to get it flaming. You might end up with more flame than you anticipated.

- Set up the smoker in a well-ventilated area that's away from any flammable structures, such as shrubbery or your home.

- Don't work in the dark. Be sure you have plenty of light.

- Use insulated mitts to transfer hot items.

- Roll up your sleeves or, even better, don't wear long sleeves or baggy clothes when working with fire.

- Don't bring an outside smoker inside. Smokers give off a good deal of smoke. You don't want the fire department making a visit because the smoke alarms keep going off. You also don't want your house to reek of smoke forever.

The Finished Product

How long you'll smoke the meat depends on the size and shape of the cut as well as the temperature of the coals and the size of the smoker. The goal is to arrive at the safe minimum internal temperature:

- 145°F (65°C) for chops, roasts, and whole cuts of beef, veal, and lamb
- 160°F (70°C) for all pork, ground beef, ground veal, and ground lamb
- 165°F (75°C) for all poultry

Smoking Fish

Unlike meats, which should be lean, you want fish to be the high-fat varieties. This means salmon and trout smoke quite well. Fat absorbs smoke more readily than lean tissues, so lean fish can be dry and tough when you smoke them. For fish, think fat!

Preparation

Fresh. That's the first rule of working with fish. If you've caught the fish, keep them iced until you're able to clean them—and don't wait too long to clean them. Fish to be smoked should be in excellent condition, without rips, bruising, and other damage to the flesh. As with any other means of preserving foods, the process of preserving won't improve on the quality of what you've started with. As soon as you can, prepare the fish for brining. (See Chapter 21.)

When brining is complete, remove the fish from the brine, rinse them in cool water, and let them dry—skin side down—on greased racks. The grease keeps the skins from sticking to the rack. Fish should be dry within a couple of hours. You'll know they're ready for the smoker when the flesh has a shine, known as a "pellicle."

Method

Hot smoking uses a short time in the brine followed by a short time in the smoker. In any case, you're looking for a uniform brown color on the fish. For hot smoking, you'll set the temperature at 90°F (35°C) for the initial 2 hours and then raise it to 150°F (65°C) until the fish is finished (anywhere from 4 to 8 hours). Hot smoking will kill parasites that fish are notorious for harboring. The fish will need to be refrigerated after the smoking process and should be used within a few days.

If you won't be using the fish immediately, it's best to freeze them. Coat the fish lightly with vegetable oil to prevent them from drying out and oxidizing during storage. Then wrap them in moisture/vapor-resistant freezer wrap and overwrap with aluminum foil or place them in freezer bags. Seal, label, date, and freeze.

Smoked fish cans beautifully and you'll have a supply that won't need to be thawed before you use it. See Chapter 12 for directions.

Be sure there's enough room in the smoker for the air to circulate around the fish. Also make sure they're not touching each other.

Storage

For smoked meats that will be used soon, refrigeration is fine, but it you've smoked a whole ham or roast or goose or 2 or 12, you'll be storing them in the freezer after the smoking process is complete. Before you reach for the aluminum foil for the big wrap, stop and think about how you're going to use this meat. What are the recipes you're likely to use? How will the meat for these be prepared? Slices? Smaller roasts? This is the time to use those good knives and cut slices off the ham or roast or whatever you've smoked, wrap them in meal-sized portions, and use your vacuum sealer before consigning them to the freezer. Then when you want to use your smoked meats and poultry for salads or soups or whatever, you won't be confronted with frozen slabs of meat the size of the Rockies. And don't forget to label and date each package.

Recipes

Smoked foods add a wonderful dimension to ordinary dishes. Flavor and aroma are enhanced, and they're a treat to be savored. Here are a couple of rub and marinade recipes to get you started, along with some recipes featuring smoked foods.

Rub Basics

Rubs are dry. They give a nice coat to smoked meats and help seal in the good juices. The basics are, well, basic. There are three words to remember: sweet, spicy, and savory. The sweet is usually brown sugar and you can experiment with light or dark. The dark is stronger. The spicy is cayenne pepper or red chili powder or flakes. Let your imagination roam with the savory section. Choose from onion powder, garlic powder, paprika (smoked is good), salt (kosher is good here; don't use iodized salt), dry mustard, ground cumin, and whatever spices you like to use in your cooking. There are no hard and fast rules.

Proportion is next. A rub is truly a matter of personal taste and the one rule is that you can always add more, but you can't add less. Sample as you go along and adjust the amounts as you like. Just remember to keep some notes so you can repeat the perfect mixture the next time.

Rub #1

Yields	Prep time	Cook time
1 cup	10 minutes	none

1 cup light brown sugar

2 tbsp paprika

2 tbsp kosher salt

1 tbsp freshly ground black pepper

2 tsp garlic powder

2 tsp onion powder

1 tsp celery salt

1 tsp ground cumin

1 tsp mustard powder

1 tsp cayenne pepper

1. In a small bowl, combine all the ingredients. Mix well.

2. Store the rub in a glass jar with a tight-fitting lid or a food-safe plastic bag with a zip closure. You can freeze the rub.

Rub #2

Yields	Prep time	Cook time
½ cup	10 minutes	none

½ cup light brown sugar

1 tbsp smoked paprika

2 tbsp kosher salt

1 tsp freshly ground black pepper

2 tbsp garlic powder

2 tbsp onion powder

1 tbsp chili powder

1 tbsp chipotle powder

1. In a small bowl, combine all the ingredients. Mix well.

2. Store the rub in a glass jar with a tight-fitting lid or a food-safe plastic bag with a zip closure. You can freeze the rub.

Marinade Basics

Marinades are liquids. Their purpose is to give meats and poultry a long, luxurious soak to tenderize and add flavor. For most marinades, overnight is perfect, but if you're pressed for time, marinate as long as you can. Even 30 minutes will work some magic.

Marinade #1 (Great for Poultry)

Yields	Prep time	Cook time
1 cup	10 minutes	none

1 cup light brown sugar

1½ tsp minced garlic

1 tsp grated ginger

⅓ cup soy sauce

1 cup water

1. In a small bowl, combine all the ingredients. Mix well, then transfer to a food-safe plastic bag with a zip closure.

2. Add the meat, seal bag, and refrigerate for at least 2 hours, although overnight is best. Turn the bag occasionally to be sure the marinade is covering the meat.

Note: You can easily double, triple, etc., this recipe to make more marinade.

Marinade #2 (Great for Beef)

Yields	Prep time	Cook time
1 cup	10 minutes	none

½ cup balsamic vinegar

1½ tsp minced garlic

2 tbsp Worcestershire sauce

¼ cup soy sauce

¼ cup peanut oil

1 tsp mustard powder

1 tbsp Italian seasoning

1. In a small bowl, combine all the ingredients. Mix well, then transfer to a food-safe plastic bag with a zip closure.

2. Add the meat, seal bag, and refrigerate for at least 2 hours, although overnight is best. Turn the bag occasionally to be sure the marinade is covering the meat.

Note: You can easily double, triple, etc., this recipe to make more marinade.

Smoked Chicken Salad

To give this old favorite a new twist, substitute smoked duck or goose for the chicken or substitute goat cheese for the feta.

Serves	Prep time	Cook time
2	20 minutes	none

romaine lettuce leaves, torn into pieces

2 cups smoked chicken, cut into 1-inch (2.5cm) cubes

1 cup shredded carrots

1 small red onion, sliced

¾ cup crumbled feta cheese

vinaigrette dressing

1. Add as much romaine lettuce as you desire to a large salad bowl. Add the chicken, carrots, onion slices, and cheese.

2. Drizzle the vinaigrette dressing over the top before serving.

Smoked Salmon Bisque

This is a good use for any leftover smoked salmon fillets. It's also an excellent first use for your smoked salmon. It's rich, hearty, and satisfying.

Serves	Prep time	Cook time
5	20 minutes	25 minutes

1 cup canned tomatoes

1lb (450g) smoked salmon,
    cut into bite-sized pieces

½ cup chopped onions

2 tbsp chopped parsley

4 tbsp butter

4 tbsp all-purpose flour

1½ cups milk of choice

1½ cups half-and-half

1½ tsp kosher salt

½ tsp paprika

1. Drain the tomatoes, reserving the liquid. Pour the liquid into a measuring cup and add enough water to make 2 cups of liquid.

2. In a large saucepan on the stovetop over low heat, combine the tomatoes, salmon, onions, parsley, and the 2 cups of liquid. Simmer for 20 minutes. Remove the saucepan from the heat and set aside.

3. Melt the butter in a separate large saucepan on the stovetop over medium heat. Add the flour, milk, and half-and-half, stirring continuously.

4. Add the salt and paprika. Continue to cook, stirring until smooth and creamy. When the mixture boils, add the salmon mixture and stir until well blended.

5. Remove the saucepan from the heat and serve the bisque with crusty bread.

Smoked Duck with Cherry Preserves

This is easy and elegant—and it tastes wonderful!

Serves	Prep time	Cook time
4	25 minutes	40 minutes

uncooked wild rice

2 smoked ducks, halved

½ cup chicken stock

1 cup cherry preserves

for the salad

spring mix greens

dried cherries or cranberries

1 small can of mandarin oranges

feta cheese crumbles

1. Prepare the wild rice according to the package directions.

2. In a large skillet on the stovetop over low heat, combine the ducks and chicken stock. Cover the skillet and cook until the ducks are heated to an internal temperature of 130°F (55°C). Remove the skillet from the heat and keep covered.

3. Warm the cherry preserves in a small pot on the stovetop over low heat.

4. Add as much spring mixed greens as you desire to a large salad bowl. Add the dried cherries, mandarin oranges, and as much feta cheese crumbles as you'd like.

5. Transfer the ducks to a serving platter. Spoon the cherry preserves over the top. Serve with the wild rice and salad.

Smoked Turkey Soup

Use the remains of the Thanksgiving turkey for this flavorful soup.

Serves	Prep time	Cook time
6	25 minutes	90 minutes

1 smoked turkey carcass

1 to 2 boxes of chicken stock
(or turkey stock if available)

assorted fresh or dried chopped
vegetables (such as carrots,
onions, and potatoes)

1. Break the turkey carcass into manageable pieces.

2. Add the carcass pieces to a large pot on the stovetop over high heat. Cover the carcass with chicken or turkey broth. Bring to a boil, then reduce the heat to low. Simmer for 60 to 90 minutes or until the meat easily falls from the bones.

3. Remove the pot from the heat and allow the carcass to cool. Remove the meat from the bones. Discard the bones.

4. Strain the liquid from the pot and into a large bowl. Refrigerate the bowl overnight. In the morning, skim the fat from the surface.

5. In a large pot on the stovetop over high heat, combine the carcass liquid and the fresh or dried vegetables. Bring to a boil, then reduce the heat to low. Simmer for about 1 hour to meld the flavors.

6. Remove the pot from the heat and ladle the soup into individual bowls.

Note: You can also add your favorite pasta to this soup.

Root Cellaring

This concluding chapter completes our look at time-honored methods of food preservation. Root cellaring is about as simple and as inexpensive a way to keep your food out of harm's way as you could imagine. It doesn't require electricity. You don't need to purchase jars, rings, and lids, freezer packaging materials, or major appliances, such as smokers. It doesn't take up room in your pantry. It's just what the name implies: storing root crops and other fruits and vegetables in the cellar, although it's a bit more involved than hurling your turnips under the house. Apples are prime candidates for root cellaring, along with root crops, such as carrots, potatoes, beets, and turnips, among others. They store quite nicely under conditions of controlled temperature and humidity. Other crops also fit this category, especially winter squash, including those giant-sized Hubbards!

The Science Behind Root Cellaring

From the moment a fruit or vegetable seed is planted in the ground, it's programmed to sprout, grow, ripen, and eventually—if not consumed or preserved in some way—rot, thus returning nutrients to the earth so the cycle might begin again. The home food preserver's goal is to delay the onset of that final step as long as possible.

Root cellaring operates on a simple premise that walks a fine line: Keep foods cold enough so they don't deteriorate but not so cold they freeze. This discovery, as with the rest of the methods described in this section of the book, was probably an accidental one. Just as someone thousands of years ago discovered that the sun could be used to dry foods and thus preserve them, someone else undoubtedly noticed that cold temperatures helped keep food edible for long periods of time.

Home food preservers, even the earliest ones, are keen observers of nature.

Observing that a certain process works usually comes before understanding *how* that process works. Early on, it's enough to know that it just does—most of the time. Until we understand the *why*, it can be a hit-or-miss affair. Eventually, scientists discover the whys and the wherefores, and this allows some refinements and adjustments to be made to help us become more successful at preserving food.

As with other methods of preserving food, root cellaring works to slow down the enzymes that are responsible for ripening and eventually overripening and rotting foods. It also keeps in check other microorganisms responsible for food spoilage. In the case of root cellaring, that means holding fruits and vegetables at temperatures generally between freezing and 40°F (0°C and 4°C).

This is essentially how your refrigerator operates. Harnessing the principles of refrigeration and putting them to use in an environment that's not dependent on electricity is the theory behind root cellaring.

Generally speaking, in the Northern Hemisphere, winter temperatures are colder than summer temperatures. They're also widely variable depending on what part of the country you call home. Elevation plays a role, as does latitude. At the heart of the issue, however, is the capricious temperament of Mother Nature. Even if your temperatures in winter average in the high 40s (8°C), that average is just that: an average. You can have days in the teens (-10°C) and days in the 50s (13°C). Consistency isn't one of nature's prime descriptive terms. That means you can't just consign your vegetables to the outdoors if you live in a cold climate and be confident they'll keep safely until you're ready to use them. They have specific requirements.

Ripening fruits and vegetables respire (breathe) and transpire (give off moisture and a certain amount of heat), so controlling the temperature and humidity of their storage environment is important. Nutrients can be lost during transpiration, so it's important to have a means of controlling the airflow to optimize your storage conditions. This is why in most refrigerators you'll see different storage options for fruits and vegetables in the hydrator compartments. Fruit compartments will have a means of allowing air and the gases given off by ripening fruits to escape. Vegetable compartments are designed to keep moisture in to prevent shriveling. They're usually ventless.

General Principles & Procedures

If you've grown a garden that's blessed you with a good harvest or if you've taken advantage of fresh produce from a local farmers' market, root cellaring can be an economical way to hold that produce until you're ready to use it. Location is the first consideration, determining the dimensions and type of root cellar is next, and deciding what you'll store is third.

You don't need to have a cellar to preserve food by root cellaring. A shed, a pit dug into the ground on a sheltered side of the house, an unheated breezeway between the house and garage, or a section of the garage that's free from fumes can work.

All types of food-preservation techniques require some effort. That's a given. With root cellaring, the time and effort revolves around preparing an area that will give you the right amount of air circulation so you can control the humidity. You also want the cellar to be dark and free from insects and rodents. Mice are notorious for their ability to slip through a hole the size of a quarter. You don't need to create a fortress, but a snug bunker is definitely the way to go.

Where do you live? More specifically, what's the winter weather like where you live? If winters are relatively mild, you have more options than folks who live in areas that receive the brunt of winter storms and subzero temperatures. It's not fun struggling to uncover your produce when the temperature is –35°F (–37°C) and the wind is whipping the snow into stinging nettles that burn your cheeks.

The USDA has an excellent resource for home food preservers interested in root cellaring fruits and vegetables: naldc.nal.usda.gov/download/CAT87213861/PDF.

Storage Options

You have two basic options when deciding where to locate your root cellar: outdoors or indoors. Outdoor storage generally entails some type of pit dug into the side of an earthen bank or barrels sunk into the earth. If you enjoy the digging and your climate allows you to retrieve your produce during the winter, this could be feasible. However, outdoor storage is more than just digging a minor hole or two. You'll need to provide for drainage, remove any rocks around the barrels (they could be frost conductors), lay in a bed of straw, and create some type of door that will allow you to get at the produce while at the same time being rodent-proof. If you enjoy a challenge, you've got one here.

Indoor storage is the other option and there are several ways to go about creating a root cellar that will serve your needs. The essential components for an indoor root cellar are the following:

- **Accessibility:** You won't use the foods if it's a pain to get to them.

- **Room:** Plan a cellar big enough to keep your vegetables and fruits separated.

- **Air:** You'll need a way to circulate the air, such as a window.

- **Coolness:** A storage area with an exterior north-facing wall can help here.

- **Thermometer:** This is helpful to keep track of the coolness.

- **Heat source:** A heat source, such as a 100-watt lightbulb, will prevent the cellar from getting too cold.

- **Humidity:** You'll need an area with between 80 to 95% humidity in general (the actual water composition of most vegetables) and a way to control that humidity. This can mean either increasing it or decreasing it. A dirt floor is a plus. However, onions and squash don't like humidity (they'll mold) and they'll need a dry environment.

- **Darkness:** When it comes to root cellaring, light is the enemy.

Just as with your freezer, a full root cellar operates better than one that isn't full. You'll also need to keep tabs on it. You can't just fill it and neglect it. There's maintenance required. If you're handy with home improvement projects and have a basement, you're already halfway there. Select a corner away from heating ducts and water pipes, preferably one with a window. You'll need a source for air circulation and this is where a window comes in handy. Without a window, you'll be forced to create a system of vents and this can get tiresome. You'll build two more walls to complete the storeroom. This is the time to decide how big to make the room because fruits and vegetables should be separated.

Finishing the storeroom involves insulating the inner walls, installing a door (insulated on the inside), and building an air duct box for the window. This box helps with air circulation—getting the cooler air down at ground level and allowing the warmer air a way to vent out. Having one vent down low will allow cool air to enter. Another vent higher up will allow warmer air an exit. If you remember your science, warm air rises and cold air sinks.

Organic Gardening (www.groworganic.com/blogs/articles/root-cellar-basics) is another good source for excellent directions for constructing a basement root cellar. You can find a wealth of information from this publication.

Even if you don't have a basement, a breezeway between the garage and the house can work well for storage. The main factor here is keeping the temperature cool and providing a means for air circulation. New shelving available at home supply stores is made of vinyl-coated metal slats and works well, as does wooden shelving with slats. The objective here is to keep your fruits and vegetables from sitting on solid wood or metal and rotting. Think *air circulation*.

Lower shelves will be cooler and higher shelves will be warmer. Situate your foods accordingly. Different foods have different temperature requirements.

For best results in root cellaring, select fruits and vegetables that mature late in the season and have been allowed to fully ripen on the tree, on the plant, or in the ground. Earlier maturing produce doesn't hold up as well.

If you've just bought a new refrigerator and still have the old one, move it to the garage, plug it in, and set the temperature gauge for 40°F (4°C). It's the perfect temperature for holding potatoes. You can keep potatoes in the refrigerator throughout the winter and they won't spoil. Toward spring, you'll notice some sprouting, but old folk wisdom says that if you remove the sprouts three times, they won't trouble you anymore. Whether or not this happens to be true, keep your spuds free of sprouts. These draw nourishment from the potatoes and can eventually cause them to shrivel up.

Root Cellaring Fruits

Apples and pears are the most commonly root-cellared fruits. You'll need to keep an eye on them and remove any fruit that's showing signs of spoiling. As with all the other types of preserving, have a plan to use your food. Nothing lasts forever!

Boxes work well for keeping apples and pears from rolling around the shelves in the root cellar. You'll need some nesting material, such as dried leaves, straw, or newspaper.

Apples

Apples are far and away the most commonly root-cellared fruit and those that ripen latest in the season are the best choices. These include Jonathan, Delicious, Cortland, Winesap, and McIntosh.

Check apples carefully before storing and be sure they're cool going into storage. Trapping any warmth will accelerate enzyme activity and shorten their storage life. Select only unblemished, firm apples and bed them down on a layer of straw or dried leaves. You can layer them as apples, straw, apples, straw, etc.

The adage "One rotten apple spoils the whole barrel" is very true. The same goes for potatoes.

Pears

Late-season pears, such as Anjou, are the best choice for root cellaring. Comice and Bosc have shorter shelf lives. You want these pears to be ready to pick but still hard and green. If they've begun the ripening process before you pop them into storage, you'll be disappointed. They'll rot from the inside out. Store them just like apples.

Citrus

Around holiday time, you'll generally find good deals on oranges and grapefruit. These can also go into the root cellar in their boxes. Keep an eye on them, and if any get moldy, toss them. Clean off any stray mold that's come in contact with the good fruit.

Tomatoes

Tomatoes are good candidates for the root cellar. They need high moisture. Harvest them before a killing frost because once they've frosted, they'll rot. They can be dark, dark green and will still ripen nicely. You'll be eating delicious, red, ripe tomatoes in December and they'll be far superior to anything available at the grocery store.

Leave the stem on—at least enough to make a handle to carry. Spread newspaper on a shelf and arrange the tomatoes so there's a bit of space between. They'll ripen gradually, so be sure to check on them frequently and remove the ones that are ready for eating. If you have an overabundance of ripe ones at any time, cover them with newspaper to help keep in the moisture.

Root Cellaring Vegetables

Keep it simple: Potatoes, beets, turnips, carrots, cabbage, cauliflower, onions, and winter squash root cellar very well, provided you house them in the right conditions. Some prefer cool conditions and some like it warmer. Some want their environment really wet and others want just a touch of moisture.

Vegetables with thin skins, such as beets, carrots, turnips, radishes, kohlrabi, parsnips, and cucumbers, need storage conditions that are cold and moist. Leave enough of a stem on these vegetables to keep moisture from seeping out. Store each variety separately. See specific directions a little later in this chapter.

Potato sacks, wooden crates, and cardboard boxes are good containers for these vegetables. If you're using cardboard boxes, line them with plastic garbage bags and cut some ventilation holes. You can alternate a layer of moist sawdust or sand with a layer of vegetables. Don't stack vegetables too high in boxes or bins or else you'll upset your neat arrangement as you dig through the container searching for your produce. The sand or sawdust doesn't need to be sopping—just damp. Check it every week or so and add some water if it appears to be drying out. Sand and sawdust are available at hardware stores, garden outlets, building supply stores, or even at the sawmill if you live close to one.

Potatoes

Potatoes need high moisture. They share moisture by huddling together in sacks or bins. You don't need to add any cushioning material, such as sawdust or sand, to potatoes. Whether you've grown your own potatoes or stocked up on grocery store specials, you'll need to be aware of the difference between new potatoes and those that have set their skins. All potatoes go through the same maturing process. As soon as the plants have finished blossoming, new potatoes can be harvested. New potatoes aren't suitable for wintering over in the root cellar. You can tell it's a new potato because the skin will rub off easily, exposing the white flesh underneath. They're delicious and much prized, but they need to be eaten quickly.

The potatoes that root cellar well are those that have been harvested after the potato plants die off. It's best to allow these potatoes to harden off in the ground for a couple of weeks before digging them. This ensures the skins have set. You can tell a hardened-off potato because the skins won't easily rub off. You'll need a potato peeler. These potatoes are good candidates for root cellaring.

Don't let potatoes see the light of day! Sunlight causes chemical changes in potatoes, turning them green. This green color indicates the presence of solanine—and it's not good for you. You can cut out a small amount of green, but if the potato is green clear through, toss it.

Potatoes for storing should be firm and without cracks or black spots. You don't have to leave space between them and can store them in cardboard boxes, wooden boxes, or burlap bags. It's easier if you do some sorting for size before you pile them into containers. Keep one box for bakers (big and smooth), another one for medium-sized and irregular shapes, and one box for the little ones, which are excellent creamed or added to soups and stews. Check them from time to time and remove any potatoes that are soft or show signs of spoiling.

Beets

Leave the tails on, trim any leaves, and leave ½ inch (1.25cm) of the crown. Pack in boxes. Lay down a layer of damp sand, then a layer of beets, then more sand, more beets, etc.

Turnips

These vegetables have a strong odor that can wreak havoc with other produce. Store them by themselves in layers of moist sand.

Carrots

Select firm carrots without blemishes. Remove the leaves, leaving ½ inch (1.25cm) of the crown. Store in layers of moist sand.

Cabbage

Cabbage has a stronger odor than turnips by far and can insinuate itself into other produce if you're not careful, so it needs its own place. Remove the roots and any browned leaves. Store in boxes and cover with moist sand. If you only have a few heads, wrap each head in newspaper and store away from other produce.

Cauliflower

Cauliflower likes it cold and moist. If you're harvesting your own, keep the roots on and nestle them back into the damp sawdust or sand in the root cellar. This will extend their storage life.

Onions

You can braid onions just as you braid garlic and they'll store nicely hanging from a peg in a cool, airy location. Otherwise, they need to be dried first before storing them on racks or in baskets. They prefer dry conditions.

Winter Squash

Winter squash, including pumpkins, stores beautifully. Leave a bit of stem and allow the cut to harden off before bringing inside to store. These don't like it too cold or too moist, so keep their storage temperature between 50°F and 55°F (10°C and 13°C).

Recipes

Treat your root cellar like a grocery store. Before you visit it to grab one acorn squash, sit down and plan your menus for the week. Then make your "shopping list." Even if you tend to be spontaneous in your meal planning, winter weather can put the brakes on your good intentions to make a daily call to your produce. You'll more than likely decide it's not worth the trouble to brave the elements, and your fruits and vegetables will pine away in isolation. A little planning before you make the trek will make good use of your hard work at harvest time.

You can create all manner of hearty meals from the produce you've root cellared. You've got all the ingredients for soups, stews, and casseroles that will warm you throughout the long, cold winter. Country folk enjoy a *homegrown dinner* and take pride in being able to put one on the table. This simply means a meal made entirely from foods they've grown or raised. How close can you come?

Scalloped Potatoes

Originally, these were called *escalloped potatoes*, a term that refers to fish scales. The potato slices were arranged in overlapping rows and resembled fish scales. Over time, the term was shortened, but we still try to arrange the potatoes in that overlapping pattern.

Serves	Prep time	Cook time
4	25 minutes	35 to 40 minutes

2 cups milk of choice

2 tbsp butter

2 tbsp all-purpose flour

4 white potatoes, scrubbed and peeled

1. Preheat the oven to 350°F (175°C).

2. In a medium saucepan on the stovetop over low heat, make a white sauce by whisking together the milk, butter, and flour. Cook until the mixture begins to thicken, whisking constantly. Remove the saucepan from the heat.

3. Thinly slice the potatoes. Add the slices to a medium saucepan on the stovetop over high heat. Cover with water and bring to a boil. Reduce the heat to low and simmer until fork-tender, about 15 to 20 minutes. Remove the saucepan from the heat and drain the potatoes.

4. Arrange the slices in an 8×10×2 inch (20×25×5cm) glass baking dish. Cover with the white sauce. Add the next layer of potatoes and cover with white sauce.

5. Place the dish in the oven and bake until brown and bubbly, about 25 minutes.

6. Remove the dish from the oven and serve the scalloped potatoes immediately.

Karen's Potato Salad

This is a good side dish for hamburgers and homemade baked beans.

Serves	Prep time	Cook time
4	15 minutes	10 minutes

2 large or 4 medium-sized russet potatoes. (Yukon Golds are also a good choice.)

½ cup mayonnaise (or enough to make mixture creamy)

¼ tsp curry powder

½ tsp mustard powder

2 celery stalks, chopped

kosher salt, to taste

freshly ground black pepper, to taste

paprika

1. Scrub, peel, and dice the potatoes into whatever thickness you prefer.

2. Add the potatoes to a medium saucepan on the stovetop over high heat and cover with water. Bring to a boil, then reduce the heat to low. Simmer until fork-tender, about 7 to 10 minutes. Remove the saucepan from the heat and drain the potatoes.

3. In a medium bowl, combine the mayonnaise, curry powder, and mustard powder. Add the potatoes and celery. Mix gently. Season with salt and pepper to taste.

4. Sprinkle paprika over the top. Keep the salad refrigerated until ready to serve.

Parmesan Potatoes

This is a simple dish with good flavor.

Serves	Prep time	Cook time
4	5 minutes	35 to 40 minutes

2 russet potatoes, scrubbed, halved, skins on

1½ tbsp butter

grated parmesan cheese

1. Preheat the oven to 350°F (175°C).

2. Place the potato halves cut side up on a baking sheet. Top each potato with about 1 teaspoon of butter. Sprinkle the parmesan cheese over the top.

3. Place the sheet in the oven and bake until the potatoes are done and the cheese has browned and has a nice crust, about 35 to 40 minutes.

Twice-Baked Potatoes

This is an elegant company dish, but it's really just baked potatoes gone mashed potatoes gone fancy.

Serves	Prep time	Cook time
4	25 minutes	60 to 90 minutes

2 russet potatoes, scrubbed

¼ cup sour cream

2 green onions, chopped coarsely

1 cup coarsely grated sharp cheddar cheese, divided

kosher salt, to taste

freshly ground black pepper, to taste

1. Preheat the oven to 350°F (175°C).

2. Place the potatoes on a baking sheet. Place the sheet in the oven and bake the potatoes until done, about 1 hour.

3. Remove the sheet from the oven and allow the potatoes to cool slightly. Use a sharp knife to cut each potato in half lengthwise. Use a spoon to carefully scoop out the cooked potato and transfer to a large bowl. Be sure to leave enough of the potato behind so the skin doesn't collapse. You're making a shell with the potato skin.

4. Mash together the potatoes, sour cream, and ½ cup of the grated cheese. Add the green onions and mix well. Season with salt and pepper to taste.

5. Spoon the mixture into the potato shells, mounding generously. Top with the remaining ½ cup of grated cheese.

6. Place the filled potatoes on a baking sheet. Place the sheet in the oven and bake the potatoes until heated through and the cheese has melted and is crispy brown, about 15 to 20 minutes.

7. Remove the sheet from the oven and serve the potatoes immediately.

Note: Try this recipe with an added 1 tablespoon of maple syrup.

John's Hubbard Squash Soup

Rich and satisfying, this is the perfect supper for a blustery winter evening. Serve with crusty bread.

Serves	Prep time	Cook time
2	5 minutes	35 to 40 minutes

1 medium-sized Hubbard squash

3 tbsp light brown sugar

1 tbsp butter

kosher salt, to taste

freshly ground black pepper, to taste

¼lb (115g) precooked Polish sausage,
    cut into ¼ inch (0.5cm) slices

sour cream

cilantro leaves

for the white sauce

1 tbsp butter

2 tbsp all-purpose flour

1 tbsp extra virgin olive oil

1½ cups 2% hot milk of choice

1. Use a sledgehammer or another destructive device to whack the Hubbard squash into manageable pieces. Remove the seeds and peel. Cut the squash into pieces.

2. In a large pot on the stovetop over high heat, combine the squash and enough water to cover. Boil for 10 minutes or until tender.

3. Remove the pot from the heat and drain the squash.

4. In a large bowl, combine the squash, brown sugar, and butter. Mash until well mixed or use a blender. Set aside.

5. In a medium saucepan on the stovetop over medium heat, make the white sauce by melting the butter and heating the olive oil.

6. Remove the saucepan from the heat and add the flour, stirring constantly to make a smooth roux. Add the hot milk and return the saucepan to the stovetop, stirring constantly until the mixture comes to a rolling boil.

7. Transfer the squash mixture to a large pot on the stovetop over low heat. Add the white sauce and sausage. Stir until thoroughly heated.

8. Remove the pot from the heat and transfer the soup to tureens before serving. Top each tureen with a dollop of sour cream and a garnish of cilantro leaves.

Cole Slaw

Cabbages store well in the root cellar. We covered sauerkraut in our chapter on fermenting, so here's another side dish to go with the potato salad recipe (page 379).

Serves	Prep time	Cook time
8	10 minutes	none

1 head of cabbage, quartered and cored

2 carrots

for the dressing

½ cup granulated sugar

½ cup apple cider vinegar

½ cup mayonnaise

1 tsp celery seeds

1. Grate the cabbage and carrot to your preferred sizes. Transfer to a large bowl.

2. In a small bowl, combine the sugar, apple cider vinegar, mayonnaise, and celery seeds. Mix dressing ingredients in a small bowl.

3. Stir the dressing into the cabbage and carrot mixture. Cover the bowl with plastic wrap and refrigerate overnight. Stir the mixture occasionally.

Note: You can double the dressing ingredients if you prefer more dressing.

Roasted Carrots with Honey Glaze

This is a pretty dish with good flavor.

Serves	Prep time	Cook time
4	10 minutes	25 to 35 minutes

1lb carrots, scraped

2 tbsp butter

¼ cup honey

¼ cup freshly squeezed lemon juice

1. Preheat the oven to 425°F (225°C).

2. Slice the carrots lengthwise, then cut them diagonally into pieces.

3. In a small bowl, combine the butter, honey, and lemon juice. Mix well.

4. Pour the honey mixture over the carrots. Transfer the carrots to a baking sheet.

5. Place the sheet in the oven and roast the carrots until they're nicely glazed, about 25 to 35 minutes.

6. Remove the sheet from the oven and serve the carrots immediately.

Root Vegetable Mash

We began this recipe section with a bit of potato. We'll finish with potatoes and a mix of other root-cellared favorites.

Serves	Prep time	Cook time
4	10 minutes	25 to 35 minutes

3 potatoes, whatever variety you have

1 parsnip, small rutabaga, or small turnip

¼ cup sour cream

1. Scrub and peel the potatoes. Cut the potatoes into quarters.

2. Scrub and peel the root vegetable of your choice. Cut them into pieces.

3. Add the potatoes and root vegetable to a pot on the stovetop over medium heat. Cover with water and cook until the vegetables are done, about 15 to 20 minutes.

4. Remove the pot from the heat and transfer the potatoes and root vegetable to a large bowl. Mash together the vegetables and sour cream.

5. Transfer the vegetable mash to a large bowl before serving.

acid foods Foods containing enough acid to result in a pH of 4.6 or below; thus, they can be processed in a boiling water bath. Includes most fruits (except for figs and Asian pears), most tomatoes, fermented and pickled vegetables, relishes, jams, jellies, and marmalades.

anaerobic Means "without oxygen." Specifically, it refers to something that can live in the absence of oxygen and to which oxygen can be toxic.

backslopping A small amount of a previously fermented batch is added to the raw food to begin the fermentation process.

bacteria A group of microorganisms, including *salmonella, clostridium,* and *Escherichia coli (E. coli)*.

blanching The process of placing raw foods in boiling water for a specific period of time in order to stop deterioration caused by enzymes.

brining The process of preserving foods by immersing them in a saltwater solution.

cake tester A piece of wire with a loop at one end. The tester is anywhere from 3 to 6 inches (7.5 to 15.25cm) long. You insert your finger into the loop handle and insert the tester into the middle of the cake or another product you're testing. When it comes out clean, the product is done.

canning A method of preserving food that uses heat and/or pressure to remove air and create a vacuum seal.

cold frame A wooden box minus the top and bottom. It's set outdoors on the ground, plants are set inside it for shelter, and the top is usually an old window that's attached with a hinge and propped up with a piece of wood during the day and closed down at night. It provides protection from wind and cold.

corning A means of preserving meat that gets its name from the large salt crystals, or "corns," that were once rubbed into the meat to cure it.

cryptosporidium   A waterborne protozoa—a parasite that can take up residence in the human intestine and cause illness. In the case of individuals with a suppressed immune system, that illness can be fatal. The parasite is found in waters contaminated with sewage and animal waste.

danger zone   Temperatures at which bacteria will grow (40°F to 140°F [4°C to 60°C]), with the most rapid rate of growth occurring between 70°F and 100°F (21°C to 38°C).

drumette   The fleshy part of the poultry wing; it's what you'll be served if you order wings at a restaurant. Many people discard the wings, not realizing there's some good meat there.

dry salting   The process of combining salt with the juices from the food being salted to form a concentrated brine.

enzymes   Substances in food that accelerate changes in flavor, color, texture, and nutrition, especially when the food's surface is exposed to air.

fermentation   Changes in food caused by the intentional growth of bacteria, yeast, or mold.

frencher   A small device that clamps onto a counter or tabletop. You feed green beans into a hopper at the top and then turn a small hand crank that feeds the beans from the hopper to internal stainless steel blades that slice the beans lengthwise.

freshening   The process of rinsing and soaking meat in cold water to remove as much salt as possible before cooking.

headspace   Also called *headroom*. In a container, this is the space between the food or liquid and the lid. During heat processing, it provides room for food to expand and also creates the vacuum as the jar cools.

hot pack   Heating raw food in boiling water or steam before filling jars.

low-acid foods   Foods with a pH above 4.6 that must be processed in a pressure canner or acidified to a pH of 4.6 or lower if they're to be processed in a boiling water canner.

marbling   The term given to the white flecks of fat in the muscle of meat. Higher grades have more marbling, which increases the tenderness and flavor of the meat.

microorganism   A life-form too small to be seen without magnification. Bacteria, mold, and yeast are examples that can be found in food.

mold   A fungus type of microorganism whose growth on food is usually visible. Molds might grow on many foods, including acid foods, such as jams, jellies, and canned fruits.

open-kettle method   An older method of processing acid foods. Food is heat-processed in a covered kettle and then packed hot into sterile jars and sealed. The seal might not hold and food might spoil by this method.

perishable foods   Foods that will spoil rapidly unless preservation or storage methods are used to prolong shelf life.

pH   The measure of acidity or alkalinity on a scale ranging from 0 to 14. A food is neutral when its pH is 7. Lower values are more acidic and higher values are more alkaline.

pickling   A method of adding enough vinegar or lemon juice to a low-acid food to lower its pH to 4.6 or lower. These foods might then be safely processed in a boiling water canner.

raw pack   Raw food that's packed into containers and then processed.

sanitize   To clean in a manner that reduces the number of bacteria to safe levels and makes a surface safe for contact with food.

shelf life   The recommended length of time a food is safe to eat or is palatable. Shelf life depends on the initial number of bacteria, storage temperature, and handling practices. Therefore, shelf life is only an estimation.

steam blanching   A method of blanching that takes longer than regular blanching, but if you prefer not to partially cook your vegetables, you might find this a good alternative. You place a single layer of vegetables in a basket and hold the basket in place over boiling water. The steam generated by the boiling water blanches the vegetables. This method works for broccoli, pumpkin, sweet potatoes, winter squash, and mushrooms. *See also* blanching.

struck through   The term used to indicate that a fish has been completely salted and won't accept any more salt.

superfine sugar   Finely granulated sugar that dissolves almost instantly without leaving a granular residue at the bottom of the bowl.

tomatillo   A relative of the tomato. It originated in Central America and has been cultivated in Mexico and Guatemala since pre-Columbian times. It's also referred to as "husk tomato," "jamberry," or "groundcherry."

toxin   Poison produced by a living organism, such as a bacterium or mold. These toxins include *Staphylococcus aureus*, *Clostridium botulinum*, and *Bacillus cereus*.

venting   In canning, the process by which air is expelled from the canner.

Syrup Chart

You can use any strength of syrup you want. The following chart gives you ingredients for making sugar syrup in a variety of strengths. The less sugar you use, the lighter your syrup will be. It will also be thinner in consistency. Heavy syrup is downright thick. It can also tend to overshadow the flavor of the fruit.

If you aren't sure what strength you want to use, try mixing up a batch of light first. If this is too sweet for your taste, you'll want to use extra light (or even fruit juice or plain water). You can always add more sugar until you find the right proportions for your taste, but you can't take it out. For example, if you find the light strength not sweet enough, add 1 cup of sugar to the mixture and bring it to a boil again. Allow the syrup to cool and then taste it. Now you'll have medium light syrup. If it's still not sweet enough, add another 1 cup of sugar, bring to a boil, allow to cool, and then taste. By this time, you'll have reached medium heavy, and there's only one more strength to sample.

Percent	Type	Sugar (in cups)	Water (in cups)	Yield (in cups)
20	Extra light	1¼	5½	6
30	Light	2	4	5
40	Medium light	3	4	5
50	Medium heavy	4¾	4	6½
60	Heavy	7	4	7¾

To make the syrup, add the sugar and water to a large pot on the stovetop over high heat. Bring to a boil, then turn off the heat. If you're going to freeze the syrup, allow it to cool before pouring it into containers. If you're going to can the syrup, pour the boiling-hot syrup into containers, using a funnel and protection for your hands.

Processing Times Reference Charts

Vegetables

Minutes in weighted gauge pressure canner at 10 pounds of pressure or dial gauge pressure canner at 11 pounds of pressure (at sea level—make adjustments for altitude)

Vegetable	Type of Pack	Pints	Quarts
Asparagus	hot & cold	30	40
Beets	hot	30	35
Carrots	hot & cold	25	30
Creamed corn	hot	85	–
Green beans	hot & cold	20	25
Greens	hot	70	90
Lima beans	hot & cold	40	50
Mixed vegetables	hot	70	90
Mushrooms	hot	45[a]	–
Okra	hot	25	40
Peas	hot & cold	40	40
Peppers	hot	35	–
Pumpkin (cubes)	hot	55	90
Soups & stews	hot	60	75
Sweet potatoes[b]	hot	65	90
White potatoes[b]	hot	35	40
Whole corn	hot & cold	55	85

[a] *Pints or half-pints*
[b] *11-pound pressure*

Fruits

Minutes in boiling water bath at 212°F (100°C) (pressure at sea level—make adjustments for altitude)

Fruit	Cold Pack		Hot Pack		Pressure Canner at 5lb Pressure	
	Pints	Quarts	Pints	Quarts	Pints	Quarts
Apple pie filling	-	-	-	-	25	25
Apples	-	-	20	20	8	8
Applesauce	-	-	15	20	8	10
Apricots	25	30	20	25	10	10
Berries, Soft	15	20	15	15	8	8
Blueberry pie filling	-	-	-	-	30	30
Cherry pie filling	-	-	-	-	30	30
Cranberry sauce	-	-	15	-	-	-
Figs	-	-	45	50	-	-
Fruit cocktail	20	-	-	-	-	-
Fruit juices[a]	5	5	-	-	-	-
Grapefruit sections	10	10	-	-	8	8[b]
Grapes	15	20	10	10	-	-
Nectarines	25	30	20	25	10	10
Orange sections	10	10	-	-	8	10[b]
Peaches	25	30	20	25	10	10
Peach pie filling	-	-	-	-	30	30
Pears	-	-	20	25	10	10
Plums	20	25	20	25	10	10
Rhubarb	-	-	15	15	8	8
Tomatoes (whole or halves)	85	85	40	45	20	20
Tomato juice	-	-	35	40	20	20
Tomato sauce	-	-	35	40	20	20

[a] Half gallon = 10 minutes
[b] Hot pack

Meats, Poultry & Game

Minutes in weighted gauge pressure canner at 10 pounds of pressure or dial gauge pressure canner at 11 pounds of pressure (at sea level—make adjustments for altitude)

Food	Type of Pack	Pints	Quarts
Beef	hot & cold	75	90
Chili con carne	hot	75	90
Game	hot & cold	75	90
Ground meats	hot	75	90
Hard sausages	cold	75	90
Lamb	hot & cold	75	90
Lamb sausage	hot	75	90
Meat stock	hot	20	25
Pork	hot & cold	75	90
Pork sausage	hot	75	90
Poultry (with bones)	hot & cold	65	75
Poultry (deboned)	hot & cold	75	90
Rabbit (with bones)	hot & cold	65	75
Rabbit (deboned)	hot & cold	75	90
Squirrel (with bones)	hot & cold	65	75
Squirrel (deboned)	hot & cold	75	90

Seafood

Minutes in weighted gauge pressure canner at 10 pounds of pressure or dial gauge pressure canner at 11 pounds of pressure (at sea level—make adjustments for altitude)

Food	Pints	Quarts
Clams (minced)	70[a]	
Clams (whole)	70[a]	
Crab	80[b]	
Oysters	75[c]	
Raw fish	100[d]	
Smoked fish	110	110
Stew	100	100[e]

[a] *60 minutes for half-pints*
[b] *70 minutes for half-pints*
[c] *75 minutes for half-pints*
[d] *Pints or half-pints*
[e] *With seafood*

For any additional information or questions, refer to the instruction booklet for your pressure canner or contact your local extension office.

Freezer Storage Chart

Properly prepared and packaged frozen foods held at a constant temperature of 0°F (-18°C) will keep indefinitely. The following storage times are relative to quality only.

Food	Storage Time
Bacon and sausage	1 to 2 months
Casseroles	1 to 2 months
Egg whites or egg substitutes	8 to 12 months
Fish: cooked	1 month
Fish: fresh	3 to 6 months
Fish: smoked	4 to 5 weeks
Fruits and vegetables	12 months
Gravy: meat or poultry	2 to 3 months
Ham, hot dogs, and lunch meats	1 to 2 months
Ice cream	2 to 3 weeks
Meat: cooked	2 to 3 months
Meat: uncooked ground	3 to 4 months
Meat: uncooked roasts	9 months
Meat: uncooked steaks or chops	4 to 6 months
Pies and pastries	4 to 6 months
Poultry: uncooked giblets	3 to 4 months
Poultry: uncooked parts	9 months
Poultry: uncooked whole	12 months
Poultry: cooked	3 to 4 months
Soups and stews	2 to 3 months
Wild game: uncooked	8 to 12 months

Source: www.fsis.usda.gov/food-safety/safe-food-handling-and-preparation/food-safety-basics/freezing-and-food-safety

Best Preserving Methods for Specific Foods

Many foods can be preserved by more than one method, but some methods produce a better product than others. Here are some recommendations.

Vegetables for Freezing

Asparagus	Okra
Beans: lima, green, or yellow wax	Parsnips
Bok choy	Peas
Broccoli	Peppers: green
Brussels sprouts	Pumpkin
Carrots	Squash: summer
Cauliflower	Squash: winter (mashed)
Corn	Sweet potatoes (diced or mashed)
Greens: beet, chard, collard, mustard, turnip	Turnips (diced or mashed)
Kohlrabi	

Vegetables for Canning

Beans: green or yellow wax	Corn
Beets	Peas
Carrots	

Vegetables for Drying

Beets	Onions
Cabbage	Peas
Carrots	Peppers: green
Celery	Potatoes
Corn	Turnips
Mushrooms	

Vegetables for Root Cellaring

Beets	Parsnips
Cabbage	Potatoes
Carrots	Rutabagas
Cauliflower	Squash: winter
Onions	Turnips

Fruits for Freezing

Apples (slices)	Melon
Apricots	Nectarines
Avocados	Peaches
Berries	Pears
Cherries	Pineapple
Currants	Plums
Figs	Prunes
Grapefruit	Rhubarb
Grapes	Strawberries

Fruits for Canning

Apples	Pears
Apricots	Pineapple
Cherries	Plums
Nectarines	Rhubarb
Peaches	Tomatoes

Fruits for Drying

Apples	Grapes
Apricots	Huckleberries
Blueberries	Peaches
Cherries	Pears
Cranberries	Plums
Figs	

Fruits for Root Cellaring

Apples	Pears
Citrus	Tomatoes

Herbs for Drying

Chervil	Rosemary
Chives	Sage
Dill	Tarragon
Mint	Thyme
Oregano	

Agencies

American Dietetic Association   This is a good resource for recipes developed for people with food allergies. Find more information on their website: www.eatright.org/cps/rde/xchg/ada/hs.xsl/index.html.

Cooperative Extension Service   The essential resource for the home food preserver is the Cooperative Extension Service, an agency of the USDA. The Extension Service certifies Food Safety Advisors/Master Food Preservers and also exists to answer your questions about food preservation and food safety. You can find your local branch through an online search. To access the national center and find information about your local Extension Office, visit www.usda.gov/topics/rural/cooperative-research-and-extension-services.

The National Center for Home Food Preservation   This provides current research-based recommendations for most methods of home food preservation. It was established with funding from the Cooperative State Research, Education and Extension Service, U.S. Department of Agriculture (CSREES-USDA), to address food safety concerns for those who practice and teach home food preservation and processing methods. Visit their website for helpful information: www.uga.edu/nchfp.

USDA   The most comprehensive resource for the home food preserver is the United States Department of Agriculture (USDA). Find out more on their website: nal.usda.gov.

Books

Ball Blue Book of Preserving. Alltrista Consumer Products, 2004.

Bubel, Mike, and Nancy Bubel. *Root Cellaring–Natural Cold Storage of Fruits & Vegetables.* Storey Publishing, 1991. Readable discussion of the joys and challenges of root cellaring, along with specific instructions for building a root cellar.

Complete Guide to Home Canning. USDA Extension Service, 2015 (Agriculture Information Bulletin (AIB) No. 539). This book can be downloaded from the National Center for Home Food Preservation at nchfp.uga.edu/publications/usda/INTRO_HomeCanrev0715.pdf.

Greene, Janet, Ruth Hertzberg, and Beatrice Vaughan. *Putting Food By*, fifth edition. Plume, 2010. One of the most-beloved books on food preservation, the first edition appeared in 1973. It's been updated for modern times.

Kowalchik, Claire, and William H. Hylton, eds. *Rodale's Illustrated Encyclopedia of Herbs.* Rodale Press, 1998.

Bulletins

Visit pubs.extension.wsu.edu/consumer-food-safety for the pamphlets used in this book—print and digital for all types of food-preservation procedures. These include:

"Canning Meat, Poultry, and Game"	"Home Canning Smoked Fish"
"Canning Seafood"	"Pickles, Relishes, and Chutneys"
"Canning Tomatoes and Tomato Products"	"Pickling Vegetables"
"Canning Vegetables"	"Salsa Recipes for Canning"
"Drying Fruits and Vegetables"	"Smoking Fish at Home—Safely"
"Fish Pickling for Home Use"	"Storing Vegetables and Fruits at Home"
"Freezing Convenience Foods That You've Prepared at Home"	"Using and Caring for Your Pressure Canner"
"Freezing Fruits and Vegetables"	"You Can Prevent Foodborne Illness"

Websites

Build It Solar   www.builditsolar.com/Projects/Cooking/cooking.htm. Good resource for information on solar dryers and root cellars.

Pick Your Own.org   www.pickyourown.org. If you want to pick your own produce, this is the website that lists just about every pick-your-own farm in the United States—and also in several other countries. The site is user-friendly. Just click on your state and prepare to take notes.

Index

A

Acid and acidity
  canning and, 144
  in jams and jellies, 279
  salsas and, 246
  vinegar and, 216
Air drying, 310–311
Anaheim peppers, 248, 249
Apple cider vinegar, 216, 232
Apple pie filling
  freezing, 55
  processing times for canning, 394
Apples
  Apple Butter, 302
  Apple Peel Jelly, 290
  for chutney, 298
  Cranberry, Apple & Orange Relish, 253
  Dried Apple Coffee Cake, 326
  drying, 318
  freezing, 51–52
  Harvest Time Apple Relish, 254
  jellies made from, 283, 286
  Linda's Crispy Cobbler, 58
  pectin in, 285
  processing times for canning, 394
  root cellaring, 373–374
  Sweet-Hot Chutney, 306
Applesauce
  Applesauce & Raisin Loaf, 112

  canning, 163
  freezing, 52
  processing times for canning, 394
Apricots
  for brandied fruit (rumtopf), 299
  canning, 157
  for chutney, 298
  drying, 318
  freezing, 48
  jellies made from, 283
  pectin in, 285
  Pickled Apricots, 219
  processing times for canning, 394
  sun drying, 311
Ascorbic acid, 33, 41, 312, 314, 318
Asparagus
  Asparagus & Beef Stir-Fry, 74
  canning, 174
  freezing, 61
  Pickled Fish Pasta, 242
  processing times for canning, 393
Avocados, freezing, 54

B

Baby beef, 82
Bacon
  Barbara's Boston Baked Beans, 333
  freezing, 86, 397
Bacteria
  canning and, 144–145
  pickling and, 207

  poultry and, 91
  vacuum-sealing system and, 38
Baked beans
  Barbara's Boston Baked Beans, 333
  freezing, 123
Baked potatoes, 125
Baking powder, making your own, 107
Bananas, drying, 318
Beans. See also Baked beans; Green beans
  Barbara's Boston Baked Beans, 333
  freezing, 62
  Minestrone with Italian Sausage, 330
  snipping tips and tails of, 62
  vine drying, 311
Beef
  Asparagus & Beef Stir-Fry, 74
  Beef Stroganoff, 99
  canning, 188–189
  corned beef, 229–231
  Corned Beef & Cabbage, 244
  Corned Beef Hash, 243
  cuts of, 83, 84–85
  drying, 320
  fat in, 85–86
  ground, 85–86
  hormones, antibiotics and additives in, 82–83
  pickling (corned beef), 229–231
  processing times for canning, 396

purchasing, 82, 84
salting, 341
Shepherd's Pie, 331
smoking, 355
terminology, 82
Beet greens, 67
Beets, 66
Beet Relish, 256
brining, 340
canning, 175–176
drying, 319
freezing, 63
Mel's Borscht, 183
Pickled Beets, 224
processing times for canning, 393
root cellaring, 375, 376
Bell pepper(s)
about, 248
Beet Relish, 256
Corn Relish, 257
freezing, 71
Oscar Relish, 255
Piccalilli, 258
Pigs' Hocks & Pigs' Feet, 231
Sweet & Sour Pork, 75
Berries. *See also* specific berries
canning, 158
freezing, 43–47
hard, 43–44
jellies made from, 283
pectin in, 285
pick-your-own, 44
processing times for canning, 394
Rice Pudding with Smashed Fruit Topping, 59
soft, 44
Berry pie filling, freezing, 55
Biscuits
Blueberry Grunt or Slump, 57
Easy Cheesy Biscuits, 113
Sourdough Biscuits, 273
warming after freezing, 107
Blackberries
freezing, 44–45
Linda's Crispy Cobbler, 58

pectin in, 285
Rice Pudding with Smashed Fruit Topping, 59
Blanching, 33
about, 40
for drying, 319
french fries, 126
steam-blanching, 68
Blanching times, 40, 61, 62, 64, 65, 66, 67, 68, 69, 70, 71, 126
Blueberries
Blueberry Grunt or Slump, 57
drying, 318
freezing, 43, 44
No-Cook Strawberry-Blueberry Jam, 291
Blueberry pie filling, processing times for canning, 394
Bluefish
canning, 193
salting, 343
Boiling water canner, 131–132, 141, 172
Botulism, 125, 144, 145, 209, 229, 232, 234, 337
Boysenberries, freezing, 44–45
Bread(s). *See* Quick breads
Breadcrumbs, 106
Brining and brine
about, 208
fermentation and, 262–263
fish for pickling, 234
percentage of salt in solution, 336
salting vegetables and, 338
vegetables, 340–341
Broccoflower, freezing, 64
Broccoli
freezing, 64
Ham, Cheese, Potato & Broccoli Casserole, 76
Pickled Fish Pasta, 242
Bruised fruit, 45

Brussels sprouts, freezing, 65
Bull (beef), 82
Butter
freezing, 103
safe at room temperature, 28
Buttermilk, freezing, 104

C

Cabbage(s)
about, 208
Beet Relish, 256
Cabbage & Salt Pork, 347
Cole Slaw, 383
Corned Beef & Cabbage, 244
drying, 319
Kimchi, 272
Piccalilli, 258
root cellaring, 376
sauerkraut, 266–269
Cakes
Cherry Upside-Down Cake, 169
Dried Apple Coffee Cake, 326
Pineapple Upside-Down Cake, 168
Calf beef, 82
California grapes, pectin in, 285
Canned foods
in contact with flood waters, 21, 22
power outages and, 28
Canning, 15, 127–203
acidity, 144
altitude and, 145–146
antidarkening solution for, 155
bacteria and, 144–145
beef, pork, or lamb, 188–190
best vegetables for, 399
birth of, 130
canners used for, 131–134, 141–143
disposal of contaminated foods from, 151–152

fruit juices, 161–163
fruit purées, 163
fruits, 155–161, 403
game, 196–197
ground meats, 189
headspace and, 146
heat and, 145
hot pack vs. raw pack, 146
liquid loss and, 149–151
meat, poultry, seafood and game, 187–203
open kettle method, 149
pie fillings, 164–165
poultry, 190–193
procedures, 155–156
Processing Times Reference Charts, 393–396
recipes, 166–170, 181–185, 198–203
science behind, 130–131
seafood, 193–196
supplies and equipment for, 129, 131–140
syrup and, 154
tomatoes and tomato sauce, 165–166
troubleshooting for, 147–151
vegetables, 174–180
Canning jars. *See* Glass canning jars
Canning lids and rings, 137–139
Cantaloupe
freezing, 54
Pickled Cantaloupe, 221
pickling, 216
Carrots
brining, 340
canning, 176
freezing, 65
Karen's Vegetable & Beef Soup, 184
Kimchi, 272
in mixed vegetables, 181
processing times for canning, 393
Roasted Carrots with Honey Glaze, 384
root cellaring, 375, 376

Casaba, freezing, 54
Casseroles
freezer storage time, 397
freezing, 120–121
Ham, Cheese, Potato & Broccoli Casserole, 76
Kielbasa & Sauerkraut Casserole, 271
Sillgratin (Herring & Potato Casserole), 348
Cauliflower
brining, 340
freezing, 64
root cellaring, 377
Charcoal, for smoking, 354
Charcoal smokers, 357
Chard, 66, 67, 178
Cheese(s), 27, 28, 105
Cherries
canning, 158
Cherry Upside-Down Cake, 169
drying, 318
freezing, 47
jellies made from, 283
Cherry pie filling
freezing, 56
processing times for canning, 394
Cherry Preserves, Smoked Duck with, 366
Chili con carne
processing times for canning, 395
recipe, 199
Chowders, 201, 328
Chuck (beef), 84
Chutneys, 298–299, 305–306
Citrus. *See also* specific citrus fruits
freezing, 52–53
marmalades from, 287
root cellaring, 374
Clams
canning, 195
Clam Chowder by the 4s, 201

freezing, 95
Cobblers
freezing, 110
Linda's Crispy Cobbler, 58
Coconut, freezing, 54
Cold smoking, 352, 353
Cold water, thawing foods in, 42
Collards, 66, 67
Concord grapes, pectin in, 285
Conserves, 297–298, 304
Cookie dough, freezing, 110–111
Cookies, freezing, 110
Cooking oil, freezing, 104
Corn
canning, 151, 176–177
Corn Chowder, 328
Corn Pudding, 329
Corn Relish, 257
creamed corn, 177
Creamy Corn Pudding, 185
drying, 319
freezing, 65–66
Karen's Vegetable & Beef Soup, 184
in mixed vegetables, 181
processing times for canning, 393
Succatosh, 346
Corned beef, 229–231
Corned Beef & Cabbage, 244
Corned Beef Hash, 243
Corning, 229, 338
Cow, 82
Crab
canning, 195, 398
freezing, 94–95
Crab apples, 285, 286
Crackers, freezing, 110
Cranberries
Cranberry, Apple & Orange Relish, 253
Cranberry & Orange Muffins, 60

Cranberry Sauce, 167
drying, 318
freezing, 43, 44
pectin in, 285
Cranberry sauce
processing times for canning, 394
recipe, 167
Creamed corn
canning, 177
Creamy Corn Pudding, 185
processing times for canning, 393
Cream, freezing, 104
Crisps, freezing, 110
Cucumber(s). See
also Pickles; Pickling
cucumbers
about, 208
4-Day Sweet Gherkins, 226-227
Kimchi, 272
for pickling, 210
root cellaring, 375
Curing (salting), 336, 341.
See also Salt(ing)
Curing fish, 234
Currants, pectin in, 285
Curried Chicken, 100
Custard/cream pies,
freezing, 109

D

Dairy products, freezing,
103-105. See also specific
types of dairy products
Dates
for chutney, 298
freezing, 54
Pear Chutney, 305
Dehydration, 309
Dehydrators, 315-317
Dill, for pickling, 208
Dill pickles, 209, 223, 264-266

Discoloration, preventing, 41
Double-wrapping meat, 80
Dry ice, 26
Drying, 309-333
air, 310-311
best fruits for, 403
best herbs for, 403
best vegetables for, 402
conditioning process, 323
dehydrators used for, 315-317
jerky made from, 320-322
oven, 313-317
in the oven, 313-315
pasteurizing and, 323
procedures for, 317-320
recipes, 326-333
rehydrating and, 325
solar dryer used for, 312
storing dried foods, 324
sun, 311-312
testing for dryness when, 322-323
Dry pack, freezing
strawberries in a, 46
Dry salt(ing), 338-339
for pickling fish, 234
sauerkraut and, 267
vegetables, 338
Duck, 92, 190, 355
Smoked Duck with Cherry Preserves, 366

E

Eggs
Dark & Spicy Eggs, 237
Deviled Eggs, 238
freezer storage time, 397
freezing, 105
hard-boiling, 235
Pickled Egg Salad, 239
pickling, 234-235
Sweet & Sour Eggs, 236
Elderberries, 285
Electric smokers, 357

Emergencies, food safety
and, 21-28

F

Farmers' markets, 11
Fell (lamb), 89
Fermentation, 261-273
brine and, 263-264
dill pickles, 264-266
origins of, 261
pickling and, 207, 208
procedure for, 262-263
recipes, 271-273
sauerkraut, 266-269
science of, 262
sourdough starter, 270-271
yogurt and, 270
Figs
canning, 159
drying, 318
freezing, 55
pectin in, 285
processing times for canning, 394
Fish
canning, 193-194
drying, 320
freezer storage time, 397
freezing, 93-94
Green Chili Fish Stew, 241
Pickled Fish Pasta, 242
Pickled Herring in Cream Sauce, 240
pickling, 232-234
salting, 343-344
Sillgratin (Herring & Potato Casserole), 348, 349
smoking, 352, 359-360
Fish loaf, freezing, 122
Fish stock, 120
Foam, with jams, 288
Food mill, 163, 164
Food preservation, 11-12
food waste and, 14-15
fresh and natural ingredients used with, 12-14
gift-giving from, 17

partnerships, 15–16
personal satisfaction from, 16
Food safety
 cleanliness and, 19–20
 in emergencies, 21–28
 green potatoes and, 179
 imported products and, 19
 poultry and, 91–92
 storage temperatures and,
  20–21
Food storage. *See* Storage
Food waste, 14
4-H, 79
Freeze & cook bags, 39
Freezer bags, 37
Freezer burn, 33
Freezer containers, 37
Freezer jam, 282
Freezing, 29–126
 baked beans, 123
 benefits of, 33
 best fruits for, 402
 best vegetables for, 399
 breadcrumbs, 106
 casseroles, 120–121
 cobblers and crisps, 110
 cooked meats and poultry,
  123
 cookies and cookie dough,
  110–111
 cooking oil, 104
 crackers and potato chips,
  110
 dairy products, 103–105
 eggs, 105
 electricity and, 17
 equipment and supplies for,
  37–39
 freezer for, 34–37
 fruits, 43–55
 gravies and sauces, 122
 herbs, 71
 meat loaf and fish loaf, 122
 meat, poultry, seafood and
  game, 79–97
 pie crusts and pastries, 108
 pie fillings, 55–56
 pies, 109

pizza, 124
potatoes, 125–126
procedures for, 40–41
quick breads, 106–107
sandwiches, 124
science behind, 31–33
seafood, 93–97
stocks, 117–120
vegetables, 61–71
vegetable stir-fry mix, 124
French fries, 126
Frenching, 174
Frozen foods, 21, 27
 storing, 41
 thawing, 41–42
Fruit(s). *See also* Fruit
 spreads; specific fruits
 best preserving methods for
  specific, 403
 canning, 154–156
 drying, 318–319
 freezer storage time, 397
 in jams and jellies, 278
 Linda's Crispy Cobbler, 58
 "perfect-looking" versus
  organic, 13–14
 pickling, 215–217
 processing times for canning,
  394
Fruit cobblers, freezing,
 110
Fruit cocktail
 canning, 159
 processing times for canning,
  394
Fruit juices
 canning, 161–163
 processing times for canning,
  394
Fruit leather, 314–315
Fruit pies
 freezing, 109
 safe at room temperature, 28
Fruit purées, canning, 163
Fruit spreads
 brandied fruit (rumtopf),
  299–301
 chutneys, 298–299, 305–306

conserves, 297–298, 304
equipment and supplies for,
 280–281
freezer jam, 282
fruit butters, 295–297, 302–
 303
ingredients, 277–279
jellies, 283–287, 290
marmalades, 287, 293
procedures for making,
 279–280
recipes, 290–294, 302–306
reduced-sugar, 288
strawberry jam, 281, 291–292
troubleshooting, 288–289

G

Game birds, 92
Game meat(s), 90
 canning, 196–197
 drying, 320, 321
 freezer storage time, 397
 processing times for canning,
  395
Garlic
 food safety and, 19
 outside air drying, 310
Gas smokers, 357
Gherkins, 208, 211, 217
4-Day Sweet Gherkins,
 226–227
Glass canning jars
 breaking, 147–148
 failure to seal, 148–149
 for freezing, 37
 lids and rings for, 137–138
 types of, 135–137
Glossary, 387–389
Goose, 90, 92, 190, 355
Gooseberries, 285
Grades/grading, of meat,
 83, 88, 90
Graham cracker crusts,
 freezing, 108
Grams, conversions from
 ounces to, 392

Grapefruit
  canning, 159
  freezing, 53
  pectin in, 285
  processing times for canning, 394
  root cellaring, 374
Grape juice, 53, 285
Grapes
  for brandied fruit (rumtopf), 299
  canning, 160
  drying, 318
  freezing, 53
  jellies made from, 283
  pectin in, 285
  Pickled Grapes, 218
  processing times for canning, 394
Gravies
  freezer storage time, 397
  freezing, 122
Green beans
  brining, 340
  canning, 174–175
  freezing, 62
  Karen's Vegetable & Beef Soup, 184
  in mixed vegetables, 181
  outside air drying, 310
  processing times for canning, 393
Green chili peppers, 248
  Green Chili Fish Stew, 241
  Roma Salsa, 252
  Tomatillo Salsa, 251
Green peppers
  keeping fresh, 250
  Sausage & Potato Skillet, 203
  Sweet & Sour Pork, 75
  Wilma's Bread & Butter Pickles, 222
Greens
  canning, 178
  freezing, 66–67
  processing times for canning, 393
Green tomatoes
  for chutney, 298

Piccalilli, 258
Tomatillo Salsa, 251
Ground beef, 80, 85–86
  Chili con Carne, 199
Ground meats
  canning, 189
  processing times for canning, 395
  smoking, 358
  temperature for smoking, 358
Guava, pectin in, 285
Guinea hens, 190
Gutting fish, 94

H

Ham(s), 86, 198
  freezer storage time, 397
  Ham, Cheese, Potato & Broccoli Casserole, 76
  salting, 342
  Split Pea & Ham Soup, 200
Hamburger
  ground beef vs., 86
  Karen's Lasagna, 98
Hard berries, freezing, 43–44
Hard sausages, 190, 397
Hard water, pickling and, 216
Hash browns, 126
Headspace
  for canning, 146, 150
  for freezing, 40
Heavy cream, freezing, 104
Heifer, 82
Herbs
  air dying, 310–311
  drying, 310–311, 315, 320, 403
  freezing, 71
Herring
  curing (salting), 344
  Pickled Herring in Cream Sauce, 240

Sillgratin (Herring & Potato Casserole), 348
Homemade ice cream, freezing, 104
Honeydew, freezing, 54
Hormones
  beef and, 82, 83
  lamb and, 90
  pork and, 88
  poultry and, 91
Hot dogs, freezer storage time, 397
Hot pack, 146
Hot peppers, 248
  canning, 179
  handling, 248
  Harvest Time Apple Relish, 254
  Oscar Relish, 255
  Sweet-Hot Chutney, 306
  types of, 248
Hot smoking, 352
Huckleberries, 43, 318, 403

I

Ice cream, freezing, 104, 397
Instant Pots, 135, 270
Iodized salt, 214, 269, 339, 360
Irradiation, 91–92

J

Jam(s)
  conserves, 297–298
  freezer jam, 282
  making strawberry, 281
  No-Cook Strawberry-Blueberry Jam, 291
  Rose Hips Jam, 294
  Strawberry Jam, 292
Jars, canning. *See* Glass canning jars
Jelly(ies), 283–287, 290

safe at room temperature, 28
Jerky, 320–322, 324

K

Kadotas, canning, 159
Kale, 66, 67
Kimchi, 272
Kohlrabi
    freezing, 68
    root cellaring, 375
Kosher dill pickles, 209, 223
Kosher salt
    canning seafood with, 194, 195, 196, 197
    for corned beef, 230
    for pickling, 210, 214, 230
    for salting, 337, 338–339
    for sauerkraut, 266, 267

L

Lactic acid bacteria, 207, 208, 263
Lamb
    about, 88
    buying, 80
    canning, 188–189
    consumer concerns about, 90
    cuts of, 88–89
    grades of, 90
    processing times for canning, 395
    Shepherd's Pie, 331
    temperature for smoking, 358
Lamb sausage, 190, 397
Leg (lamb), 88, 89
Lemon meringue pie, freezing, 109
Lemons
    freezing, 53
    pectin in, 285
    preserved, 345
    Preserved Lemon Sauce, 346
Lids, canning, 137–139

Lima beans
    brining, 340
    canning, 175
    freezing, 62
    in mixed vegetables, 181
    processing times for canning, 393
    Succotash, 346
Limes, freezing, 53
Lobster, freezing, 95
Loganberries
    freezing, 44–45
    pectin in, 285
Loin (beef), 83, 84
Loin (lamb), 89
Loin (pork), 87–88
Lunch meats
    freezer storage time, 397
    freezing, 124

M

Mackerel
    canning, 193
    Mackerel Run Down, 349
    salting, 343
Mango chutney, 298, 299, 306
Marbling, in meat, 83
Margarine
    freezing, 103
    safe at room temperature, 28
Marinades, 356, 362–363
Marmalades, 287, 293
Mason jars, 135, 136–137
Measurements, equivalencies for, 391
Meat(s). *See also* Beef; Game meat(s); Lamb; Pork; Poultry
    coloring, 86
    drying, 320–322
    freezer storage time, 397
    freezing, 80
    freezing cooked, 123
    grading of, 83
    pickling, 229–232

purchasing, 79–80
    salting, 341–343
    smoking, 352–356, 353–354
    wrapping, 80, 81
Meat loaf, freezing, 122
Meat stock, 118, 189, 397
Melons
    freezing, 54, 232
    Pickled Cantaloupe, 221
    Pickled Watermelon Rind, 220
    pickling, 215
Milk, freezing, 104
Mixed vegetables
    canning, 181
    Dutch Oven Rabbit Dinner, 202
    Pickled Mixed Vegetables, 228
    processing times for canning, 393
    Shepherd's Pie, 331
Muffins
    Cranberry & Orange Muffins, 60
    freezing, 107
    Old-Fashioned Muffins, 327
    warming after freezing, 107
Mushrooms
    canning, 178
    drying, 310, 319
    freezing, 68
    processing times for canning, 393
Mussels, freezing, 96
Mustard, 66, 67
Mutton, 88

N

Nectarines, 48
    for brandied fruit (rumtopf), 299
    canning, 157–158
    freezing, 49–51
    jellies made from, 283
    processing times for canning, 394
    Sweet-Hot Chutney, 306

O

Okra
  brining, 340
  canning, 178
  dry salting, 339
  freezing, 69
  processing times for canning, 393
Onion(s)
  brining, 340
  keeping fresh, 250
  outside air drying, 310
  in relishes, 255, 256, 257, 258, 259
  root cellaring, 377
  for salsas, 249, 251, 252
Orange(s)
  canning, 159
  Cranberry, Apple & Orange Relish, 253
  freezing, 53
  Orange Marmalade, 293
  pectin in, 285
  processing times for canning, 394
  root cellaring, 374
Oven drying, 313–317
Oysters
  canning, 196, 398
  freezing, 96–97

P

Papaya, 298
Parsnips, 319, 375, 399, 402
Root Vegetable Mash, 385
Pasta
  freezing, 121
  Pickled Fish Pasta, 242
Pasteurization, 211, 266, 323
Pastries. See Pies and pastries
Peaches, 48
  for brandied fruit (rumtopf), 299

canning, 156–158
for chutney, 298
drying, 318
freezing, 49–51
jellies made from, 283
Linda's Crispy Cobbler, 58
Oscar Relish, 255
Peach Conserve, 304
pectin in, 285
Pickled Peaches, 219
processing times for canning, 394
removing skin of, 49–50
sun drying, 311
Sweet-Hot Chutney, 306
Peach pie filling
  freezing, 56
  processing times for canning, 394
Pearl onions, in Peas & Pearl Onions in Cream Sauce, 77
Pears
  for brandied fruit (rumtopf), 299
  Broiled Pears, 170
  canning, 160
  drying, 318
  Easy Pear Salad, 170
  freezing, 52
  jellies made from, 283
  Linda's Crispy Cobbler, 58
  Pear Chutney, 305
  pectin in, 285
  Pickled Pears, 219
  processing times for canning, 394
  root cellaring, 374
Peas
  brining, 340
  canning, 179
  drying, 319
  freezing, 69–70
  Peas & Pearl Onions in Cream Sauce, 77
  processing times for canning, 393
Pectin, 278
  in conserves, 297

for jellies, 285–286
Peppers. See also Bell pepper(s); Green chili peppers; Hot peppers
  canning, 179
  drying, 319
  keeping fresh, 250
  processing times for canning, 393
  for salsas, 248
  Sausage & Potato Skillet, 203
  Stewed Tomatoes, 182
Perfect Scallops, 97
Pheasant, 92
PH scale, 144, 263
Pickles
  brined or fermented, 208–209
  dill pickles, 209, 223, 264–266
  fermented, 262–266
  4-Day Sweet Gherkins, 226–227
  Quick Kosher Dill Pickles, 223
  quick-pack pickles, 209, 210, 215, 217, 223
  Reduced-Sodium Pickles, 225
  shelf life of, 212
  storing, 212
  vegetables for, 208
  Wilma's Bread & Butter Pickles, 222
Pickling
  eggs, 234–235
  equipment and supplies for, 210
  fish, 232–234
  fruits, 215–217
  meats, 229–232
  procedures, 211
  recipes, 217–228, 236–244
  science behind, 207–208
  storing products from, 212
  troubleshooting, 213–214
  vegetables, 217
Pickling cucumbers, 208, 210

fermented dill pickles, 264–265

Pickled Mixed Vegetables, 228

Quick Kosher Dill Pickles, 223

Reduced-Sodium Pickles, 225

Pickling salt, 210, 214, 337, 338–339

Pie crusts
freezing, 108
No-Fail Pie Crust, 111

Pie dough, freezing, 108

Pie fillings
canning, 164–165
freezing, 55–56

Pies and pastries
Chicken Pot Pie, 332
Cranberry & Cherry Scones, 115
freezer storage time, 397
freezing, 108, 109
Shepherd's Pie, 331

Pigeon, 190

Pigs' feet , 231–232

Pigs' hocks, 231–232

Pineapple
for brandied fruit (rumtopf), 299
canning, 160–161
for chutney, 298
freezing, 55
Pineapple Upside-Down Cake, 168

Pizza, freezing, 124

Plums
for brandied fruit (rumtopf), 299
canning, 161
for chutney, 298
dried, in Peach Conserve, 304
drying, 318
freezing, 52
pectin in, 285
processing times for canning, 394

Pomegranates, pectin in, 285

Pork. *See also* Ham(s)
antibiotics in, 88
Breaded Pork Chops, 102
canning, 188–189
cuts, 86, 87
processing times for canning, 395
salting, 341, 342
smoking, 355
Sweet & Sour Pork, 75

Pork sausage, 190

Potato chips, freezing, 110

Potatoes
canning, 179–180
Clam Chowder by the 4s, 201
Corned Beef Hash, 243
drying, 319
Dutch Oven Rabbit Dinner, 202
freezing, 125–126
green, 179
Ham, Cheese, Potato & Broccoli Casserole, 76
Karen's Potato Salad, 379
Karen's Vegetable & Beef Soup, 184
Parmesan Potatoes, 380
processing times for canning, 393
root cellaring, 375–376
Root Vegetable Mash, 385
Sausage & Potato Skillet, 203
Scalloped Potatoes, 378
Shepherd's Pie, 331
Sillgratin (Herring & Potato Casserole), 348
Twice-Baked Potatoes, 381

Potato patties, 126

Poultry, 90–92
about, 90
antibiotics in, 91
bacteria associated with, 91
canning, 190–193
Chicken Breasts in French Dressing Sauce, 101
Chicken Pot Pie, 332
Curried Chicken, 100
drying, 320
freezer storage time, 397

freezing, 92
freezing cooked, 123
irradiation and, 91
processing times for canning, 395
Smoked Chicken Salad, 364
Smoked Duck with Cherry Preserves, 366
Smoked Turkey Soup, 367
smoking, 355
temperature for smoking, 358

Poultry stock, 119

Power outages, 25–28

Pressure canner, 132–134, 142–143, 171

Prunes
drying, 318
Peach Conserve, 304
pectin in, 285

Pudding pies, freezing, 109

Pumpkin
canning, 180
processing times for canning, 393
Pumpkin Butter, 303
root cellaring, 377

Purification, water, 23–24

Q

Quail, 92

Quick breads. *See also* Muffins
Applesauce & Raisin Loaf, 112
freezing, 106–107
Zucchini Bread, 73

Quick-pack pickles, 209, 210, 215, 217, 223

Quince, pectin in, 285

R

Rabbit
canning, 193
Dutch Oven Rabbit Dinner, 202

processing times for canning, 395

Radishes, 375

Raspberries
freezing, 44-45
Linda's Crispy Cobbler, 58
pectin in, 285
Rice Pudding with Smashed Fruit Topping, 59

Recipes
butters, conserves and chutneys, 301-306
fermentation, 271-273
fermented dill pickles, 264-265
fruit spreads, 290-294
marinades, 362-363
pickling, 217-228, 236-244
pickling solution, 233
rubs, 360-361
salsas and relishes, 250-259
using canned foods, 166-170, 181-185, 198-203
using dried ingredients, 326-333
using fermented ingredients, 271-273
using foods from the root cellar, 377-385
using frozen foods, 57-60, 73-77, 97-102, 111-115, 236-244
using pickled foods, 217-228
using salted foods, 345-349
using smoked ingredients, 364-367

Red currants, 299

Refrigerator(s)
food safety and temperature of, 26, 27
maximum temperature of, 20
maximum time perishable foods left out of the, 20
raising during floods, 21
thawing foods in the, 42

Relishes, 209, 245-259.
See also Salsas
Beet Relish, 256
Corn Relish, 257

Cranberry, Apple & Orange Relish, 253
Harvest Time Apple Relish, 254
Oscar Relish, 255
Piccalilli, 258
Summer Squash Relish, 259

Resources, 403-404

Rhubarb, 396, 402, 403

Rib (beef), 85

Rice Pudding with Smashed Fruit Topping, 59

Roe, freezing, 93

Roma tomatoes, for salsa, 247, 252

Root cellaring, 369-385
best fruits for, 403
best vegetables for, 402
fruits, 373-374
location for, 371-373
recipes, 377-385
science behind, 369-370
vegetables, 375-377

Rose hips, in Rose Hips Jam, 294

Round (beef), 85

Rubs, 356, 360-361

Rumtopf (brandied fruit), 299-301

Rutabagas
brining, 340
Root Vegetable Mash, 385
salting, 339

S

Safety. *See* Food safety

Salmon
crystals in home-canned, 194
Green Chili Fish Stew, 241
Pickled Fish Pasta, 242
Smoked Salmon Bisque, 365
smoking, 359

Salmonella enteritidis, 91

Salsas
ingredients, 247-250

onions for, 249
peppers for, 248
Roma Salsa, 252
Tomatillo Salsa, 251
tomatoes for, 247

Salt(ing), 15, 335-349
canning vegetables and, 173
fish, 343-344
historical perspective on, 335-336
lemons, 345
for making jerky, 321
meats, 341-343
medical issues related to intake of too much, 337
for pickling, 210, 233
pickling and, 207
recipes, 345-349
science behind, 336-337
smoking and, 352
varieties of, 337
vegetables, 338-341

Saltpeter, 229

Salt pork
Barbara's Boston Baked Beans, 333
Cabbage and Salt Pork, 347
Clam Chowder by the 4s, 201
Corn Chowder, 328

Sandwiches, freezing, 124

Sauces, freezing, 122

Sauerkraut, 266-269
Kielbasa & Sauerkraut Casserole, 271

Sausage(s)
canning, 190
freezer storage time, 397
Kielbasa & Sauerkraut Casserole, 271
Minestrone with Italian Sausage, 330
processing times for canning, 395
Sausage & Potato Skillet, 203

Savoy cabbage, 208

Scaling fish, 93

Scallops
freezing, 95

Perfect Scallops, 97
Pickled Fish Pasta, 242
Scones
Cranberry & Cherry Scones, 115
freezing, 106
Scoville Heat Unit Scale, 428
Seafood. *See also* specific seafood
canning, 193–196
freezing, 93–97
processing times for canning, 396
Seafood stock, 119–120
Shellfish
canning, 193, 194–196
freezing, 96
Shortcakes, 114
Shoulder (lamb), 89
Shoulder (pork), 87
Shrimp
canning, 196
freezing, 96
Smoked fish
canning, 194
freezing, 93
Smokehouse, building your own, 353–354
Smokers, 352, 356–358
Smoking, 15, 351–367
cold smoking, 352, 353
fish, 359–360
hot smoking, 352, 359
portable smokers for, 356–357
recipes, 360–367
safety concerns, 358
science behind, 352
temperatures for, 358, 359
woods used for, 354
Snap beans. *See* Green beans
Snap peas, 69, 70
Snow peas, 69, 70
Soft berries, 44–45, 158

Solar drying, 312
Soups and stews, processing times for canning, 393
Sour cream, freezing, 104
Sourdough starter, 270–271
Sourdough Biscuits, 273
Spice bags, 217
Spices
in chutneys, 299
for pickling, 216–217
rubs, 356
for salsas, 250
Spinach, 66, 178
blanching, 67
Karen's Lasagna, 98
Split peas, in Split Pea & Ham Soup, 200
Squash. *See also* Zucchini
canning winter, 180
freezing summer, 71
John's Hubbard Squash Soup, 382–383
root cellaring, 369, 375, 377
Squirrel
canning, 193
processing times for canning, 395
Steam-blanching, 68
Steer, 82
Stocks, freezing, 117–120
Storage
of dried foods, 324
of emergency supplies, 21
of foods for earthquakes, 25
of frozen foods, 41
outdoors, 27
of pickled products, 212
safety and, 20–21
of smoked meats, 360
temperatures, 20–21
Strawberries
drying, 318
freezing, 46–47
No-Cook Strawberry-Blueberry Jam, 291

pectin in, 285
Strawberry Jam, 292
strawberry jam, 281
String beans. *See* Green beans
Stuffed potatoes, 125
Sugar
in jams and jellies, 278
reduced, in fruit spreads, 288
Sugar pack, freezing strawberries in a, 46
Summer squash, freezing, 71. *See also* Zucchini
Sun drying, 311–312
Sweet potatoes
canning, 180
processing times for canning, 393
Syrup chart, 391
Syrup pack, freezing strawberries in a, 46–47

T

Table salt, 337
Thawing foods, 28
berries, 45
methods to avoid, 41
methods to use, 42
before smoking, 356
Thickening agents, 164
Tomatillo, for salsa, 247, 251
Tomatoes
canning, 144, 165–166
Chili con Carne, 199
drying, 318
Karen's Vegetable & Beef Soup, 184
keeping fresh, 250
in mixed vegetables, 181
Oscar Relish, 255
processing times for canning, 394
root cellaring, 374
for salsa, 247
Stewed Tomatoes, 182

Tomato juice
canning, 166
canning game and, 197
processing times for canning, 394
Tomato sauce
canning, 166
processing times for canning, 394
Trout
canning, 193
salting, 343
smoking, 359
Turnips, 66
blanching, 67
brining, 340
drying, 319
root cellaring, 375, 376
Root Vegetable Mash, 385
salting, 339

U-V
Upright freezers, 36

Vacuum sealer, 32
Vacuum sealer packaging machines, 38
Veal, 82, 358
Vegetables. *See also* Mixed vegetables
see also specific vegetables
best, for freezing, 399
best preserving methods for specific, 399–400
blanching, for freezing, 40
brining, 340–341
drying, 319
freezer storage time, 397
pickling, 217
processing times for canning, 393
for root cellaring, 369, 375–377, 402
salting, 338–341
Vegetable stir-fry mix, freezing, 124
Vegetable stock, 120

Vine-drying, 311
Vinegar, pickling and, 216, 217, 232, 234

W
Water bath canner (boiling water canner). *See* Boiling water canner
Watermelon
freezing, 54
Pickled Watermelon Rind, 220
pickling, 215
Water supply, purifying your, 23–24
Waxed foods, pickling and, 210, 215–216
Websites, 406
Wild game. *See* Game meat(s)
Winter squash
canning, 180
root cellaring, 369, 375, 377
Wrapping meat, 80, 81

Y
Yogurt
freezing, 104
making, 270
Youngberries, 43

Z
Zucchini
freezing, 71
in mixed vegetables, 181
Summer Squash Relish, 259
Zucchini Bread, 73